Projections of Power

AMERICAN ENCOUNTERS / GLOBAL INTERACTIONS

A series edited by Gilbert M. Joseph and Emily S. Rosenberg

This series aims to stimulate critical perspectives and fresh
interpretive frameworks for scholarship on the history of the
imposing global presence of the United States. Its primary
concerns include the deployment and contestation of power,
the construction and deconstruction of cultural and political
borders, the fluid meanings of intercultural encounters,
and the complex interplay between the global and the
local. American Encounters seeks to strengthen dialogue
and collaboration between historians of United States
international relations and area studies specialists.

The series encourages scholarship based on multiarchival
historical research. At the same time, it supports a
recognition of the representational character of all stories
about the past and promotes critical inquiry into issues
of subjectivity and narrative. In the process American
Encounters strives to understand the context in which
meanings related to nations, cultures, and political economy
are continually produced, challenged, and reshaped.

Projections of Power

The United States and Europe in
Colonial Southeast Asia, 1919–1941

Anne L. Foster

Duke University Press ‖ *Durham and London* ‖ 2010

© 2010 Duke University Press
All rights reserved
Printed in the United States of America
on acid-free paper ♾
Typeset in Charis by Tseng Information Systems, Inc.
Library of Congress Cataloging-in-Publication Data
appear on the last printed page of this book.

Contents

Acknowledgments

From the earliest conception of this book in my first graduate seminar until the last days before submitting the final version of my manuscript, I have received instruction, support, friendship, and insightful readings from so many people. First I thank my professors, now friends: Bob Beisner, Alan Kraut, Valerie French, and Peter Kuznick from my undergraduate days at American University, and Takashi Shiraishi, the late David Wyatt, Sherman Cochran, Ted Lowi, Mary Beth Norton, and Michael Kammen from my graduate days at Cornell University. My graduate mentor, Walter LaFeber, stands alone as a wonderful teacher, scholar, example, and advisor. His wisdom, support, and care helped me become the scholar and teacher I am today.

During the research and writing of the dissertation which became this book I received support from friends made in graduate school, especially Mary Callahan, John Fousek, Jojo Abinales, Donna Amoroso, Shawn McHale, Jeff Hadler, Elizabeth Remick, Jim Siekmeier, Sayuri Shimizu, and Mike Montesano, a wonderfully distracting office mate. During research I met Mark Bradley and Chris Goscha, who have been wonderful readers and better friends. In the years during which the dissertation became a book, I benefited from the help and friendship of Cary Fraser, David Langbart, Frank Costigliola, Paul Kramer, Andy Muldoon, Geoff Smith, Sam Walker, and Bill Walker. Frank has been a constant support and source of encouragement. Cary read several versions of the introduction, and his suggestions helped me every time. Thanks for supportive words at crucial moments from Al McCoy and Ian Tyrell. I appreciate as well Emily Rosenberg's continued faith, and last-minute help when I really needed it.

Financial support enabled multiple trips to archives in Europe and the United States, and some much needed time for writing. I received support from the John D. and Catherine T. MacArthur Foundation's Fellowship in

Peace and International Cooperation, the Faculty Summer Research grant at Saint Anselm College, and the University Research Grant at Indiana State University.

Archivists and librarians performed wonders and tolerated my unusual requests, sometimes in less-than-colloquial Dutch or, especially, French. Thanks in particular to David Langbart of the United States National Archives for his suggestions of new places to look for things of interest. The librarians of Cunningham Memorial Library at Indiana State University, especially Steve Hardin, and of Geisel Library at Saint Anselm College patiently and quickly found even the most obscure of my interlibrary loan requests.

Valerie Millholland and Miriam Angress at Duke University Press have been patient and helpful well above the normal expectations. I appreciate as well the perceptive and sympathetic readings from two anonymous readers, whose comments improved the book. I remain responsible for any errors or lack of clarity.

My colleagues at Saint Anselm College and now at Indiana State University have made professional life a pleasure. Thanks especially to Silvia Shannon for friendship and mentoring. Chris Olsen, Dave Nichols, Ann Chirhart, and Barbara Skinner have contributed to this book in ways that only they will recognize. My students at both institutions have listened to many more stories about rubber and tin than they thought existed, tolerated them with good humor, and helped me write about those subjects more accessibly.

For hospitality and friendship during research trips, thanks to David Aldridge and Diane Gross, Tom Jacobsen and Mabel Shaw, Mark Bradley and Anne Hansen. Friends have provided critical support during the writing too, cooking for me, sometimes even cleaning my house. Such help enabled the final push. Naomi and Susan have often been the welcome distraction, reminding me that dancing in the living room and bike rides to the park are necessary for a well-rounded life. My parents, Chuck and Jan Foster, first taught me history through the telling of family stories. Their support and encouragement have been unceasing, and I rely on that.

Preface

The imperial system of Southeast Asia in the early twentieth century was dynamically formed by an international process. By placing the imperial experiences of Europeans, Americans, and Southeast Asians within one analytical frame, this book explains aspects of that imperial system previously difficult to understand. For instance, how did European governments work to maintain political control as economic control slipped away to other countries and, to some degree, to indigenous actors? How did the increasing power of the United States simultaneously strengthen and threaten the imperial system in Southeast Asia? How did ideologies such as nationalism and communism work to create sentiments of common identity for Southeast Asians as a group, as well as for Europeans and Americans? What were the effects of growing exposure to consumer culture from the United States? The Introduction to this book suggests some ways in which answers to these questions enhance understandings of Southeast Asian history, imperial history, and the history of United States foreign relations. A key argument sketched in the Introduction and elaborated throughout the book is that the presence of the United States in Southeast Asia as a colonial power was instrumental in creating the type of imperialism which existed during the period 1919–41.

Chapter 1 explores political relations and developments from 1919 to 1929, and focuses on the initial fears of Europeans after the First World War that the United States would lead, at least rhetorically, a wave of challenges to European colonial rule. Then, in the face of challenges from both Japan and nascent communist movements in the region, Europeans and Americans made common cause against these external threats even while United States officials attempted to hold themselves aloof from public displays of support for European colonial rule. United States political actions and policies during the 1920s explicitly aimed to uphold imperialism in Southeast Asia, with United States officials acting decisively alongside European officials to combat the primary political and strategic threats to the existing order.

Chapter 2 covers the same years, but explores economic relations. In this arena competition between Europe and the United States shaped the relationship more than cooperation did, especially during the 1920s. Americans, whether officials or businessmen, believed that the American way of conducting business would be most transformative for the region, and aggressively pursued policies without regard to their impact on traditional European methods of conducting business. These Americans also took pride in their belief that their involvement in Southeast Asia's economy tended to be more beneficial for Southeast Asians than what Europeans did. They predicted that a more Americanized economy would be an important part of helping Southeast Asians become sufficiently modern and self-reliant to be able to think about ruling themselves one day in the future. The region's economic and strategic importance for American industry meant, though, that United States officials and businessmen worried most about how to ensure sufficient and inexpensive supplies of critical raw materials from Southeast Asia, especially rubber, oil, and tin. The economic policies and practices of the United States often worked against the interests of Europeans in the region, who thought that United States actions therefore threatened imperial structures. Involved Americans demonstrated little concern about these European worries, believing that newly emerging economic relationships would over time foster beneficial political structures. During the booming 1920s these Americans were remarkably unconcerned about the future of imperialism one way or the other.

Chapter 3 explores cultural relations during the whole interwar period, taking a broad view of cultural relations. American culture in Southeast Asia was represented perhaps most forcefully by Hollywood movies, which United States observers saw both as a way to partially correct the overwhelming trade imbalance that the United States ran with Southeast Asia and as a way to promote American economic, cultural, and political values in the region. Since Hollywood movies were very popular, Europeans worried that they might have exactly the effect hoped for by Americans, and worked to censor them. Yet movies were not the only representations of American culture. Christian missionaries also had an important presence in most Southeast Asian colonies, and were perceived by both Southeast

Asians and Europeans to be preaching an "American doctrine" as much as any religious message. Equally important, Southeast Asians learned to read and write in the mission schools, many of which did not follow the European curriculum. Finally, the presence of American consumer products was a critical part of cultural relations. For United States observers, acquiring these products and using them correctly was a way for Southeast Asians to make the transition to modernity, with growing potential for self-rule. In promoting an American way of life, involved Americans often appeared to explicitly condemn European colonial rule and advocate new freedoms for Southeast Asians, who often interpreted this advocacy to mean that Americans supported an end to colonial rule. But these Americans rarely had an ideological commitment to ending colonialism and rarely worked to that end. The demise of colonialism would come naturally, someday, when Southeast Asians demonstrated their readiness, in part by producing and consuming properly.

Chapter 4 returns to economic relations, covering the years 1929–41, and explores the impact of the Depression. Initially it investigates the worldwide impact of the Depression, looking closely at the implications for Southeast Asians of having entered, as Americans believed they should, the modern world economy. The Depression was hard on Southeast Asia: the region was primarily a producer of raw materials, the prices of which dropped precipitously as industrial production in Europe and the United States fell sharply below their former levels. The primary response by European governments was to attempt to regulate and restrict production in the hopes of propping up prices somewhat. This strategy benefited Europeans much more than Southeast Asians, and initially was opposed as well by most United States officials and American businessmen. But in the face of the continuing and pervasive economic downturn, these Americans came to see some restrictions as a necessary evil, and lobbied hard for some ability to influence their implementation. Thus the 1930s represent a shift not merely in how Americans viewed the role of government at home but also in what types of intervention in the world economy were deemed acceptable. These maneuvers revealed the bedrock commitments of the United States: survival of an economic system led and controlled by Europe in the Southeast Asian colonies, which incidentally undergirded European imperialism, was substantially more important than promoting unfettered free markets or Southeast Asian entrepreneurship.

Chapter 5 returns to political relations, covering the years 1929–41. The

1930s opened with two major, long-lasting, and threatening rebellions against European colonial rule, one in Vietnam and the other in Burma. Although each lasted approximately one and a half years, involved thousands of peasants, and required massive military might to suppress, the supposedly communist-inspired one (in Vietnam) was considered much more threatening by the region's colonial powers. The chapter begins by exploring why that assessment was made, and its implications for nationalist movements and cooperation by the colonial powers. The rest of the chapter explores the tensions growing in the region from increasingly determined nationalist movements, even if apparently ineffectual at the time, and the growing threat that Japan presented. It concludes by arguing that the beginning of the Second World War solved none of the colonial powers' broader problems, but only placed them in abeyance until the end of the war. As the challenges to the imperial system grew during the 1930s, and even as the United States moved slowly to grant more self-rule to the Philippines, the United States reluctantly continued the policies it had pursued in the preceding decade: supporting European imperialism against both Japan and nationalists, although haltingly and with much advice about needed reforms.

The Conclusion returns to large themes in the existing historiography, pointing to how this exploration of the role of the United States in creating early-twentieth-century imperialism in Southeast Asia calls into question some long-standing assumptions. Attention to the ways people, products, ideas, and surveillance systems crossed borders suggests that Southeast Asia's regional identity has multiple sources. The high levels of colonial government cooperation to combat perceptions of communist threat indicate that the cold war grew out of conflicts deeper than struggles over Eastern Europe at the end of the Second World War. The methods and strategies of United States officials reveal continuities in the United States exercise of power throughout the twentieth century. Imperialism in Southeast Asia was contested, complicated, and resilient in ways revealed only through this exploration of the interactions of Europeans, Americans, and Southeast Asians.

Introduction

The United States, uniquely among modern states, began as part of a colonial empire (actually three colonial empires—British, Spanish, and French), gained independence, and itself became a major colonial power. Imperialism is at the core of the historical development of the United States, and the range of that experience has been critical to the shaping of modern ideas about imperialism, as well as resistance to imperialism.[1] The history of colonial America has long attracted accomplished and innovative scholars both in the United States and abroad, and the now-well-established field of Atlantic history has situated the American colonial experience within a broader regional, comparative context.[2] This history of colonial America is a constituent part of the history of seventeenth- and eighteenth-century imperialism. Yet studies of the imperialism of the late nineteenth century and the early twentieth more rarely consider United States imperialism alongside the canonical empires emanating from Europe, especially Britain and France.[3] This book aims to look broadly at Southeast Asia during the era of high imperialism, and to explore how participation by the United States, with both colonial and anticolonial traditions, influenced both justifications for the European imperialist systems in that region and the way they functioned.

In Southeast Asia the United States entered the terrain of apparently thriving, robust, and fully elaborated imperial systems. Initially its officials sought primarily to learn from and fit into European-led imperial orders, although within a short time they began to assert the superiority of United States methods of colonial rule. By the end of the First World War the United States was a full partner with European powers in efforts to create and maintain a viable colonial order in Southeast Asia. Its methods did sometimes differ from European methods, but all imperial powers in the region actively worked to support colonial rule regionally, just as all imperial powers took some steps toward granting autonomy to colonial subjects. The participation of the United States in this effort meant that European colonial rulers felt more pressure than they might have liked to encourage Southeast Asians to embrace consumer culture and industrial capitalism. Similarly, however, Americans in the region adapted to trade regimes that they did not believe were beneficial, after coming to understand the value of those trade regimes for European imperialism. Both Americans and Europeans agreed easily on the need to repress radical nationalism.

Just as it prompted change by its presence, the United States itself changed as a result of its participation in the colonial order. An outpouring of recent scholarship on United States imperialism, which draws on insights from scholars of European imperialism who have explored the ways the metropole has been profoundly altered by empire, has examined transnational contexts such as the creation of national identity, immigration, cultural exchange, and imports of "exotic" goods which become staples.[4] This book draws attention to a continuity as well as a change in United States projections of power, relating both continuity and change to the historic ambiguities in the relationship of the United States to imperialism.

In the United States colonialism has been simultaneously embraced and viewed with unease. Theodore Roosevelt, speaking as a former president in 1910, worked to justify United States colonial rule in the Philippines: "a people that shows itself totally unable to govern itself from within must expect to submit to more or less government from without."[5] Roosevelt's standard for self-government was behavioral. Nations could govern themselves when they met certain behavioral standards established by other, more powerful, presumably superior nations. That notion has long informed United States attitudes toward other nations, from decisions in the early nineteenth century about whether to support independence movements in Spain's South American colonies to choices in the early twenty-first century about when United States troops could leave Afghanistan and Iraq. Such a standard is an imperial notion. If nations fail to meet it, the United States, and other countries in the position of passing rather than receiving judgment, have rights to intervene. The incorporation of new continental territories by the United States was justified in part by this imperial notion; United States westward expansion was itself imperial.

What changed in 1898 was the decision to impose a government "from without," as Roosevelt said. United States continental expansion had been imperialistic, using the behavioral test to determine unfitness for continued self-rule as well as to decide when to allow self-government within the United States political system for acquired territories. The acquisition of Puerto Rico and the Philippines introduced colonialism. The reason for denying self-rule in those territories was also behavioral, but statehood was no longer the proffered goal. The Philippines could strive for independence. Puerto Rico has been denied even that. The continuity of imperialism and the change represented by formal colonial rule help to explain why government officials and other involved Americans worked easily within existing imperial structures and simultaneously offered an often biting critique of European colonial rule.[6] The firm imperialistic belief of these Americans that they had authority to instruct people in other nations how to govern themselves remains a constant. Imperialistic thought and behavior represent a continuum, with formal colonial rule at one end and contingent independence at the other end. Nearly all Americans were somewhere on the continuum.

The period from 1919 to 1941 might in retrospect be seen as the age of late high imperialism. Several characteristics of imperialism in those decades suggest the usefulness of examining the era more systematically. That the period would be the last gasp of modern imperialism, for instance, giving way after 1945 to a system with imperialistic characteristics but organized on somewhat different principles, was at best dimly perceived. Still, officials, scholars, interested observers, and most of all the colonized understood that modern imperialism had in many ways reached an apogee by the time of the First World War. In the period after 1919 the colonized had new organizational approaches to resisting colonial rule and a new rationale for that resistance. This resistance took many forms, from direct, violent confrontation to collaboration with intent to undermine from within, and a host of positions in between. The actions of the United States in the Philippines during the move toward autonomy, as well as the rhetoric of self-determination emanating from the United States, encouraged resistance. United States collaboration with European powers in tracking and arresting radical nationalists ensured that resistance would be suppressed.

Although colonial officials still largely believed in the ideology of the civilizing mission which defines high imperialism generally, they had begun to question where this notion was leading. Some increasingly saw formal colonial rule as an outmoded concept and looked forward to a day, admittedly far off, when it would end. Others wondered whether the genie of education, tutelage, and modernization could be put back in the bottle. They perceived that perhaps the emphasis on civilizing had itself prompted some of the new and worrying resistance. Colonial officials too, as well as foreign policy makers of the colonial powers, perceived that the geopolitical situation had been irrevocably altered by the First World War. Britain no longer held hegemonic power; power centers were more diffused. A jockeying for the leadership position among Britain, the United States, Japan, and (to a much lesser extent) the Soviet Union, to name only those involved in the particular disputes in colonial Southeast Asia discussed here, led to unsettled geopolitical conditions. This instability led to increased collaboration and cross-colony learning among officials from colonial powers, but also to increased economic, political, and cultural competition. Both colonial subjects and those from the colonial powers had to imagine themselves in a future which would be distinctly but perhaps not yet radically different from the world of pre-1914. This book explores the context in which that imagining took place, and some of the possibilities which Europeans, Southeast Asians, and Americans perceived as necessary, desirable, frightening, and unacceptable.

The role of the United States in how these imaginings took place is the least-studied component. In the fine and growing scholarship on late colonial Southeast Asia, even comparativists have only begun to pay serious attention to the United States as a regional colonial power, or as a cultural, political, economic, or military force in the region.[7] The United States hides in plain sight. Scholars have generally ignored its influence and power during the years after the First World War, even though it was the most important purchaser of key Southeast Asian products, the primary source of important cultural imports, and a nation increasingly committed to maintaining the political order in the region. Failure to include the United States is more than a simple geographical omission. It leads to reified notions of American exceptionalism.

Scholars have become accustomed to reading into silences, and finding in those silences the experiences of the oppressed, of the subaltern. But what has happened here is an odd case of power begetting silence: the United States has been overlooked not because it was or is oppressed, but because of the way people have perceived its status and considerable power. Remnants of the notion that the United States is exceptionalistic influence scholars to the extent that many remain stubbornly resistant to subjecting the United States to comparison, except as the case against which others may be measured. And, in a way pertinent to the story here, lingering notions of exceptionalism have meant that scholars have taken at face value stories which claim that the United States acquired colonies for different reasons than the European nations, governed differently, had different intentions. The perhaps unconscious but still powerful assumption drawn from the belief in those stories has been that the United States therefore played no meaningful role in maintaining the colonial order in Southeast Asia during the 1920s and 1930s.[8]

Scholarship on the United States in the Philippines has certainly complicated ideas about the nature of United States colonial rule there, but so far with little impact on that powerfully held assumption that the United States held itself aloof from the European imperial system more generally. Emphasis on the dyad of colonizer and colonized, for example the United States and the Philippines, tends to reinforce notions that that relationship is the only important one. The chapters which follow demonstrate how deeply the United States as a country, and many citizens of the United States as both private and public individuals, were involved with that imperial system. Neither Americans nor the United States government uncritically and enthusiastically supported the imperial system at all times and in all places. Americans held diverse opinions about imperialism. Significantly, interested Americans were generally supportive of imperial rule while being less supportive of some of the economic and cultural implications of the political system. By the 1920s most interested Americans shared a sense that formal colonial rule was outmoded, requiring new forms, models emanating from the United States, for knitting dependent parts of the world to more powerful parts of the world. Many Americans increasingly saw the intransigence of Europeans on issues of limited self-government as part of the problem with the imperial system. Americans were more likely than Europeans to advocate active transformation of the existing imperial system, whose backbone was colonial rule, into a new order of autonomous or independent states educated to support European and United States values, and held to those values through the deployment of economic and political rewards and punishments. Even the most optimistic Americans believed that a new order was years or perhaps decades away.[9] In the meantime these Americans both supported the existing imperial system and sometimes infuriated Europeans by supporting steps by their government which might undermine the system. Thus to subject the United States to comparative treatment does not mean that we are required to see only its similarities to other imperial powers, although similarities exist. Difference is a basis for comparison as well.

The United States Role in Late High Imperialism

The United States presence in colonial Southeast Asia played a formative role in shaping late high imperialism in the region. The economics of imperialism rested on the purchasing power of the United States after the First World War, as it became the primary purchaser of colonial exports from British Malaya, the Netherlands Indies, and the Philippines.[10] A key component of the shift in the importance of the United States was the growing prevalence of rubber in the region. Cultivated rubber from Southeast Asian plantations began to reach world markets during the First World War, and the United States purchased about half of the entire world's rubber supply throughout the 1920s and 1930s. As discussed in chapters 2 and 4, struggles over the production and sale of rubber were often fierce during these years. The United States used its economic power to attempt to shape policies regarding the production and export of major colonial products, with varying degrees of success. The United States had other key roles in the economics of imperialism as well. Many involved Americans believed that capitalistic economic activity by Southeast Asians was both good preparation and a sign of readiness for self-government. These Americans then encouraged and facilitated economic behavior by Southeast Asians, such as entrepreneurship and factory work, which Europeans found potentially problematic. For instance, indigenous smallholder rubber producers threatened to undercut European plantations on price, but were also gaining access to a source of wealth which provided some independence from the colonial state. Both United States government officials and involved Americans operated on the assumption that American methods, American investment, and American purchases would produce prosperity, modernity, and natural evolution toward an end to formal colonialism in the context of shared commitments to a particular, mutually beneficial economic arrangement.

Cultural relations and policies in the region's colonies also shifted during the years under consideration, and while the changes had many sources, the presence of a variety of American cultural products was an important one. Perhaps the two most potent forces were American missionaries and Hollywood movies. Although American missionaries often shared with supporters of imperialism a belief in racial hierarchy, by the early twentieth century the structures and programs of the American missions, and some-times the sentiments of missionaries, provided an opportunity for South-east Asians to become educated, usually with English as the language of instruction, and to experience democracy and self-rule, however limited, as they participated in running churches, schools, and hospitals. Hollywood movies contributed to changing notions of entertainment and leisure, but they were also part of a nascent movement toward consumerism, one en-couraged especially by Americans. American cultural products, in the as-sessment of involved Americans, had the potential to transform Southeast Asian lives. These products especially could convey a type of modernity that would encourage Southeast Asians to participate enthusiastically in the American vision for the world. Even Europeans could, according to United States observers, benefit from American cultural products. There was a ten-sion between modernity and tradition, but the Americans who introduced their country's cultural products had few compunctions about advocating choices that tilted toward their vision of modernity. The meanings of these cultural products were contested in a variety of ways which reflected and shaped other struggles within the imperial system.

Even in a traditional political sense United States activities had crucial importance. Historians cannot but look through the lens of hindsight: com-pared to United States involvement with Southeast Asia after or during the Second World War, the interwar period appears of limited importance. Al-though the United States commitment to using force to uphold a particu-lar political order in Southeast Asia dramatically increased after the early 1940s, the earlier years saw considerable political activity as well. United States officials often saw themselves as pursuing a common endeavor with European colonial officials, and acted accordingly. Colonial officials from all the imperial powers engaged in cross-colony learning, sending study mis-sions and advice. The governors general of all the colonies visited each other several times during these years. Both colonial and foreign relations officials from the United States took steps to combat communism in the region, in-cluding the sharing of secret information. They perceived communism as a threat to the whole region, and began to devise region-wide approaches. United States officials also consulted regularly with European colonial offi-cials about a variety of colonial governance and security matters. These policies appear insignificant in relation to what came after 1941, but they reflected a serious engagement in a part of the world that Americans had had little to do with before 1898. They also reflected the interwar belief that

American interests were generally best served when government promoted the kind of economic and cultural relations discussed above, that beneficial political relations would follow from increased American economic and cultural influence.

Imperialism in Southeast Asia in the 1920s and 1930s took the particular shape that it did in large measure because of the presence of the United States as a colonial power. The magnitude and nature of its economic involvement in Southeast Asia posed a threat to the power of European governments within their colonies, offered entrepreneurial opportunities to Southeast Asians, and during the Depression prompted new levels of intervention in colonial economies by European and United States governments alike. Cultural exports from the United States to Southeast Asia promoted ideas about modernity and living standards to both Europeans and Southeast Asians, suggesting that the United States was no less important than Europe as a source of modern ideas. And already during these years, the transnational or international projects that the United States found compelling, such as the fight against communism, were pursued more vigorously by all the powers than those that United States officials found less urgent, such as concrete measures against radical Buddhists or the Japanese. A full understanding of late high imperialism in Southeast Asia depends on systematic attention to when, how, and why the United States and Americans acted in the region.

Perceptions of the United States Role in Southeast Asia

My work is situated at the intersection of three separate but related fields: United States foreign relations with Southeast Asia, United States imperialism, and imperialism in Southeast Asia. Scholarship on the history of United States foreign relations as a field is dominated by the period since 1945, and particularly so in examinations of United States relations with Southeast Asia. Overemphasis on the more recent period, especially for areas of the world under imperial control before 1945, obscures continuities in what motivated the United States to exercise power overseas and the means that it used to do so. Studies of United States imperialism have traditionally focused on a dyadic relationship (the United States and Puerto Rico, for instance) and situated themselves firmly within either the field of United States history, in which case they examined the particularities of United States colonial forms, or the appropriate area studies field, in which case they often explored indigenous efforts to assert or regain control of their country. Inadvertently or not, this approach has reinforced exceptionalistic perceptions of United States imperialism. Comparative explorations of global imperialism too have privileged the comparison of European empires, neglecting not only the United States empire but the Japanese empire as well. These three omissions have distorted understandings of how United States power is exercised in the world as well as the nature of modern imperialism.

Nearly all works on United States relations with Southeast Asia have traditionally started their analysis with 1945, or perhaps 1941.[11] Only rarely, mostly in works on relations with Vietnam, is there even mention of what happened before 1941. One story has become familiar: the lost-opportunity tale, about Ho Chi Minh's attempt to persuade Woodrow Wilson to support Vietnamese independence. But the way even this story is told represents a reading backward from post-1945, in that the tellers of this tale mean it to demonstrate that United States policies toward Vietnam had been as flawed in 1919 as they were in the cold war. Scholars of United States foreign relations who have told this story have typically lacked interest in its broader context at the time, and have focused on Ho Chi Minh, not because he was necessarily interesting or important in 1919 but because he later became so.[12]

Many scholars of relations between the United States and Southeast Asia have wanted to explain United States policies during the cold war, so it is neither surprising nor particularly problematic that they should have confined their research and analysis to that period. Broadening the focus has several benefits, however, as some scholars have begun to discover. Frances Gouda has written a relatively traditional diplomatic history of the United States and Indonesia which takes seriously the policies and images developed during the 1920s and 1930s as a factor in post-1941 relations.[13] She argues that United States officials often had positive images of Dutch colonial officials and Dutch colonialism during the 1920s, but that these positive images were tarnished during the 1930s by what the United States officials perceived as intransigent Dutch policies toward incipient Indonesian nationalism. This complicated and contradictory set of images informed United States policy after the Second World War. Gouda finds that the legacy of the interwar period was part of the reason why the United States pursued a more flexible policy toward Dutch rule in Indonesia than it managed to conceive for French rule in Vietnam. Gouda has offered a valuable, persuasive answer to a vexing question about why the United States fought a devastating war in Vietnam but not in the apparently more important country of Indonesia. Yet her question is still a cold war question. Her chapters on the 1920s and 1930s function primarily to set up an analysis of the 1940s.

At first glance, Mark Bradley's work on United States relations with Vietnam from 1919 to 1950 appears similar to Gouda's, but Bradley offers a more far-reaching analysis.[14] His questions are not so deeply rooted in the cold war but rather come largely from the context of Vietnamese history. He explores how the United States, its presence, its history and culture, and its policies provided part of the context for how the Vietnamese could both conceive of and carry out their anticolonial struggle. Bradley's different set of motivating questions has led him to reconceptualize the chronology. His book covers the years 1919–50, but the pre-1941 chapters are not mere background fodder for the chapters on the Second World War and the early cold war. Instead, the important break in how Vietnamese and Americans began to imagine themselves in relation to each other came in 1919, not 1941 or 1945 or even later. The simple shifting of chronological focus had profound implications for what Bradley saw in the relationship between the United States and Vietnam.

The works of Gouda and Bradley have done much to help reorient histories of United States foreign relations away from the relentless assumption that everything changed in the mid-1940s, but merely shifting the chronological focus is insufficient. Other artificially drawn analytical lines, particularly those which separate the study of colonialism from foreign relations, also need to be redrawn or erased. Some scholars are tentatively surveying these traditional boundaries. Since about 1990, perhaps not coincidentally as the cold war was ending, historians of the United States have called insistently for "internationalizing" the field of United States history.[15] This effort has focused primarily on comparing developments in the United States, such as slavery, temperance, and suffrage, among many others, with similar ones elsewhere. In the field of the history of foreign relations, there has been an even more insistent call for "international history," especially by scholars in the realist tradition. It is now expected that most scholars of foreign relations will learn one or more foreign languages, and conduct research in the archives of at least two nations. But the work of many who call themselves international historians has often remained traditional in focus and conception: they study powerful men in powerful nations, and what these men said and did to shape and execute foreign policies.[16] Thus efforts to internationalize the history of the United States have continued to pay remarkably little attention to the United States as a colonial power.

That claim may sound strange, since titles with variations of the word "empire" in them abound, but the focus has largely been on "internal colonialism"[17] or the imperialistic characteristics of the United States in the postcolonial era. The era when the United States most resembled a traditional European colonial power because it ruled from across the ocean colonies that it had no intention of incorporating, ever, into its body politic, has been comparatively neglected by those most interested in the internationalizing project. The neglect has not been complete. Amy Kaplan noted in 1993 three absences in the study of United States imperialism: the absence of culture from the study of United States imperialism, the absence of imperialism from the study of United States culture, and the absence of the United States in postcolonial studies generally. She made this observation in the introductory essay of the influential *Cultures of United States Imperialism*, and the essays which followed it attempted to begin filling the absences. Still, even in that volume only two of the twenty-four essays explore United States rule in its colonies as a way of thinking about United States imperialism and culture.[18] The fourth absence, unnoted by Kaplan, is the absence of study of what United States imperialism means for both the future of colonialism and foreign relations after 1898.

Kaplan's manifesto, and other developments, prompted scholars to explore United States rule in its colonies, resulting in a body of work which has transformed understandings of many aspects of United States history. In many ways the twentieth-century culture and politics of the United States were formed in its experience as a colonial power. Paul Kramer demonstrates how racial conceptions in both the United States and the Philippines developed in the transnational setting of imperial rule, as well as how colonial rule (and its end) were shaped by ideas about race and nation. His fascinating study firmly sets what it has meant to be both Filipino and American in a transnational crucible, forged in the imperial relationship. He prompts reconsideration of the traditional narratives of race formation, United States anticolonial thought, immigration reform, and even ideas about representative democracy.[19] Works in the burgeoning field of United States imperialism studies, to provide a handful of examples, have demonstrated how the United States state developed as a result of the need to govern well in the Philippines, how Puerto Rican, Filipino, and American élites in cooperative and contentious relationships shaped ideas about political education throughout the empire, and how the field of public health in the United States developed as it did partly because important early projects began in United States colonies.[20] These explorations of the meaning of United States imperialism are among the most exciting recent developments in the field of United States history, but they maintain an exclusive focus on the dyad of colonizer and colonized, with comparisons at best occurring across the United States empire, and then only rarely.[21] This tight focus provides insight into the national histories of the United States, the Philippines, and Puerto Rico, but the international history of empire remains relatively untouched. With no comparative context, United States imperialism appears sui generis. This book, by contrast, places the United States as an imperial actor into the Southeast Asian imperial system, and demonstrates how United States imperialism both shaped and was shaped by that participation.

Scholars of European imperialism in Southeast Asia have tendencies to focus on dyads of colonizer and colonized as well; they might, for example, study British imperialism in Burma, possibly making comparative statements about British rule in India or Malaya or even Ghana, but rarely investigating how it resembles or differs from the experience of the French in Cambodia. Until recently scholars were attracted to the most elaborated parts of the colonial state, focusing their studies of British imperialism more on Singapore than on Sarawak, their studies of French imperialism more on Cochinchina than on Tonkin. This focus led to perceptions of European imperialism as highly formal, bureaucratized, and intrusive, and facilitated a superficial comparison with what was perceived to be an informal, ad hoc, and fleeting United States imperialism. Scholars of European imperialism more recently have begun to look at empire from the edges, seeing a broader range of imperial projects.[22] Studying United States imperialism alongside these European projects provides a richer, more complex picture of the breadth and depth of imperialism. A key focus of this new scholarship has been on cultural constructions of empire, as exemplified in the work of Ann Stoler on how the construction of colonial knowledge and ultimately governance rested on particular but shifting sexual and familial relations, and of Victoria de Grazia, who has reconceptualized the old notions of "informal empire" to explore how European acceptance of key elements of the "American way of life" led to foundational shifts in the governments and economies of European nations.[23]

The focus on culture in these works helps to explain the manifestation of

power and control in the lives of those living in empire, but the basic institutions which allowed colonial states to exercise that power, and through
which they did so, are not fully understood. Key parts of what actually allowed colonial states in Southeast Asia to exist are not part of the set of
assumptions held by scholars about the Southeast Asian imperial system.[24]
The narrative which follows cuts across those assumptions by focusing on
the particular ways in which United States power—economic, cultural, and
political—undergirded that imperial system.

‖‖‖‖‖‖

If we still lack knowledge and understanding of the basic functions and
structure of the imperial system in Southeast Asia, then we must turn our
attention to fundamental institutions of state power, such as trade regimes,
education systems, tax collection methods, and such policy-making bureau-
cracies as foreign and colonial ministries. Some of the subject matter in
this book therefore might appear traditional, even old-fashioned. But in the
end the picture of the imperial system in play, of the various types of foreign relations conducted, and of the construction of colonial knowledge and
power, is anything but traditional. The United States projected its power
during these years in ways which have eluded the gaze of traditional diplomatic historians, but which structured the choices, dreams, and possibilities
perceived by Southeast Asians and Europeans.

From 1919 to 1941 Southeast Asia increasingly became a coherent geographical region, in large part because of interactions among Southeast
Asian political activists as well as among the Europeans and Americans who
ruled over the colonies which made up the region. Its politics, economics,
and culture were dramatically shaped as well by forces emanating from
outside the region, and notably by the efforts and policies of Americans,
whether in government, in private business, or as representatives of cultural
institutions. Examining these boundary-crossing contacts and encounters
elucidates both the choices and the limits faced by all who worked to shape
Southeast Asia in their own interests. It also illuminates the complex, sometimes contradictory ways the United States projected its power to serve both
colonial and anticolonial goals in the region.

1

||||||||||||||||||||||||||||||||||||||||||||||||||||||||||||||||||||||||||||||||||||||||||||||||||||||||||||||||||||||||||||||||||||||||||||

New Threats and New Opportunities

Regional Cooperation in Southeast Asia, 1919–1929

The United States had had a presence in Southeast Asia at least since acquiring the Philippines as a colony in 1898. Its importance in the region grew after the First World War, amid a variety of changes in the relationship between Southeast Asian and European colonial rulers, in global economic relations, and in the role of the United States in the world. The First World War saw a reorienting of perspective, with the idea of a separate region of Southeast Asia, defined in opposition to both Europe and the United States, becoming possible. Although this idea would not be fully realized until the Second World War, elements of it were present in these interwar years, as Europeans worried about the political changes that the First World War had begun, Southeast Asians searched for ways to overturn political and economic structures they found oppressive, and Americans believed that their ideas about the future could reconcile the apparently contradictory impulses of the other two groups. The ideology of self-determination which Woodrow Wilson held up as an ideal challenged traditional imperialism in Southeast Asia. Yet Wilson had not much thought about the possibility of self-determination for places such as Burma and the Netherlands Indies.[1] When Southeast Asians began to make claims for independence based on political theories from Europe and the United States, Europeans and Americans reacted swiftly and cooperatively but could not find a way to quell the growing demands.

The political changes occurring in colonial Southeast Asia during the 1920s exemplify the characteristics of and tensions within the United States style of imperialism. United States officials worked easily with European officials on many political issues, relying both on a shared outlook and a sense of common identity. United States and European officials, in both colonial and foreign ministries, cooperated against communists, radical nationalists, and other perceived political threats to the existing order in the region. But European officials did not see the United States as a consistent, reliable ally in defense of the colonial regimes. Its participation was too often informal, even ad hoc, and Europeans grew frustrated with its failure to see that its actions sometimes undermined parts of the carefully constructed colonial system. Both Europeans and Americans did begin to see, with varying degrees of fear, that colonized peoples were forming groups with their own agenda and demands. Colonial powers found themselves in a defensive position, as Southeast Asians took the political initiative, offering increasingly persistent and organized resistance to colonial rule. In response, the United States throughout the 1920s projected its power in support of the colonial powers often enough to ensure that they maintained the upper hand.

Fighting the Public Opinion Battle

As part of the British government's preparations in 1918 for the peace conference at Versailles at the end of the First World War, Arnold J. Toynbee, member of the British delegation, wrote a memorandum in which he noted that the United States, with its talk of self-determination, had won the "public opinion" battle. It is not completely clear which public he had in mind, but he was very clear about the consequences of this United States victory. From that point on Britain would have to "consider" self-determination in governing its colonies. The idea of self-determination had been introduced, and the question could never again be whether it would arrive, but only when. Toynbee also thought that the United States public opinion victory carried some responsibilities: the United States, through the League of Nations, should take the lead in administering the mandate nations of the Mideast. The Arabs might trust the United States more because of that public opinion victory, but Toynbee also suggested that the United States would do a better job than the British in leading what he envisioned as a radically reformed, if not completely new, world.[2]

The French vice-consul in Manila, Maurice Paillard, shared some of Toynbee's enthusiasm. He predicted that the United States would grant independence to the Philippines at the end of the war. Paillard was not worried about the future of an independent Philippines, because the new peace treaty had provisions to ensure the independence of small nations, like the future independent Philippines but presumably also like a potentially independent Indochina, without "fear for their future."[3] In 1918 both Toynbee and Paillard seemed remarkably willing to grant to the United States leadership of a world in which international relations would work very differently than in the past.

The First World War was not worldwide in the same sense that the Second World War would be; fighting was less global. Yet it deserves to be called a "world war" because the resources of the world were necessary to fight it, and the political consequences reverberated widely. No battles occurred in colonial Southeast Asia, but some Vietnamese fought in the war, some Indonesians made money from increased direct trade with the United States in strategic war materials, and Woodrow Wilson's 14 Points offered a new basis for anticolonial movements. The Vietnamese anticolonial movement, members of which arranged to be in Paris during the peace conference, carefully prepared a list of demands (*revendications*) based on the 14 Points. The list is now famous, since it was signed by Nguyen Ai Quoc, who became better known as Ho Chi Minh. The drafters acknowledged that "the principle of national states" was making the transition from an "ideal" to a "reality," and put forth their modest demands for "a government of law, not decrees," freedom of education, the press, and assembly, and equality of legal rights as a means of creating democracy in Vietnam in eventual preparation for independence.[4] The group of Vietnamese meeting in Paris designed their demands specifically to meet the conditions of Wilson's self-determination rhetoric: they were radical only in the sense that all anticolonialism was radical. The demands were gradual; they acknowledged the universality of the ideals of the American and French revolutions. Toynbee was right. Wilson's self-determination had won the public opinion battle, even among Southeast Asian anticolonialists.

President Woodrow Wilson's postwar vision did include the possibility that the United States would provide military backing for the type of world order he proposed, as well as the certainty that the United States would provide political leadership of the League of Nations. He wanted to create what Gordon Levin has called a "liberal-capitalist internationalism."[5] The participation of the United States in the First World War demonstrated Wilson's willingness to fight for that order, while his commitment, minimal though it may have been, of troops to the anti-Bolshevik cause in Siberia in 1918–20 indicated that the First World War had not been an exception. But Wilson's vision did not prevail. The U.S. Senate, in the belief that it was following the wishes of the American people, rejected the Treaty of Versailles. The reason most often cited for the rejection was article X, the very article which acknowledged the responsibility of league members to back their commitments with military force.

The defeat of the treaty in the Senate only confirmed what had become clear about the applicability of self-determination rhetoric to Vietnamese, Indonesian, Burmese, Malaysian, or even Filipino anticolonial movements: not only did the United States government have no plans to support such movements with military or political power, it also had no plans to support them with more than a minimum of gradualist, tutelary rhetoric about the possibilities for self-rule *some day*. Still, the battle for public opinion that Toynbee referred to in his memorandum was not completely lost. First, hopes had not been raised so high as to have been dashed by the failure of the United States to support anticolonial movements. Second, in the statements of United States policymakers, the rhetoric of anti-imperialism coexisted with promises to maintain order in the world. Southeast Asians took some hope from the former, while colonial officials took their hope from the latter. U Nu, later to be a prime minister of independent Burma, learned about the American Revolution as a teenager and later claimed that he "drew sustenance" from its example during his participation in Burma's struggle for independence.[6] The French ambassador to Washington, Jules Jusserand, acknowledged in 1921 that American ideals were appealing to colonized peoples, and that as a result colonial rule increasingly rested on the "good will" of the colonized, but he also reported that all the colonial powers in Southeast Asia recognized Japan as a serious threat to order in the region. Jusserand predicted that the United States would cooperate with Britain, France, and the Netherlands to restrain Japan.[7]

Washington Conference and a New Politics for Southeast Asia

The election of a Republican president in the United States in 1920, Warren G. Harding, who pledged a "return to normalcy," confirmed that the Senate's defeat of the Versailles treaty, and the subsequent failure of the United States to join the League of Nations, were representative of United States foreign policy, not exceptions to it. But policymakers of the 1920s knew that a "return" to the foreign relations of the nineteenth century was neither possible nor desirable.[8] Although Southeast Asia rarely attracted the attention of the secretary of state or president, it was in many ways the ideal location for practicing the type of global foreign policy which the State Department of the 1920s wanted to conduct. It was also considered a natural location for the exercise of United States power, both because the United States had a colony in the Philippines and because it was a "Pacific power." Finally, it was an area where the exercise of United States power promised to be efficacious.

The Washington Conference of 1921–22 embodied two important components of United States foreign policy during the interwar period: a desire to shape the world by the American example rather than by force, and a Euro-American perception of the threat that Japan posed to the traditional order in Asia. The results of the Washington Conference included abolition of the Anglo-Japanese alliance and its replacement with the Four-Power Treaty, a loose agreement that the signatories would consult with one another should their "insular possessions and insular dominions" in the Pacific be threatened.[9] Akira Iriye has found that the importance of the Four-Power Treaty stems from an attempt by the United States, ultimately successful in his eyes, to end the diplomacy of imperialism. Perhaps, but officials from the European colonial powers at the time thought it much more important that the United States had finally come very close to guaranteeing the colonial order.[10]

Curtailing the Japanese naval buildup and attempting to enmesh Japan in a multilateral foreign relations organization, thereby restraining it from further expansion in China, are commonly cited reasons for British and United States participation in the Washington Treaty system. The United States briefing book for the conference identified the threat of Bolshevism in the region to be as great as the threat from an expansionistic Japan.[11] Communist parties had recently been founded in the Netherlands Indies (1920) and China (July 1921). The Comintern, holding its Third Congress when the Washington Conference opened, immediately recognized the public relations opportunity, and in January 1922 sponsored the first Congress of the Toilers of the Far East, attended by representatives from Japan, China, Korea, India, the Philippines, the Netherlands Indies, and Indochina. These chronologically overlapping but ideologically opposed conferences suggest that the struggle between the United States and Soviet visions for Asia had begun by 1921.[12]

The United States and Soviet Union were not the only countries to see Southeast Asia as a potentially fruitful area for the exercise of power. It was the one part of the world where all the great powers were present and actively attempting to shape the region's future. The relative success of each power had implications for its ability to realize whatever vision it had for its place in the world. In this way interwar Southeast Asia functioned almost as a laboratory in which the great powers tested formulas for cooperating with and competing against one another.

The Washington Conference raised the stakes in the public opinion battle that Toynbee evoked back in 1918. To avoid a naval arms race and in hopes of promoting a new kind of international relations in Asia, the United States had joined forces with the European colonial powers in Asia. Washington policymakers saw no reason for these policies to undermine their efforts in the public opinion battle. In the same briefing book for the Washington Conference, the United States presence was held up as an example for others: "This memorandum deals with the great social, cultural, educational, moral and religious contribution which America has made and is now making to the Orient, together with the large investments in money and life which this contribution has occasioned and the profound influence which it exerts."[13]

The various foreign policy goals of the United States might appear contradictory: anticolonialism alongside endorsements, secret or not, of the colonial order, concern about Japan's economic expansion voiced by those aggressively advocating an Open Door for United States investment and trade,[14] the rhetoric of self-determination in the same sentences with denunciations of Bolshevism as an illegitimate challenge to existing colonial governments. A Dutch newspaper article in April 1919 claimed that some Americans found it "hypocritical" to denounce Japan's activities in Asia while using the Monroe Doctrine to claim Central and South America as a sphere of influence for the United States.[15] In the administrations of Harding, Coolidge, and Hoover, however, these policies appeared completely compatible. As will be discussed in chapter 2, the Open Door was always more a policy to defend the interests of United States corporations than an idealistic statement about how foreign economic relations should work.

In no way could United States policy toward European colonialism during the 1920s and 1930s be considered anticolonial, if by anticolonial one means that United States policymakers should have been denouncing British, French, and Dutch rule and helping Southeast Asians to throw off the yoke. Washington officials can be said to have been anticolonial only in the sense that they wanted no further expansion of colonialism, and that they believed colonialism was ultimately an inefficient way to organize the world economy and political system. They saw only one desirable end to colonialism, and that was one which guaranteed to the United States access to investment and markets, and which did not enhance the security of its rivals, namely the Soviet Union and increasingly Japan. Thinking about United States foreign policy in this way makes it clear that for policymakers of the time, anticolonial rhetoric, calls for an Open Door for investment and trade, and refusals to formally join security alliances could coexist logically with a foreign policy principle of respecting the territorial status quo in the region, keeping the door closed to most foreign investment and trade in the United States colony in the Philippines, and maintaining informal agreements among regional powers to simultaneously restrain Japan and the Soviet Union and transform international relations in ways that Washington officials believed promoted peace.

The Washington Conference set up a structure of foreign relations in Asia, including Southeast Asia, which would last until approximately 1930. It identified the two threats to regional stability, Japan and Bolshevism, and tried to co-opt Japan by bringing it into the international system as an almost equal player. The policy for Japan had promise, because it envisioned that Japan would act like the Euro-American powers and over time would come to be treated like them in the international system. The threat posed by Bolshevism initially proved more difficult to address. The colonial powers of Southeast Asia during the rest of the decade grappled with how best to identify and resolve the problems that Bolshevism posed to colonial regimes and regional stability.

Threats to the Political Order in Southeast Asia

To colonial officials the years after the First World War were a period of burgeoning threats to their rule. As will be discussed below, international trade relations had shifted, providing colonies with more autonomy from Europe.[16] Anticolonial movements were nothing new, but after the First World War they seemed to be better organized, to reflect greater knowledge of European political theory, to appeal to a broader segment of society, and to be more resilient.[17] Official colonial responses to this political threat took two paths. The first was conciliation in the hope of cooptation. To this end colonial governments established, or expanded indigenous representation on, legislative councils in several of the Southeast Asian colonies during or soon after the First World War.[18] This practice was within the traditional pattern of colonial rule, in which "the colonial powers in Asia isolated each colony from its neighbors. . . . In each case the sovereign Western power wove a web of practically exclusive influence over and around the colonial nation, creating firm cultural and institutional bonds with it, and decisively cutting it off from significant communication with its regional neighbours."[19] Colonial governments had been islands, whether geographically or not, and the important lines of political (and economic) communication ran between colony and mother country. This also meant that the discourse of political dissent took place between Vietnamese and French, Burmese and British, Javanese and Dutch, and Filipino and American.

By the early 1920s colonial officials realized that new routes of communication had developed for Southeast Asians involved in the anticolonial struggle. Bolshevism provided a general rather than a particularistic explanation for why Southeast Asians had been colonized; they therefore had reason not only to feel solidarity across colonial state boundaries but also to seek personal contacts. The Comintern provided one structure for that cross-boundary contact. Southeast Asian communists could and did meet other Southeast Asian communists at the University for the Toilers of the Far East in Moscow, at centers in China and Singapore, and at Communist Party congresses. Colonial officials perceived Bolshevism as an international threat and decided that cooperation was the only way to meet the threat.[20]

Responding to Threats Cooperatively

Initially intercolonial cooperation took the form of visits by the governors general of the Southeast Asian colonies to their counterparts. The stated rationale, especially for the early visits, was for the governors "to establish personal and friendly relations with one another"[21] and to learn about methods of governance in the other colonies. The governor general of the Philippines, Leonard Wood, visited Java in 1923 for eight days. When his visit was initially proposed the United States secretary of state, Charles E. Hughes, heartily endorsed it, regarding the visit as potentially of "particular political service." The United States consul in Batavia, Charles Hoover, emphasized the eagerness of the Dutch to have the visit and of the Dutch governor general, D. Fock, to make a return visit.[22]

In the invitations and the reports of the governors to their superiors in The Hague and Washington there was no hint that the visit had a political agenda. Yet the reports of the United States consul, Hoover, and the vice-consul in Soerabaya, Rollin R. Winslow, indicate that both participants and the media covering the visit were mindful of colonial politics and foreign relations. Winslow particularly noted that the local media discussed at some length what the visit implied about the impact of potential independence for the Philippines on anticolonial movements in the Netherlands Indies, and how the Netherlands Indies could draw closer to the United States without risking involvement in a potential war with Japan.[23]

Fock's return visit to the Philippines in the following year was more explicitly political. Governor Wood, no fan of independence for the Philippines, told Fock of his belief that Philippine independence held two dangers for Dutch rule in the Netherlands Indies. First, it would encourage Indonesian nationalists. As noted above, many Dutch in the Netherlands Indies were already worried about that. Second, the Philippines would never be able to defend itself, and so would quickly fall under Japan's influence, if not under its direct rule. The Dutch would naturally find it more difficult to defend the Netherlands Indies, since they often perceived Japan as a potential enemy, a problem that they did not have with the United States. Wood informed Fock of his theories for a reason: he wanted Fock to communicate them to the Dutch minister in Washington, A. C. D. de Graeff, and request that de Graeff drop a subtle hint about the Dutch desire for the United States to remain in the Philippines. Wood believed that Washington officials held the Dutch in high regard, and that this hint would therefore be effective.[24]

Fock was intrigued, and although he told Wood that he was not involved in foreign policy, he strongly recommended consideration of this plan in his report to the Dutch colonial minister in The Hague on his visit. Wood's other proposal was more problematic. Wood proposed that the governors general of the colonies in Asia meet once a year to discuss common interests, but Wood envisioned that the Japanese governor of Formosa would not be invited. In fact Wood clearly believed that common action against Japan might be one of the main points of discussion among the European and American governors. Fock worried that such an exclusion would offend Japan, which the Netherlands did not wish to do. But during his meetings with Wood, Fock was as noncommittal about this proposal as he had been about the other, for which he had more enthusiasm.[25]

Although Wood's proposal to exclude the Japanese governor of Formosa indicates his belief that concern about Japan was one of the "common interests" of the colonial governors in Asia, a more pressing one was the spread of Bolshevism. During later exchanges of visits colonial governors did discuss the communist threat in their colonies, but these discussions only supplemented an ongoing exchange of information, assistance, and personnel in response to the threat of "communist propaganda."[26] Official concern about the impact of communism in Southeast Asian colonies developed quickly after the First World War, but regular exchanges of information and personnel, both formal and informal, took longer to evolve.

In January 1920 the Dutch foreign minister, H. A. van Karnebeek, and the United States chargé discussed the threat to the "eastern possessions" of the Netherlands posed by the "continual pressure of the Bolshevik material and intellectual forces constantly moving eastward." In 1920 solutions focused more on possible intervention in the Soviet Union and monitoring Bolshevik influence in Europe than on proposals for Southeast Asia.[27] By 1923 the Dutch had new worries, about organization campaigns in the Netherlands Indies run by the "bolshevist Kuomintang." Officials in Batavia and The Hague, fearing that these "undesirable elements" had "penetrated" the Netherlands Indies, tried to begin a dialogue with British authorities about, at minimum, more carefully monitoring the Kuomintang, and Sun Yat-sen especially, in Shanghai and Hong Kong. The British replied, as reported by the Dutch ambassador in London, that they did not find either Sun Yat-sen or the Kuomintang "such a danger" as the Dutch did.[28]

Dutch concern did not diminish, and British concern about communist influence in Singapore and Malaya slowly grew. In October 1924 Fock wrote to the Dutch colonial minister, de Graeff, about the general problem of "colonial propaganda, which the Soviet government desires to continue spreading in the British, French, and Dutch colonies." This letter prompted another attempt by the Dutch government to get the British and French authorities to participate in "an exchange of reports about communist propaganda." During the early spring of 1925 Fock sent letters to his counterparts in French Indochina, the Straits Settlements, and India. They all responded quickly and expressed their willingness, given certain conditions, to participate in exchanges of information.[29]

Dutch authorities in the Netherlands Indies initiated all the negotiations for cooperation; they had reason earlier than other colonial officials to worry about communism, since the first recognizably communist-influenced movement in the region, the Indies Social Democratic Association, was founded there in 1914 by the Dutch Marxist Henk Sneevliet. The Netherlands Indies was also the site of Asia's first communist party, the Perserikataan Kommunist di India (PKI), founded in 1920. By 1925 British and French officials also had reason to worry about communism. Thanh Nien, predecessor to the

Indochinese Communist Party, was founded in French Indochina in 1925. Communist parties were not formally established in India (December 1925) or the Straits Settlements (1930) until after Britain had provisionally agreed to participate in information exchanges, but organizations and trade unions sponsored by the Comintern, not to mention the Kuomintang, were active in these colonies.[30] By 1925 the three European colonial powers had found common interests powerful enough for them to begin creating their own cross-boundary structures, which would come to have a function similar to the Comintern's, providing colonial officials with opportunities to forge personal relationships and create bureaucratic structures across the region.

Strikingly absent from these proposals for cooperation by the colonial powers is the United States. Netherlands Indies officials apparently did not invite United States officials in the Philippines to participate in the regional information exchanges. Both the French and British governments did have arrangements to share information with the United States about communists in North America and Europe, and naturally considered extending them to Asia.[31] Aristide Briand, the French foreign minister, assessed the likelihood of participation by various countries in the inevitable international accord. He claimed that Britain, the Netherlands, Siam, Portugal, and France had no objections to cooperating to combat communism, while Japan was interested only in surveillance of Koreans, not other Asians. Briand regarded China as little better than Japan's pawn, and therefore believed it unlikely that China could meaningfully contribute. The United States, he thought, would not wish to join an international accord, because public opinion in the United States opposed "imperial cooperation," and because police in the Philippines effectively controlled radical groups there already.[32]

Briand did not claim that United States officials themselves were opposed to the idea of secret police cooperation. They appear to have favored it, and participated in it informally and ad hoc. In 1925 and 1926 United States officials showed interest in collecting information about communism and communists in and from Asia. In September 1925 F. W. B. Coleman, from the United States legation in Riga, sent a report with invented spellings of the names of two not-yet-famous Communists: the Comintern representatives "Tom? Tam Mallakka [Tan Malaka] and Iguen-Ai-Kvak [Nguyen Ai Quoc]" had helped to form the League of War against American Imperialism, with headquarters in Mexico.[33] The wide-ranging activities of Asian communists confirmed the beliefs of United States authorities that communism was a global and undifferentiated threat. In September 1926 the United States consul in Batavia, C. Porter Kuykendall, reported that contact between PKI members and the Comintern in Moscow "have increased to such an extent" that the police were instituting extreme suppression measures. The PKI attempted to escape surveillance by moving its headquarters to Singapore, but the Dutch were prepared, since they have "had eight secret service men in Singapore."[34] The apparent ease with which PKI members shuttled between Batavia, Moscow, and Singapore reinforced suspicions that communism posed a worldwide threat. Kuykendall's knowledge of Dutch agents in Singapore demonstrates the extent to which officials from the State Department had already forged relationships with colonial authorities willing to share secret information gathered by local intelligence agencies.

During 1925 and 1926 information sharing and cooperation among all the colonial powers of Southeast Asia was equally informal; details about the mechanics of sharing information had yet to be worked out. Netherlands Indies authorities proposed that consular officials in the colonies could be the conduits for intelligence sharing, much as information was shared by colonial governments with United States consuls in Batavia, Saigon, and Singapore. Foreign ministry officials from France, Britain, and the Netherlands rejected this method, because they had "natives" working in their consulates, to whom they did not wish to grant access to secret information. Officials in Paris thought that the solution was an international accord, which would formalize and standardize procedures among all participants. British officials, whether in London, India, or Singapore, were reluctant to commit to such an organization and instead proposed that the intelligence bureaus (police) in each colony share information and personnel directly as needed.[35] By late 1926 authorities in the Netherlands Indies, Singapore, and India had almost completed negotiations for formal exchanges, although informal exchanges of information and personnel had already taken place.[36]

These international cooperation arrangements had grown out of European and American fears about the possible consequences of communist organizing. The founding of only one communist party (two if China is considered part of the region), communist influences in a few anticolonial groups, and a couple of reasonably well organized strikes sufficed to prompt colonial officials to reconsider how best to serve their countries' interests as related to their colonies. Traditionally, colonial powers had defended their Southeast Asian colonies with little or no help from allies, and expected therefore to reap the bulk of the financial benefits as well. As the growth of communism, however tentative it was in the 1920s, prompted a rethinking of the nature of the threat the colonies faced, colonial authorities began to realize that they could meet this threat more effectively by cooperating. During the 1920s, moreover, the European colonial powers and the United States found that their political and strategic policies were more compatible than they had previously imagined. The success of those policies also seemed more assured if they cooperated than if they competed with or ignored one another.

An Impetus to Formal Cooperation

Before Britain and the Netherlands had finalized their formal arrangements for exchange of information and personnel, however, the PKI rebellion erupted, fulfilling the fears which had prompted colonial power cooperation initially. The PKI rebellion was actually two uprisings, one in West Java in November 1926 and the other in West Sumatra in January 1927. In Banten, a region in West Java, the uprising began during the night of 12 to 13 November, when several hundred men in the town of Labuan attacked the home of the assistant *wedana* (native official), kidnapping him and killing one of the policemen guarding his house while seriously wounding two others.[37] Similar outbreaks had been planned for the entire island of Java, but Dutch police intercepted the message, sent the day before in a code they had long since broken, and immediately instructed the Veldpolitie to arrest as many of the PKI leaders as they could.[38] They had more success in East and Central Java, where they prevented serious outbreaks, than in West Java, where the rebels attacked and killed a wedana and a Dutch railway official in Menes, seized a railway station, sabotaged railroad tracks, severed telephone and telegraph lines, and attacked government buildings. In Batavia hundreds of rebels attacked the Glodok prison in hopes of freeing the inmates, and instigated a strike among the *andong* (horse carriage) drivers. In both Banten and Batavia rebel attacks and street fighting lasted only one day to a week before the Dutch overwhelmed the poorly armed, frequently disorganized rebels. But two weeks later many Indonesians continued to stay off the streets at night, for fear of being arrested on suspicion of playing a part in the rebellion.[39]

The PKI leadership in West Sumatra had decided not to participate in the revolt of November 1926, because the local committee in Batavia, rather than the party's central committee in Bandoeng, had given the order to revolt. The PKI in Sumatra continued to meet and organize quietly as usual, but the membership grew frustrated and wanted to act rather than attend an "endless string of meetings." Local leaders acceded to their followers' demands and set the date for 1 January 1927. The rebellion followed a course similar to the one in Java. Initially the rebels killed one European and several native officials, destroyed some railroad tracks, and cut through telephone lines. Many were armed with swords and a few with revolvers, but these proved no match for the colonial police and army. Calm reigned by 12 January.[40] In the two rebellions a small number of people on the side of the colonial government were killed and a few dozen were wounded, but the poorly armed rebels suffered hundreds of casualties and an unknown number of deaths. Some of the wounded later died in overcrowded, unsanitary jails. More than ten thousand people were arrested for participation in the two uprisings, or for membership in the PKI or its feeder organization the Sareket Rayat (SR), or for being in the vicinity of the rebellion even if they did not take part. Some of the latter two groups were released after interrogation, but more than one thousand received jail sentences or were exiled to Boven Digoel, New Guinea.[41]

The rebellion never posed a physical threat to Dutch rule in the Netherlands Indies, but it quickly gained an importance out of proportion with its relative lack of success. It was the first communist-inspired rebellion in the colonies of Southeast Asia, and colonial governments feared that it would be the first of many. Initial responses to the rebellion by Dutch officials were particularly alarmist. The resident of Soerakarta, Nieuwenhuys, expressed his "opinion [that] it is now a struggle of life or death between the P.K.I. and the government. The Third International has spoken clearly on this matter: unlimited help." And the resident of the Preanger, Mühlenfeld, reported that the rebellion's goal was to establish a "Soviet Republic of Indonesia."[42] The fears of these officials were aroused by the instructions, monetary help, and inspiration which they believed, on the basis of little hard evidence, that Indonesian rebels had received from the Soviet Union.

The assistant resident of Pati, Ranneft, reported in late November that PKI and SR propaganda had been effective in persuading the "little people," presumably meaning Javanese peasants, to support the party. In interviews peasants told Ranneft of having been told by propagandists that the revolution would soon occur, and that afterward PKI or SR members would no longer have to pay taxes, would have their own land and stone house, would be able to ride public transportation for free, and occasionally would be permitted a ride in an automobile. Ranneft did not mention the scant resemblance of these promises to the theories of Marx and Lenin, but found it "ingenious" that the communists told each group of people only as much about communism as they were capable of grasping.[43]

This unquestioning acceptance of both the communist nature of the revolt and of Soviet assistance to Indonesian communists was echoed in the responses of Dutch officials in Batavia and The Hague. Governor General A. C. D. de Graeff almost immediately ordered a compilation of government-held information about the PKI. The resulting *Politieke Nota over de Partij Kommunist Indonesia* (Political Note concerning the Communist Party of Indonesia) was issued in January 1927, in a public but limited edition to the Volksraad and in a secret and strictly limited edition to government officials and selected foreign governments, including Britain, France, and the United States. Harry Benda has noted that "the compilers were governed by an evident desire to paint the uprisings as the product of a well-directed plot by Moscow in their selection of materials to report."[44] The *Politieke Nota* traced the history of the PKI from 1925, emphasizing instructions sent by Moscow to party members, quoting from political leaflets written by Tan Malaka and other party leaders, and reporting propaganda spread by the PKI through song, newspapers, and speeches. It also provided information about the PKI leaders, some of whom had visited Moscow and many of whom lived in Singapore, the Philippines, China, and the Netherlands. Their contacts with communists in those countries were also well documented. With all that as background information, it was not difficult for readers to believe the report's claim that PKI members had decided to rebel in "rigid compliance" with instructions from the Comintern.[45]

International cooperation to combat communism had in one sense failed when the PKI rebellion broke out. The rebellion was exactly what such cooperation was supposed to prevent, yet its outbreak also provided sufficient justification, especially in Dutch eyes, to continue tracking communists throughout the region. The Dutch and British quickly concluded their negotiations, and agreed on formal procedures for intelligence sharing in the Netherlands Indies and Straits Settlements by February 1927.[46]

French, British, and American consuls in the region were less alarmed by the PKI rebellion than Dutch authorities had been, but found it troubling nonetheless, and agreed that communism played some role, although their assessments of its importance varied. The French consul general in Batavia most closely echoed the assessments of Dutch officials. Initial telegrams reported "communist troubles" organized "according to a well-coordinated

plan developed in several localities." After the January uprising in Sumatra, a report by the French Foreign Ministry claimed that the PKI's "money
came from Russia; the arms were collected in Singapore; Semaoen and Tan
Malaka personally provided the liaison with Moscow and Southern China."
The revolt had occurred only after Moscow "gave the nod."[47]

British and United States consular officials acknowledged communist influences on the rebels but looked for less simplistic explanations. The British
consul general in Batavia, Fitzmaurice, emphasized that the leaders of the
PKI were definitely communist, reported their contacts with Moscow, and
asserted that these leaders probably did plan the rebellion, because it was
too secret and too well organized to have been planned by local leaders. The
"Communist rank and file," in his opinion, were "mostly ignorant coolies
quite incapable of appreciating the meaning of communism or of any ab-
struse political doctrine." The *Malayan Bulletin of Political Intelligence* came
to a similar conclusion, noting that if the Dutch authorities paid too much attention to communism they risked ignoring the discontent which had fueled
participation by "unthinking coolies" in the rebellion, and allowing "a new
and stronger nationalist party," which had learned from the PKI's failures,
to emerge. British assessments acknowledged the danger that communism
posed to colonial rule in the region, but recognized that other threats remained.[48]

The United States consul general, Charles Hoover, had a similar if more
colorful assessment. Worried that the overly dramatic Dutch descriptions
of the rebellion might have been reaching the United States, he took the
unusual step of sending a telegram to the U.S. Department of State to give
assurances that "Americans are in no danger." Almost immediately Hoover
had decided that the Java uprising was a "minor insurrection," definitely
not communistic but "merely another instance of what has been transpir-
ing periodically since the arrival of the Europeans here four hundred years
ago." It was an "anti-foreign" rebellion, typical of "reverts to savagery" who
had little or no knowledge of political matters. The leaders, Hoover stated,
may have known something about communism, but the "average ignorant
'orang'" probably had "no idea that such a place as Russia exists and . . . no
knowledge whatever of the communistic system."

At that early date Hoover could not have had much specific information on which to base his judgment; he seemed primarily to be extrapo-
lating from what he knew about the Indonesians' "close kinsmen" in the
Philippines. Hoover's language may have been more emotion-driven than

analytical, but he believed that he, rather than the Dutch officials, had a rational understanding of the rebellion. They had accepted the "convenient and fashionable appellation for all subversive movements throughout the world," while he believed that the rebellion had been caused by misguided discontent. The United States minister in The Hague was less willing to make sweeping judgments, but he did think that press reports stressing the communist nature of the rebellion were "alarmist." Both he and Hoover hastened to assure Washington that Dutch authorities had the situation well in hand, that the region was safe, and that complete suppression would take only a few weeks.[49]

Although to the French consul general the Dutch had an "extremely liberal" colonial policy, to the United States consul "caciquism" was as great a threat to the Netherlands Indies as communism, and to the British consul general, J. Crosby, communism was only the "immediate, . . . not the only or the ultimate cause of the rising,"[50] the skepticism of all three toward the Dutch insistence that the rebellion resulted directly from the influence of international communism was expressed only in secret reports to their own governments. When foreign or colonial ministry officials met with their counterparts from other countries, their discussions and actions reflected their common assessment that international communism posed a threat, and perhaps a more serious one in the wake of the PKI rebellion.

Overseas Policing: Cooperation against Communists Abroad

The Straits Settlements government had allowed the Algemeene Recherche Dienst to send two Indonesian spies, Soekandar and Soerosoedikdo, to Singapore in July 1926. Before their identity was unmasked in late September, these spies made several contacts with the PKI in Singapore, and discovered that PKI leaders planned to have a meeting there to discuss a possible rebellion. The meeting was being held up because Alimin and Moeso had not returned from their trip to Moscow.[51] After the PKI rebellion the police chief of the Straits Settlements proposed that the Netherlands Indies government "send over unofficially at least two men . . . who could board vessels coming from Java and Sumatra, etc., and warn the police of the presence of extremist leaders or well known communists."[52]

The Indies government agreed with this proposal and sent the assistant commissioner of the Batavia City Police, M. Visbeen, and two Indonesian detectives to Singapore in early December. One of their highest priorities was finding and arresting PKI leaders living abroad, especially those known to have taken a lead in planning the November rebellion. Visbeen had success remarkably quickly. On 21 December he met with the chief of police in Johore Baroe, Dalley, who told him that three days earlier the police at Kota Tinggi (twenty-seven miles from Johore Baroe) had held two men who looked very much like the pictures Visbeen had provided of PKI leaders. Visbeen immediately traveled to Kota Tinggi and at the police station found Alimin and Moeso, "who were noticeably startled" when they saw him.[53]

The British authorities took Alimin and Moeso to Singapore and held them in prison there. At this point the inadequacy of the informal arrangements between Straits and Indies authorities became obvious, because British and Dutch officials disagreed about what should happen to Alimin and Moeso next. The Dutch wanted them to be deported from Singapore to the Netherlands Indies, where they would be held by Dutch authorities preparatory to being banished to the island internment camp, Boven Digoel. Dutch regulations required no trial for banishment, only a decision by the governor general that the internee posed a threat to public order.[54] The attorney general of the Netherlands Indies, H. G. P. Duyfjes, reported that Singapore authorities "would not readily proceed with a [formal] arrest [of Alimin and Moeso] on the strength of the banishment-act." The Singapore attorney general was willing to hold them for a while, because he believed that they posed "a danger to the peace and order in the region of the Straits Settlements," but the sticking point was that Alimin and Moeso had broken no law in the Straits Settlements.[55]

The governor general of the Straits Settlements, L. N. Guillemard, "was disposed to regard sympathetically the request of the authorities of the Netherlands East Indies," but ultimately he was bound by British law, which required that only people who had directed their "communist or anarchist" propaganda against the British government could be deported. Guillemard did submit the case to the Executive Council of the Straits Settlements, which by a vote of 4–3 advised that Alimin and Moeso not be banished. Guillemard accepted this advice, acknowledging that "as the law stands at present the banishment of Alimin and Moeso would have been difficult to defend." He was nevertheless anxious to continue cooperating with Dutch authorities against communism, and proposed to London that the law in the Straits Settlements be changed. Guillemard argued that "the weapon directed against the Dutch to-day may be turned against [Britain] to-morrow," so he wished to have "power to expel from the Colony persons who are found to be active propagandists of communist or anarchist doctrines."[56]

Officials in London had "no objection" to amending the law, from the more restrictive requirement that deportation be "necessary for the public safety or welfare," to the more lenient requirement that it be deemed "conducive to the public good" by the secretary of state. They also noted, however, that deportation meant only that deportees were required to leave, and remain out of, British territory. The British government could not guarantee that they returned to their home country unless the other government chose the lengthier, more complicated process of extradition rather than deportation.[57] Upon being released from prison, Alimin and Moeso decided to leave Singapore, perhaps not surprisingly since their movements were being closely watched by both British and Dutch police. They were reluctant to visit the Dutch consul general, Kleyn Molekamp, to get passports, so the director of the Special Branch of the Singapore Police, R. Onraet, provided them with travel certificates for Swatow via Hong Kong, on the condition that they not return to Singapore. Dutch authorities did not believe that Alimin and Moeso had disclosed their true intended destination, and so informed Dutch Foreign Ministry officials in Bangkok, Manila, Shanghai, and Hong Kong to request that local government officials in those cities watch for their possible arrival.[58] The cordon proved too loose; Alimin and Moeso slipped through to Canton.

This episode stretched to its limits British willingness to engage in colonial power cooperation, but not in the way which initially appears most obvious. Information, including secret information gathered by intelligence agents, was shared without question between the British and Dutch authorities, and subsequently with United States and French authorities. The Straits police also did not hesitate to detain communists, as recommended by authorities from the Netherlands Indies. The limit arose when the Dutch asked the Straits authorities to take an action which circumvented British law. Deporting communists was not offensive to Straits officials, and they worked subsequently to change the law to allow any communists detained in the future to be deported.

But British officials in the 1920s felt that they were engaged in a power struggle in which their hegemony in colonial Asia was threatened by ideological and political developments. Bolshevik threats came from the Soviet Union, jeopardizing relations between colonial subjects and the mother country. Expansionist threats came from Japan, whose cries of "Asia for the

Asiatics" were less strong in the 1920s than they had been earlier or would be again, but still appealed to some. And self-determination threats that were in many ways more unsettling emanated from the United States, as its political and economic influence in the region grew. British power in the region depended on the Royal Navy acting as a stabilizing force, its strength discouraging the expansion of other great powers in the region. Within that context the British Commonwealth, and the sense of justice and fair play on which it rested, could inspire colonial subjects to strive toward member-ship and provided a model for other colonial powers to follow in governing. Given these ideas about the basis of British power, and perceived threats to that power, officials in the Straits and London alike believed that following legal procedure was more important than imprisoning two Indonesian com-munists. They perceived a connection between persuading Southeast Asians to believe in the superiority of British law and obeying the law themselves.

Communists in Manila and Informal Cooperation from the United States

Officials in Manila and Washington seem to have been less concerned about the apparent contradiction between advocating a government of law and ignoring laws in an effort to combat communism. In dealing with Tan Ma-laka, another PKI leader living abroad in whom the Dutch were interested—tracking him to Manila, tracking him within Manila, and then deporting him—United States authorities displayed little of the concern for laws and procedures that the British had displayed in their efforts with Alimin and Moeso.

The United States government, as noted above, had not formally agreed to participate in exchanging information, as the other colonial governments had done. Still, the United States consul general in Singapore, Addison Southard, seems to have been participating. He had close contacts with the Political Intelligence Bureau of the Straits Settlements. The Singapore police informed Southard that they had a letter from a man they believed to be Tan Malaka, from Manila, to Alimin and Moeso, who confirmed that Tan Ma-laka was in Manila. On 31 January 1927 Southard conveyed this information provided by the Political Intelligence Bureau, as well as photographs of the letter and of Tan Malaka, to the governor general of the Philippines. South-ard noted that the British and Dutch governments had worked together to capture Alimin and Moeso, and that Indies officials, who were "most eager" to find and arrest Tan Malaka, would be grateful for any assistance from officials in the Philippines. He recognized that the Philippine government might "find legal or other difficulty in arresting Tan Malaka," but suggested that Philippine authorities could "find some means of causing Tan Malaka to leave the Philippines," and then provide "prompt warning" to British and Dutch authorities about his destination.[59]

Dutch authorities were not far behind in requesting assistance from the Philippine government through the medium of the Dutch consul general in Manila, Bremer. Initially they asked only for assistance in locating Tan Malaka, and placing him under surveillance if he were found.[60] The "Secret Service" was more obliging than expected; it not only immediately instigated a secret search for Tan Malaka but asked Bremer to be ready to telegraph Batavia for instructions as soon as Tan Malaka was arrested. It took some time to find Tan Malaka. By early March the Philippine constabulary had questioned several informants who had seen Tan Malaka in the past, although they did not know him by that name. The informants promised to continue looking, and the governor's secretary, C. W. Franks, promised that when found, Tan Malaka would be deported. Franks further promised to notify Southard of his "destination and all intervening ports at which the ship will call."[61]

Communication among officials of the colonial powers in Southeast Asia proved better than that between Southeast Asia and Europe or the United States. In early June 1927 the Dutch minister in Washington, J. H. van Royen, requested assistance from the U.S. Department of State in locating not only Tan Malaka but six other PKI leaders whose photographs he enclosed. William R. Castle, assistant secretary of state, forwarded van Royen's request to the attorney general, John G. Sargent, and the secretary of war, Dwight B. Davis, who quickly replied that "the War Department does not engage in the surveillance of individuals in time of peace" and would therefore "be unable to furnish any information as to the parties in question." But a note attached to the front of this letter stated that the "interesting information" in van Royen's letter had been "informally" brought to the attention of the Military Intelligence Division, which would convey it to authorities in the Philippines through the Bureau of Insular Affairs.[62] By late June, of course, the Philippine authorities had already been searching for Tan Malaka for approximately five months, and according to State Department records the Military Intelligence Division had been so informed in March 1927.[63]

On the night of 12 August 1927 Tan Malaka was arrested in Manila as he left the editorial offices of *El Debate*, the newspaper for which he had been writing while in Manila. Tan Malaka wrote in his memoirs that he told the Filipino policemen who arrested him, "You've made a mistake in arresting me. Independence for my country will bring good for yours too." In response, one of the policemen "looked nervous and covered his ears," begging Tan Malaka, "Don't say anything more." Tan Malaka stayed in jail for only three days, during which he was interrogated about his Bolshevism, his entry into the Philippines, and his contacts with radicals in the country. During the week between Tan Malaka's release on bail and his deportation Filipinos protested in the streets and press against both his arrest without a warrant and the government's denial of his rights as a political refugee. Philippine authorities were not as interested as the British had been in defending legal principles, and on the night of 22 August the acting governor general, Gilmore, ordered Tan Malaka's deportation, before his trial had begun. Tan Malaka left early the next morning, on the S.S. *Susana*, for Amoy, China.[64]

The suddenness of Tan Malaka's departure was intended to thwart the growing protests in Manila, but it also hindered the Indies government's efforts to intercept Tan Malaka. Bremer, the Dutch consul general in Manila, was notified immediately of the decision by the United States, and sent a telegraph to Batavia with all the pertinent information. The United States consuls general in Batavia, Hoover, and in Singapore, Southard, were also immediately informed. The Dutch consul in Amoy did meet the *Susana* when the ship arrived, but Tan Malaka had escaped onto another ship in harbor with the help of a Chinese friend, who then put him up for a few months. This was only one of many escapes from seemingly impossible situations which enhanced Tan Malaka's reputation.[65]

Two things are particularly striking about this episode. First, all the decisions about tracking Tan Malaka, arresting and deporting him, and informing officials in Batavia, Singapore, and Amoy were taken by relatively low-level officials in the United States government, apparently without regard to the secretary of war's statement that it was not United States policy to engage in surveillance in peacetime. The consuls and colonial bureaucrats who took these initiatives did not expect to be reprimanded, and they were not. The United States government engaged in whatever surveillance it deemed necessary, whether or not in compliance with publicly stated policy. Southard in fact complained to Washington that an article in a newspaper in Manila about Tan Malaka's capture, which mentioned Southard's role, would "handicap his office" in collecting political intelligence and "weaken its standing" with intelligence bureaus of the Straits government. In response the secretary of state, Frank Kellogg, wrote requesting that the secretary of war, Dwight Davis, conduct an inquiry into this "unfortunate" revelation. The governor general's office apologized, explaining that the dangers of their actions "were not foreseen" and that they had believed Southard's actions "reflect[ed] credit" on the consular service.[66] The exchange confirmed that the collection of political intelligence, including from the Dutch and British secret police, was an expected part of the job of United States consuls in colonial Asia.

Second, United States officials searched several months for a man suspected of no crime in the Philippines, arrested him without a warrant, held him for three days before charging him with a crime, deported him on the eve of his trial, and informed Dutch officials of all the ports of call of the ship on which he was deported. With all the publicity surrounding Tan Malaka's arrest, why did United States officials so blatantly subvert the principles of justice which they believed demonstrated the superiority of United States colonial rule and of its vision for the region? The reason is that Tan Malaka's demonstrable connections with international communism made him too great a threat to the political order in the Philippines. Colonial administrators decided that Tan Malaka's continued presence was more dangerous than the potential criticism they would receive for failing to follow proper procedures. A key measure for United States colonial officials of the success of their country's anticolonial form of imperialism was that Filipino subjects had been educated into choosing the right kind of government.[67] As when Woodrow Wilson famously talked about teaching South Americans to elect good men, Filipinos also would demonstrate that they were ready for self-rule by choosing to run their government along lines acceptable to the United States.[68] The United States would rule in the Philippines until Filipinos passed this particular class, or test. But it would be easier for United States colonial officials to teach the proper lessons about democracy if Filipinos did not have to confront inappropriate choices. By keeping out communism, the United States had made the Philippines safe for democracy. International communism threatened to introduce dangerous new choices. In the interest of preserving the safe space for democratic choice, United States officials were willing to bend, even break, some laws.

New Allies, Permanent Enemies

Communism may have been, as the British consul general in Batavia reported, "almost extinct" in the Netherlands Indies after the PKI rebellion, but the colonial and foreign policies of the region had been permanently changed by this brief, unsuccessful, unexpected uprising.[69] The hesitant, informal steps taken in 1925 and early 1926 by the colonial powers to collaborate in combating the "communist menace" seemed, to the horror of colonial officials, to have been shown by the PKI rebellion, inadequate to combat the communist threat in their colonies. In spite of the swift, harsh repression that the Dutch immediately instigated, officials from all the colonial powers believed that repression merely treated the symptoms of a disease whose causes and course they only dimly understood.

Further information gathering was a first, necessary, insufficient step. Not surprisingly the Dutch led the way. In March 1927 they began summarizing intelligence gathered throughout the colony about anticolonial movements, particularly if radical or communist. These secret, monthly reports, called *Politieke Politioneele Overzichten* (police political overview), were sent to selected Dutch officials throughout the colony as well as to Dutch consuls and ministers in Peking, Tokyo, Bangkok, Washington, Cairo, Singapore, Shanghai, Hong Kong, Calcutta, Manila, Sydney, Saigon, and Jedda. It was left to the discretion of the diplomatic representatives whether and how much of the secret information to share, but the attorney general asked each to make it a first priority that "no Dutch interest be harmed," and to consider how likely it was that the other country would in return share information of use to the Netherlands Indies.[70]

Information exchanges among French, British, Dutch, and United States officials throughout Asia became more routine after the PKI rebellion. The distribution list for the secret *Malayan Bulletin of Political Intelligence* included the director of the Sûreté Générale in Hanoi and the advisor for Chinese affairs in Batavia, among other officials from regional colonial governments and British diplomatic representatives.[71] The United States consul general's office in Batavia had a "standing request" with the government of the Netherlands Indies for information about communism in the region, as he noted in his transmission to Washington of information about Filipino communists gathered by a Dutch official in Shanghai.[72] French police in Shanghai kept the Dutch equally well informed, and in November 1928 provided the Dutch consul general with Tan Malaka's address in Amoy.[73]

In October 1928 the Straits police sent a report to the attorney general in the Indies that the Anti-Imperialist League had become active in Singapore, apparently led by Alimin and receiving propaganda assistance from Tan Malaka.[74]

Not since its first appearance in the region had organized communism been so weak. The failure of the PKI rebellion, the subsequent repression and surveillance of the PKI by the Dutch, greater surveillance in other colonies, disputes between the Kuomintang and the CCP in China, and factional struggles in the Soviet Union combined to dramatically decrease the viability of communist parties throughout Asia in the late 1920s. And never had the anticommunist forces in the colonial governments been so well organized and coordinated. They had spies, information-exchange systems, friendly personal relationships between the various police forces, and island prisons, all prepared to meet the communist threat.

Yet even with this disparity of resources, colonial governments continued to imagine that the Soviet Union, China, and India successfully sent agents to organize Southeast Asians into communist parties, that local communist leaders had sufficient freedom of movement in the region to recruit party members, that propaganda circulated secretly, and that governments could easily be caught unaware by an uprising.[75] Choosing to emphasize secret police, spies, and intelligence gathering as necessary to contend with communist influence in their colonies merely underscored for these officials the mysteriousness of life in the colonies. They lived daily with a sense that things were not as they seemed to the Europeans and Americans, as well as a sense that a whole world existed about which they simply did not know. Communism appealed somehow within that unknown world, and they could never be sure that even the best spies, and intelligence, and cooperative systems had penetrated that world adequately.[76]

The effect was to reinforce at intellectual and administrative levels the growing sense, as F. Marshal of the Union Coloniale Française wrote, that members of the "white race" should support one another when up against "asiatic peoples."[77] Asian radicals were beginning to have experiences of their common interests as well, when they fled to other Asian countries, met other Asians at Communist Party congresses, or hid fellow Asians from political authorities. Few colonial officials questioned the value of "white race" cooperation, but its goal of standing in opposition to Asians, stated with increasing clarity, undermined the justifications that colonial officials offered for their rule, namely that it was "civilizing" and tutelary.

The United States claimed most vigorously to conduct its colonial policy solely for the benefit of the colonized, and therefore it might seem to have been the nation most likely to reject the vision of colonial powers ("white race") versus colonized ("asiatic peoples").[78] United States officials held up their efforts to improve education in the Philippines, the concrete steps already taken to include Filipinos in governing their own country, and promises made to grant independence as soon as possible as signs that the United States had "different aims" in the region than the European colonial powers did. When the governor general of the Netherlands Indies in 1929 indicated his desire to include the Philippines on a round of visits he was making to British Malaya, Siam, and French Indochina, the United States consul general in Batavia expressed concern to officials back in Washington that the "natives" would view such a visit as evidence of colonial power solidarity, while Assistant Secretary of State Nelson T. Johnson argued that the United States should not align itself with colonial policies, "either in approval or dissent."[79] These American officials wanted to continue what had until then been the relatively successful United States policy of remaining aloof and setting the best example, in their minds, of colonial rule.

Other officials in Washington, in an opinion eventually signed by the secretary of state, thought that the United States could have prestige and cooperate with the other colonial powers. "[The] strength of our position," they wrote, stems from "knowledge there that our purpose is promotion of their interests and local self-government," and therefore de Graeff's visit would not lead Filipinos to see "Western solidarity" between the United States and the Netherlands. In the end de Graeff did not visit the Philippines, although in 1931 the governor general of the Philippines, Dwight F. Davis, did visit the Netherlands Indies. It might have been possible to maintain for another two years the appearance that the United States was not in solidarity with the other colonial powers, but in important ways the United States decision to participate regularly, if informally, at all levels of the secret police efforts against communism had already restricted United States foreign policy options in the region. Not only had United States officials already by the 1920s decided that communism and legitimate nationalism were mutually exclusive, but they had also proved willing to subvert their country's principles and laws to prevent the spread of communism and communist influences. The scale was small compared to what would later become routine during the cold war, but these first steps set an important precedent for how anticolonial movements were evaluated both before and after the Second World War.

The politics of imperialism promoted cooperation among the imperial powers during the 1920s, including the United States. Officials from France, the Netherlands, Britain, and the United States perceived communism as a common, dangerous threat to the colonial order. That perception, and not surprisingly the cooperation, would persist throughout the interwar period and into the cold war. It was a measure of the degree to which United States officials perceived their purposes as similar to those of the Europeans that United States policies for the region were sometimes said to further an eventual end to formal colonial rule, while concrete actions generally supported the existing structures of colonial rule.

Officials in Washington were willing to discard, quietly, their policy of staying aloof from the other colonial powers to combat what all colonial officials saw as the common menace of communism. The collaborative structures initiated during the 1920s would provide interpretive frameworks which policymakers could draw on when colonial regimes faced much more substantial threats after the Second World War. Yet American officials were willing to collaborate in these limited political areas only because they believed that the economic power and the stature of the United States remained a still more persuasive example of the superiority of the United States system. So even while political cooperation in the region increased, economic competition remained fierce, not least because United States officials believed that this was the more effective strategy for creating a world friendly to the United States.

2

||||||||||||||||||||||||||||||||||||||||||||||||||||||||||||||||||||||||||||||||||||||||||||||||||||||||||||||||||||||||||||||||||||||||||||||||||

"The Highways of Trade Will Be Highways of Peace"

United States Trade and Investment in Southeast Asia

If Europeans and Americans involved in Southeast Asia increasingly shared perceptions of the political threats to their desired order in the region, and acted in concert to combat those threats during the 1920s, they parted company over economic policies for colonial Southeast Asia. Americans, in both private and official positions, unhesitatingly promoted American business. They believed that United States investment in colonial Southeast Asia and trade with it benefited Americans and Southeast Asians alike, and had the potential to make irrelevant the aspects of colonialism that Southeast Asians chafed under. If Europeans were enlightened and forward-thinking, these same Americans believed, they would perceive that capitalism American style was the future not merely for the region but indeed for the world, and would acquiesce. Failure to do so simply meant that Europeans were backward-looking themselves, and deserving of whatever ill consequences ensued. With this confidence that their brand of capitalism was both beneficial and profitable, Americans marched into Southeast Asia impatiently demanding to be accommodated. The confident demands on behalf of western capitalism have sometimes been understood as intended to undermine colonialism, at other times as supporting a form of colonialism. Those making these demands usually had no strong opinions about the morality of colonialism one way or the other. Rather, they believed that if the requisite economic changes were made, the problems of colonial rule would resolve themselves, because the rising economic tide would lift all boats and submerge the issues which caused conflict.

It was not inconsequential that Southeast Asia was a source of key raw materials necessary to fuel United States industries. Often these raw materials were not available elsewhere in sufficient quantities. The foremost was rubber, a commodity of relatively recent importance. Southeast Asia before the First World War had been a region of modest interest at best to United States businessmen. After the war it was the source of more imports than China by far, and as a trading partner it was on a par with Japan, Central America, and South America.[1] Even if United States economic involvement in colonial Southeast Asia was clothed in the language of improving Southeast Asian lives, and even if involved Americans believed the rhetoric, the involvement was a necessary underpinning to United States world power during the interwar period. United States officials pursued United States interests, particularly regarding oil and rubber, ruthlessly. Europeans often scrambled to devise policies which would protect their own interests and also be acceptable to the United States. Struggles over both rubber prices and oil concessions, the two most prominent struggles in which Europeans and Americans engaged in these years, demonstrate the perception which Americans had of the relationship between economic and political power, a vision which Europeans generally found as unsettling as it seemed inexorable.

Neither United States officials nor American businessmen expressed much interest in the issue of imperialism, positively or negatively. In the 1920s no one yet argued that independence might lead to better economic conditions in Southeast Asia for United States companies. The European colonial governments often imposed policies that United States businessmen did not like, but this merely prompted involved Americans to work toward changing the European laws and policies, not explicitly undermining European rule. These Americans accepted as a given the basic structure of imperialism and did not worry that their actions might weaken or eventually overturn it. Both United States officials and American businessmen viewed capitalism along American lines as a positive good and a model for the rest of the world. Imperialism was useful only so long as it was compatible with the spread of American economic power.

The Meaning of United States Economic Power

The First World War had a tremendous impact on economic structures in colonial Southeast Asia. Traditionally, colonial produce had been shipped in British, Dutch, and to a lesser extent French bottoms from entrepots in each colony to the major commercial hubs of Europe, especially London and Rotterdam. European trading companies purchased the colonial goods in Southeast Asia and sold them in Europe to Americans and other Europeans. Virtually all the profits from colonial products accrued to citizens of the colonial powers, since they owned the plantations, mines, and import-export companies. They also controlled the import business into the colonies, such as it was, of manufactured or luxury goods from Europe, though before the First World War the colonies were unimportant markets, since there was little incentive to provide the mass of people with sufficient funds to buy imported goods.

The disruption of shipping during the war changed the situation dramatically. As J. S. Furnivall, colonial bureaucrat and scholar of the region, wrote, Europeans living in Southeast Asia began to take more interest in "colonial policy" and to "participate in the direction of colonial affairs." As a consequence, they oriented themselves toward Asia rather than Europe.[2] They began to develop regional markets for colonial produce, and to realize that local manufacture could be cost-effective. A critical part of this development was increased direct trade with Japan, China, and the United States. The *Straits Times*, the major English-language newspaper in Singapore, called this the "American invasion" during the First World War, and reminded readers of their need to "resist" it.[3] Direct trade, accompanied by increased direct investment, fit well with United States plans for economic activity in the region after the war.

The general principles of United States economic activity in the 1920s were self-sufficiency, advocacy of an Open Door for trade and investment, and emphasis on the "civilizing influence of commerce," or to be more specific, the Americanizing tendencies of United States trade and investment.[4] Herbert Hoover, as secretary of commerce from 1921 to 1928 and to a lesser degree as president from 1929 to 1933, worried most about self-sufficiency. He believed that one of America's strengths was its ability to depend substantially on its own produce and a domestic market. But he recognized the dangers of economic isolation, not least because the United States had no sources within its borders of key products such as tin and rubber, the bulk of which came from Southeast Asia. Hoover's policy then was to avoid as much as possible being dependent for these products on sources that were foreign-owned or controlled by foreign governments. In Southeast Asia this policy would profoundly alter the rubber market, and to some extent United States attitudes about oil concessions.[5]

The policy set forth in John Hay's Open Door Notes (1900–1901) regarding China had a relatively specific meaning. It was supposed to guarantee that neither the European powers nor the United States would institute exclusionary economic spheres of influence in China. But United States policymakers quickly found the general concept appealing for economic policy worldwide, as a way of arguing for greater access for United States companies. The Open Door as applied in Southeast Asia did not mean equality of access for all countries, or "fair field and no favor." It did mean a demand from Washington that United States imports encounter no higher trade barriers, and that United States companies face no greater obstacles to direct investment than those faced by any other country, including the colonial ruler. The European colonial powers had been accustomed to treating their colonies' economies as extensions of the domestic economy, and to reserving certain trade and investment privileges for their countrymen. Even Dutch officials, who proudly touted their country's long history of "open door" trade policy in the Netherlands Indies, were somewhat taken aback by demands for oil concessions for United States companies in the Indies, since none were held by non-Dutch companies. When United States officials demanded acquiescence in the Open Door policy as envisioned in Washington, it often looked to European officials like a scheme for creating a wedge between the colonies and their rulers, a space which American companies would then fill.

In an unguarded moment, many in positions of power in Washington might have responded that this was precisely their intent, because encouraging the spread of American enterprise was a positive good for the world. In colonial Southeast Asia, American business had a double opportunity. The superiority of American methods—already evident, they believed, in the way the United States ruled in the Philippines—would be further demonstrated in the organizational and labor policies of United States factories and plantations, while the abundance promised by the American way of life was powerfully evident in the well-made, relatively inexpensive American consumer goods on sale in the colonies, and on view in the Hollywood movies showing there. For Washington officials, though, the issue went beyond an altruistic desire to spread the American bounty throughout the world. They believed that United States products, United States business methods, and United States labor policy would Americanize the world, even the "backward areas" like Southeast Asia.[6] Economic interdependence alone would not necessarily create a peaceful international order, but an interdependent and Americanized world would have the same interests as the United States, making peace imaginable. In this imagined world formal imperialism might be irrelevant. Yet most United States businessmen had little concern about imperialism for its own sake. They worried merely that political structures must be sufficiently stable and predictable for their business plans to flourish. Given their racist assumptions about the incapacity of Southeast Asians, most Americans believed that colonial rule was necessary for at least the foreseeable future.

For Washington officials this link between an economic system friendly to America and good governance was strong, and often explicitly drawn. One of their justifications for the continued delay in granting promised independence to the Philippines was that Filipinos as yet owned few businesses and showed little entrepreneurial spirit. The best Filipinos, which for American observers meant the best-educated and the most comfortable in American company, were likely to want secure positions in the colonial government rather than to begin a company and make their own fortune. That decision was seen as a weakness.[7] Colonial powers were judged by the same standard. Washington officials praised Dutch rule more frequently than either British or French rule, citing Dutch commitments to free trade and a relatively liberal foreign investment policy, as well as the fact that Indonesians could and did become planters, some of them becoming quite wealthy growing pepper, copra, and rubber.[8] Dutch economic policy in the Indies fit Washington's vision for how colonialism could benefit its subjects, and slowly develop them.

The three principles—self-sufficiency, Open Door, and the civilizing, Americanizing influence of United States trade and investment—guided United States officials, whether in Washington, Batavia, Saigon, Singapore, or Manila. European officials also recognized United States power, but naturally did not see it as benign. They had different visions of Southeast Asia's present and future, and they fought throughout the 1920s to realize their own visions, not American ones. For Europeans the loss of profits and control which the expansion of United States business seemed to presage was only part of their concern. They worried also that the informal, ad hoc, uncommitted style of United States political policies for the region, particularly on security issues, when combined with economic hegemony, was an invitation to unsatisfied powers like Japan and the Soviet Union to expand their military and political reach. This European concern provided an additional tension to the economic struggles, one which United States representatives often failed to perceive.

The First World War and Direct Trade with the United States

In April 1918, toward the end of the First World War, the French vice-consul in Manila reported that during the war the United States and Japan had to a large extent replaced France as leading importers into French Indochina. Initially he had not been concerned about this situation, but in conversations with some United States officials in the Philippines he learned that they expected United States companies to continue importing products into Indochina and expand the scope of the trade, particularly the direct trade between Indochina and the Philippines. If the United States, Indochina, and the Philippines expanded their mutual trade, it would hurt French "national commerce," he wrote, particularly because the Philippines government was then promoting a policy of self-sufficiency in rice and cattle production, Indochina's two main exports to the Philippines.[9] If the trade had developed as the vice-consul predicted, there would have been reason for concern in France, because Indochina sold most of its rice—its major export by far—to other countries of Asia, while it purchased most of its imports from France, which meant a small but certain profit for French manufacturers and the French government.

The Philippines never developed self-sufficiency in rice, and high French tariffs helped prevent the trade between the United States, the Philippines, and Indochina from achieving its potential, but the French vice-consul's concern for France's "national commerce" was similar to the concern of other European officials about the United States economic presence in Southeast Asia. British and Dutch officials also worried about their "national commerce," as well as their hold on their colonies. As the proportion of Netherlands Indies and British Malayan exports sold to the United States grew, which it did almost every year in the 1920s, and United States officials pushed for greater access to markets and investment in those colonies, European officials began to worry that given the chance, Americans would gladly control the economies of Malaya and the Indies, and leave only the messy governing to the British and the Dutch.[10] The assessment by the United States consul general in Singapore in a confidential report in 1919 to the Department of State that the British concern stemmed from "jealousy" because of United States "prominence . . . as a world power" and from "the certain recognition . . . that the United States is to become a formidable rival in foreign trade and commercial affairs in outlying British colonies" would only have confirmed what European colonial officials suspected.[11]

Table 1

	1913	1923	1925	1927
Malaya	24,600	153,000*	361,117	261,753
Netherlands Indies	5,359	52,457	100,961	86,664
Philippines	16,561	80,000	109,397	115,586
Indochina	> 50	2,000*	1,000	1,283

*Indicates average for years 1921–25.
All figures in thousands of U.S. dollars.

Trade statistics bear out assessments that United States economic strength in colonial Southeast Asia mirrored its growth in Europe during the First World War. On average the value of international trade for all the Southeast Asian colonies increased during the 1920s. Those colonies producing important industrial products, such as rubber, tin, and oil, saw their trade with the United States increase dramatically, as table 1 demonstrates.[12]

In addition to these increases in the value of United States trade with colonial Southeast Asia, the United States share of the international trade of the Netherlands Indies and British Malaya, the primary rubber- and tin-producing colonies, also shot up. For the Netherlands Indies, for example, the United States share of its exports increased from only 2.2 percent in 1913 to 9.9 percent in 1923 and 15.9 percent by 1926. Only the Netherlands (16.6 percent) and Singapore had greater percentages, and many of the exports to Singapore were transshipments, often to the United States. Malaya shipped 12.1 percent of its exports to the United States already in 1913, but the percentage increased to 36.1 by 1923, and 47 by 1926. Britain's share in 1926, by contrast, was approximately 16 percent.[13] The United States was quickly replacing Britain and the Netherlands as the most important trading partner of their colonies.

These figures represent the "American invasion" which so worried European colonialists, but United States officials read them differently. From Herbert Hoover as secretary of commerce to Rollin R. Winslow, the United States consul in Soerabaya, the Netherlands Indies, they urged United States companies to establish their own purchasing agencies throughout the colonies and thereby do away with the European middleman. A greater share of the profit to be made from these goods would then go to Americans. An even better solution, of course, would be for Americans to buy rubber plantations, acquire tin and oil concessions, and control entire markets overseas by "integrating backward" from United States factory to Indies rubber plantation.[14] Hoover took the Bureau of Foreign and Domestic Commerce (BFDC) "under [his] own wing" and "encouraged American rubber manufacturers to plant rubber" to evade British attempts to raise the price of rubber by restricting production.[15] Winslow, in Soerabaya, deplored that there was "not a single American purchasing agency or firm in all of Netherlands India," especially since not only England and the Netherlands had plenty but Germany and Japan also bought directly for their own use, and often earned the middleman profits on products purchased for the United States. Profit was not the only loss, according to Winslow. American prestige suffered, as when the only United States bank in the colony closed after a period of no profit. The British bank "in a similar position . . . [gave] no indication that it will give up 'under fire.'" Winslow reported Dutch concerns that a "war in the Pacific is imminent and inevitable," and worried that the lack of commitment by the United States to purchasing agencies, banks, and direct investment would be seen by the Dutch as a sign that the United States would provide no help against the Japanese in the event of war.[16]

Hoover and Winslow urged the same policy, but for slightly different reasons. Hoover wanted "fair prices" for the raw materials not produced in the United States and a steady supply of them, sought exports to the United States of "commodities which were less competitive with American industry," and used BFDC agents as "hounds for American sales." Direct purchasing and investment were for Hoover means to the end of strong United States exports and fair prices for anything the United States had to import.[17] Winslow, and many other foreign service officers, hoped for all that plus a bit more. Winslow had mentioned Dutch fears of a war in the Pacific, and implied that a stronger United States economic presence in the Indies would prod the Dutch into preparing to side with the United States in that eventuality. The economic advisor in the Department of State, Stanley K. Hornbeck, mentioned that the department could use the leverage of a loan request from the Indies government to "open up the oil resources of the Dutch East Indies to American capital." The presence of American capital might have the additional benefit of helping the Indies government "feel that this would tend to lessen the possibility of aggression by Japan."[18]

It was not departmental policy to use foreign loans as the kind of leverage Hornbeck had suggested, although the Dutch were allowed to think that it might for a little while. Hornbeck's other suggestions were less controversial within the department. Washington officials believed that pro-

moting direct trade and investment in colonial Southeast Asia, apart from
the inherent good of increasing the economic strength of the United States,
could serve other purposes that might not be so easily achieved if pursued
explicitly. The United States consul in Batavia, Charles Hoover, in 1923 suggested that these other benefits were a reason for continuing efforts to help
Standard Oil of New York acquire oil concessions in the Indies. The United
States policy of "non-interference in old world affairs," combined with the
predominance of British capital in the Indies, convinced the Dutch that they
would have to rely on Britain, not the United States, upon the outbreak of
what the Dutch believed was an inevitable war with Japan. Hoover hoped
that the planned visit by the United States fleet to the Netherlands Indies in
1923 would persuade the Dutch that the United States was also strong and
willing to assist allies, but he also urged continued economic efforts in the
realm of oil concessions and further loans to the Indies government.[19]

Washington officials understood that the Dutch hoped to use their colony's
riches to attract protectors, and seemed to believe that was the right policy
for a "small country." Foreign service officers, during their training sessions
in Washington, heard that the Dutch willingness to grant concessions in the
Indies to foreigners was prompted by their desire to obtain "their moral,
political, and perhaps, if necessary, military protection against possible ag-
gressions by Japan."[20] British officials also believed that Japanese "prestige"
would "increase . . . throughout Asia" if the United States pulled out of the
Philippines, because that would diminish the United States commitment to
the region. F. Ashton Gwatkin, of the British Foreign Office, declared that
for the United States to grant independence to the Philippines would be a
"calamity to the British Empire."[21] British, Dutch, and United States officials
all understood how security issues, investment policies, and trade mechanisms had become intertwined in the Pacific after the First World War. The
increase in United States economic and military power meant that colonial
governments usually saw it as being in their best interest to welcome American companies, purchases, and capital. Often they worked to entice Americans to buy and invest more, knowing that this was one of the few ways
to possibly secure protection from the United States against the perceived
common enemy.

Commitments were slow in coming from Washington, however. Dutch
and British officials had to make do with their mutual assurances of protection, which neither side believed would suffice. Wariness about the United
States commitment was often manifested when the British and Dutch de-

signed policies to protect their own economic interests at the expense of the United States. British and Dutch policies for rubber and oil provided the best opportunity for London and The Hague to attempt to assert their remaining powers. Economic competition among the imperial powers within the imperial system was nothing new, but the growing economic dominance of the United States threatened not merely the range of colonial control by other imperial powers. It seemed possible that United States economic methods might undermine the traditional structures of imperialism. Europeans did all in their power to attempt to curtail or co-opt the United States challenge.

Rubber Restriction and the Decline of British Economic Hegemony

Rubber, which became a profitable plantation crop in Southeast Asia around the turn of the century, had the potential to be enormously profitable for those who controlled its production and marketing. The traditional tropical products of Southeast Asia had for decades produced riches for European imperialists, and the United States bought a large quantity of these products. It was the primary purchaser of Indies tobacco, tapioca products, kapok, sisal, pepper, and quinine.[22] Malaya traditionally had sold much of its tin, and the Philippines virtually all of its sugar, coconut products, and hemp, to the United States.[23] But the United States did not need any of these products, perhaps with the exception of tin and quinine, for its industrial plants to thrive.

Once British botanists discovered that rubber trees grew well in Malaya and Ceylon, and rubber plantations in those colonies could easily surpass the level of production possible from tapping wild rubber trees in Brazil and central Africa, the race to control rubber began. The stakes were high, since rubber was a key component in the manufacture of important products for industrializing America, like tires for bicycles and cars, insulation for electric wires, rubber flooring, and the hoses, belts, and packing which enabled motors to run and plumbing to work. Before the First World War the nature of the race was not clear. In the early years of the century supply and demand seemed to work as they were supposed to do, with high prices for rubber leading to vast increases in planted areas and subsequent price declines.

Two factors would shape the race for the control of rubber after the First World War. First, the United States, which consumed approximately three-fourths of the world's rubber supply, had only one potentially suitable location for growing rubber under its control—the Philippines. The consuming interests, from the United States, and the producing interests, primarily the British in Malaya and Ceylon, fought bitterly for advantage. Second, the lag of approximately five years from the planting of a rubber tree until the time when it can be profitably tapped for rubber guaranteed that market forces would never efficiently organize rubber production, because supply could not be immediately responsive to demand.[24]

Rubber manufacturing in the United States was not the only industry to suffer in 1920–21 from having borrowed too much money at high interest rates to fulfill plans for rapid and unending growth. A general depression settled on the country after the war and affected raw materials producers around the world, not least rubber growers. Prices for rubber plummeted after the war, and by 1920 the price reached a low point for that year of approximately one-third the level that had prevailed in 1918. The situation did not improve: in June 1922 rubber sold for less than one-fourth the wartime price.[25] American manufacturers simply were not buying, relying instead on stocks they had built up. Rubber plantation owners pleaded with the British government for assistance. As James Lawrence, an American involved in the rubber industry, wrote, they found a more ready ear in Parliament than other producers in trouble did, because "any burden imposed upon rubber consumers in order to help rubber producers would rest lightly upon England and heavily upon the United States."[26]

The British government's offer of help to rubber growers took the form of the Stevenson Plan, named after Sir James Stevenson, appointed head of the committee to investigate the rubber situation by the secretary for the colonies, Winston Churchill. This plan proposed to stabilize the price of rubber by restricting the amount allowed to be sold whenever the price dropped below a certain level. From the beginning Churchill did not hesitate to point out that British producers and the British government benefited from this plan, while American consumers paid the price. Restriction, he said in September 1922, had the "double object of saving the rubber planters, and, by making the Americans pay, contribute[ing] materially to stabilizing the dollar exchange [against sterling]."[27] Rubber was also, according to Churchill, Britain's "principal means of paying" its "debt to the United States," and higher prices were one way of making the United States carry the costs of Britain's debt.[28]

With sales of rubber initially limited under the Stevenson Plan to approximately two-thirds of "standard production," which was supposed to be the production of 1919–20, prices began to increase sharply. By 1924 average prices had regained and surpassed the levels of 1920, and by 1925 were back nearly to the wartime averages. The peak of $1.21 per pound reached in 1925 was more than double the price in 1918. By 1925 stocks of rubber, especially in the United States, also were falling dangerously low. Hoover, the secretary of commerce, refused to allow the United States rubber manufacturing industry to be held hostage to British rubber producers, and he launched a campaign to undermine the Stevenson Plan. With his usual eye to public relations, Hoover devised slogans such as "Help Hoover against the English Rubber Trust" and "1776–1925," as well as articles in magazines about how people could participate in conservation and reclamation programs by learning ways to make their car tires last longer, and recycling them when they did need to be replaced. Hoover credited these efforts when prices for rubber dropped back to $0.40 per pound in 1926 and continued to fall for the rest of the decade. He later recalled the campaign with pride: restriction "so stimulated production in other countries, and new substitutes at home . . . [that rubber was] overproduced and sold at a loss by the producer. While such low prices were not in world interest, they at least demonstrated that the United States could protect itself."[29]

In this case Dutch and Indonesian rubber growers probably did more to "protect" United States interests than did the U.S. Department of Commerce. In 1922 British interests in Malaya and Ceylon controlled approximately 70 percent of the world's rubber production. After British-owned plantations in the Netherlands Indies, which were supposed to voluntarily adhere to restriction, were included, Britain controlled virtually all rubber production. The Indies government did not agree to participate in the Stevenson Plan, however, citing the difficulty of controlling production on "native" rubber plots, which were small, with production extremely sensitive to price. Privately they admitted that restrictions on Indonesian producers could have adverse political effects at a time when nationalist feelings were already running high.[30] Dutch officials also saw no reason to effectively underwrite British superiority in rubber production by participating in a restriction plan which would preserve Britain's position. French planters in Indochina, Dutch planters, and to a greater degree Indonesian smallholders in the Indies responded to the price increases under the Stevenson Plan by increasing the tapping of existing trees and the planting of new ones. By 1928 Britain controlled only 53 percent of world exports and "no longer had sufficient weight to control the market."[31]

Early in 1928 the British government announced that the restrictions on rubber production and sales imposed by the Stevenson Plan would end on 1 November 1928. The price of rubber plummeted on both the London and New York markets, dropping by $0.065 per pound on the day of the announcement. Stocks hoarded by rubber producers throughout the period of restriction flooded the market, effectively blocking any recovery in rubber prices.[32] Britain's attempt to control the rubber market had failed.

Rubber and the Power of American Consuming Interests

Herbert Hoover and the American rubber manufacturers celebrated their victory. For them the end of the Stevenson Plan was both a vindication of their policies and an illustration that the American approach to international economic relations was superior.

The initial United States response to British attempts to control the market had come before the Stevenson Plan was envisioned. The U.S. Rubber Company in 1910 acquired a lease in Sumatra, Netherlands Indies, for a rubber plantation of 83,000 acres. Goodyear followed in 1914, initially acquiring 17,000 acres, and three years later Intercontinental (also a United States firm) leased 22,000 acres.[33] All three companies added to their holdings over the next few years; the property of the U.S. Rubber Company was the largest rubber plantation in the world until Firestone's plantations in Liberia began producing. The companies' investments were prompted by price rather than concerns about potential restriction, since before the First World War demand for rubber frequently outstripped supply, leading to astronomically high prices, as in 1909 when it reached $3.00 per pound. With their own plantations these rubber manufacturers would be protected from price fluctuations in the raw material, and might earn profits from crude rubber in times of high prices.[34]

Goodyear and U.S. Rubber continued to expand their rubber holdings in Southeast Asia through the 1920s, but the investments of United States firms never amounted to more than 5 percent of the total for rubber.[35] Investment in British-controlled territory like Malaya and Burma was not profitable, because those plantations were subject to the Stevenson Plan, even when all production was to be used by the company. The Philippines had a law limiting the amount of land that non-Filipinos could own to 2,500 acres, effectively barring foreign-owned plantations. Indochina made it difficult for (non-French) foreigners to acquire rubber plantations. That left only the Indies. American rubber planters and Washington officials believed that the presence of plantations owned by United States firms had salutary effects. The Goodyear and U.S. Rubber plantations did provide a measure of security for United States rubber manufacturing interests, and more importantly, they meant that a small group of Americans were in a position to learn early about British and Dutch plans for restriction. This small group also had the right to demand representation on producer boards, which shaped British and Dutch governmental policies. They rarely succeeded in getting representation in matters relating to restriction, but they did serve as intermediaries between producing and consuming interests.

Herbert Hoover strongly urged United States rubber manufacturers to explore the possibility of acquiring their own rubber plantations, but even he believed that it would be acceptable to rely on foreign sources if restrictions were ended. United States ownership of rubber plantations in colonial Southeast Asia had an additional benefit: company executives and Washington officials believed that they served as a model for Europeans and Southeast Asians of progressive, modern, scientific, efficient production. American-owned plantations sponsored scientific research into rubber production, leading to improved budding techniques, higher productivity, and disease-resistant trees. Rubber company officials and United States diplomats in the region were equally proud of the American-owned plantations' superior treatment of their workers. They commended themselves for the high quality of the housing they provided to workers, the well-equipped hospitals, and the universal schooling offered to workers' children.[36]

The purchase of rubber plantations by United States manufacturers was a way of beating the British at their own game: Americans would demonstrate that their plantations could be as profitable, as well as more scientifically and humanely managed. Smallholder production, primarily by Indonesians, and smuggling also undermined the Stevenson Plan. Neither United States officials nor United States rubber manufacturers explicitly endorsed smuggling or the expansion of "native production," but they did report on both, often approvingly. The *Saturday Evening Post*, in a series of four articles in 1926 on "alien commodity control," noted that production of "Dutch native rubber . . . increased with remarkable speed," and reached eighty thousand pounds in 1925. It was "a serious competitor of the British-grown article."[37] These smallholder producers, from the perspective of the United States, were the perfect check on the market, because they rarely relied on rubber as their sole source of income. They planted rubber trees on abandoned land, or interspersed with other crops like tapioca, and tapped their rubber trees only when the price reached a certain level. That price, moreover, was below the price desired by plantation producers. An American, Fred Waterhouse, who purchased only "native rubber," claimed in 1924 that the British attempt to maintain a price of 50 cents a pound for rubber meant that "the [Indies] native production is being subsidised" by British producers, who were effectively putting themselves out of business.[38]

The proximity of the Indies' unrestricted rubber market to Malaya, which was under restriction, meant that smuggling was an easy way for Malayan rubber growers to benefit fully from the increased price of rubber. In June 1923, only eight months after the rubber restriction began, the United States consul at Penang, Straits Settlements, Renwick McNiece, reported on the "defects of restriction." The most prevalent was what McNiece called the "abuse of coupons." Growers received coupons which they had to turn in when they sold their rubber; no rubber could be sold unless accompanied by a coupon. According to McNiece, the "small Malay holder[s]" found it profitable not to tap their trees but rather to sell their coupons, at approximately half the market price for the rubber they represented. They then received a cash income for doing no work. But Malayan and Chinese smallholders soon discovered that they could sell their coupons and then tap their trees anyway, smuggling the rubber to the free ports at Penang and Singapore, or across sixty to seventy-five miles of ocean to Sumatra. Smuggling represented a serious challenge to the Stevenson Plan. In April 1923 alone the total exports from British Malaya were four thousand tons higher than official figures, based on coupon sales, suggested they should be.[39] In this way restriction subsidized smallholder production in Malaya, as in the Indies.

This vigorous pursuit of the free market by Indonesian, Malay, and Chinese smallholders meant low rubber prices for American companies, which naturally approved. But the large rubber companies did not wholeheartedly endorse unregulated supply and demand for the rubber market. On the contrary, in October 1926 Goodyear, Goodrich, U.S. Rubber, Firestone, Fisk Rubber, and General Motors agreed to form a rubber-buying pool to purchase 44,000 pounds of rubber which they would use to help keep rubber prices stable, and low.[40] The massive price fluctuation had hurt them as much as it hurt rubber growers, since typically they committed to purchase rubber months in advance of delivery, often paying more than the prevailing price at delivery time. Secretary Hoover helped the rubber pool to obtain the necessary government permission for the cooperative purchases, and led the campaign in 1927 to get Congressional approval. The combination of restriction and the buying pool kept prices relatively stable for a few months. But the British government announced in February 1928 that it was "studying" the Stevenson Plan, and its further announcement in early April that restriction would end on 1 November spelled the end of stability. The rubber buying pool held 35,000 tons of rubber it had purchased at 41 cents a pound, while prices stood at 19 cents a pound. Member companies of the buying pool began to dump their stocks to avoid losing their entire investment just as massive quantities of rubber held back by producers began entering the market. Still, average prices in 1928 remained at approximately 20 cents a pound.[41]

The world did "struggle with rubber" during the 1920s, as James C. Lawrence wrote in 1931. Participants in the struggle had different goals. Hoover, and many other Washington officials, wanted to end Britain's ability to dominate production of an important raw material. Rubber plantation owners wanted high, steady prices. Rubber manufacturers wanted low, steady prices. British officials wanted prices high enough to guarantee good tax revenues in the colonies, and a burden for United States manufacturers. The struggle persisted until all the participants dropped, exhausted, because none had sufficient power to control the market completely. Unrestricted rubber production continued until 1934, and prices dropped steadily. In 1931 crude rubber sold for only 3 cents per pound. The crisis brought the Dutch and British together for another attempt to restrict production in the hope of raising prices.

At the end of the 1920s, though, most Americans involved with the rubber issue believed that efforts by the United States to enforce what they believed to be a more realistic price for rubber benefited all involved, with the exception of some staid Europeans, too inflexible to produce efficiently. United States actions and power, they believed, had been sufficient to prevent British control of this important commodity, and Southeast Asians had shown themselves to be encouragingly entrepreneurial. Rubber manufacturers did want less volatility in prices, but they placed the blame for price fluctuations on European governments and plantations. For the interested Americans, allowing freer markets and more production by Southeast Asians promised a rosy future for both rubber markets and the region. With such benefits on offer, they believed it to be in everyone's interest to facilitate those free markets and that increased production by calling on the power of the United States government.

It is tempting to view the American critique of European rubber policies as anti-imperial. Indeed, sometimes President Hoover's rhetoric did castigate the British Empire, making common cause with the eighteenth-century struggle against it and efforts by the rubber industry to free itself from the British Stevenson Plan. Yet United States officials and businessmen were generally quite satisfied with the Dutch empire. Dutch imperial goals, at least as understood by these Americans, were compatible with United States economic goals. An empire like that of the Netherlands, which permitted free trade and investment, and allowed its colonial subjects to develop their own economic interests, might prove helpful to United States economic aspirations in the region.

Indies Oil and Rising American Hegemony

Hoover led United States rubber manufacturers in their fight to get more favorable prices for rubber. He helped them kick open the doors for foreign investment in the colonies; he assisted their efforts to circumvent United States anti-monopoly laws; he made British restriction policies an official point of contention between Britain and the United States. The rubber growers did not always follow Hoover, though. They did not necessarily want to buy rubber plantations to become self-sufficient in rubber. Nor did they want to antagonize British and Dutch rubber producers. In the 1920s rubber production was, for perhaps everyone but Hoover, an issue of economics, not national security. That assessment limited what rubber manufacturers would ask of the United States government, and what the government would be willing to do to support the rubber industry.

Oil was a different matter. During the First World War it had become obvious that strategic struggles over control of oil resources would color relations among the great powers. A Dutch newspaper observed, "the war has shown that the statement, that the party which controls the oil rules the world, contains a great foundation of truth."[42] The United States would not be left out of this game. One State Department official in England emphasized that "oil has become a vitally important fuel for our Navy and Merchant Marine . . . [and] a most necessary item for various other purposes in connection with our national defense." Concern on the part of the United States was compounded by the belief, prominent in the 1920s, that "our own supplies of this fuel are rapidly becoming exhausted."[43] The magnitude of governmental concern created an atmosphere in which governmental assistance to oil companies, also worried about acquiring control over finite oil resources, evolved from being acceptable to being encouraged.

Colonial Southeast Asia looked promising as a field of United States oil development, in terms of strategic benefit, available resources, and political situation. Strategically two considerations shaped the American thirst for oil in Southeast Asia. First, the U.S. Navy wanted sources of oil controlled by the United States in the Pacific, preferably close to the Philippines. Such sources would be necessary in the event of a war between the United States and Japan, in which it was assumed that the Philippines would be a major battleground. Equally important, the Navy also wanted some guarantees of access to oil in the event that Britain remained neutral in this possible war. Continued British control over naval oil supplies in the Pacific would, in the view of naval officers, guarantee the superiority of the British navy.[44]

These strategic considerations were well articulated within government circles, but government-to-government negotiations and public discussion of the matter focused on the availability of oil in the region. The two known oil-producing regions of Southeast Asia were in Burma and the Netherlands Indies. United States oil companies, notably Colonial Oil Co., a subsidiary of Standard Oil of New Jersey, had been attempting unsuccessfully to acquire oil concessions in Burma since the turn of the century. As one historian has argued, many British officials were "so suspicious of Royal Dutch-Shell's foreign connections [to the Netherlands]" that the India Office decided in 1902 to grant oil concessions in Burma only to all-British companies.[45] The British Foreign Office never admitted that such a decision had been made, but a report in April 1921 prepared in the Foreign Office for Parliament noted that in Burma "prospecting or mining leases have been, in practice, granted only to British subjects." The justification given was that the Burma fields did not produce enough oil even for India's use, and that the British Empire had to import substantial amounts of oil.[46]

During the world's struggle over rubber, at times the justifications for pursuing a particular rubber policy included its beneficial effects for imperial subjects, or the ways that the policy supported a particular form of imperialism. The struggle over oil, which was truly global and at least as contentious as that over rubber, was traditional geopolitics. Officials from the contending states, most of which were also empires, viewed the disputes through the lenses of strategy, potential military conflict, and state power. The constituent parts of the empire were important as sources of oil and as places that needed to be defended. The word "empire" was therefore more common in the documents produced as the result of the oil struggles than in the struggles over rubber, but the nature, purpose, and especially the future of imperial rule were not matters of discussion. Despite this important difference from the situation with rubber, the struggle over oil was again primarily between the United States and Britain, although they perceived a likely common enemy in Japan.

The scurry in 1921 to explain British policy toward Burma was the result of the passage in 1920 of the General Leasing Law by Congress. This law contained a reciprocity provision, stipulating that citizens or companies owned by citizens of a country which did not grant "similar or like privileges" of mining and oil concessions to United States citizens would not be able to acquire leases for mining or oil wells on federally owned land in the United States. British officials believed that equating the United States and Britain in the case of oil production was unfair. The British memorandum of April 1921 argued that "in regard to a 'closed door' policy no real parallel can fairly be drawn between the British Empire, with its small and scattered production, and a country like the United States, which at present produces two-thirds of the world's output within her home territory."[47] It was that very situation which worried United States officials, since the belief was prevalent that United States reserves would be exhausted within twenty to thirty years, after which the United States would be dependent on foreign-controlled sources of oil.[48]

British mandates in what is now called the Middle East[49] were the real battleground between the United States and Britain in the fight for oil resources, and although the U.S. Department of State continued to lodge complaint after complaint against Britain for its treatment of United States oil companies in Burma, the reciprocity clause of the General Leasing Law was not invoked against Britain for its discriminatory policies in Burma.[50]

The oil fields of the Netherlands Indies seemed much more promising to United States oil companies, and the U.S. Department of State insisted that the Netherlands open the door to United States oil companies wishing to drill. As in Burma, a subsidiary of Standard Oil of New Jersey (in the Indies the Nederlands Koloniale Petroleum Maatschappij, or NKPM) had been making efforts to acquire petroleum concessions in the Indies since the early twentieth century. This company met the requirement under Dutch law that any company desiring to obtain oil concessions in the Indies had to be incorporated in either the Indies or the Netherlands. In 1912 and 1913 NKPM purchased four small oil concessions from private companies. These concessions included the right to explore and drill for oil.[51]

In 1920 the Dutch government was preparing to grant the Djambi oil concession in Sumatra. These fields were commonly believed to be the richest in the Indies. The NKPM wanted the Djambi concession, or at least a part of it, and requested assistance from the U.S. Department of State. In a meeting on 5 June 1920 the United States minister in The Hague, Phillips, requested that the Dutch minister of foreign affairs, van Karnebeek, help him "assure Americans that their cooperation is welcomed by the colonial authorities," because "fears are expressed . . . of possible discrimination against American enterprise."[52] Phillips reported that "neither [van Karnebeek nor the economic advisor in the Foreign Office] seemed thoroughly acquainted with the situation but promised me full information."[53]

When the Dutch answer came about three weeks later it was not satisfying for NKPM. The Dutch chargé in Washington, de Beaufort, reported that "American citizens have with respect to the law the same facilities as Netherland subjects" regarding oil concessions, so long as the companies in question incorporated within the Netherlands or the Indies. He asked that this information be conveyed to whoever decided the reciprocity provisions of the General Leasing Law. But the Netherlands government planned to "themselves develop the deposits in question or else do so by contract with persons or private companies." This "government reserve" policy, as Phillips called it, did not seem to discriminate against United States citizens, although State Department officials did not like it. They initially concentrated on whether United States oil companies did have the possibility of receiving available oil concessions. In July 1920 Phillips received instructions expressing "the view of the Department that the Netherlands has not accorded the same degree of freedom to American citizens . . . [given] to Netherlands nationals in the United States and . . . therefore, has not granted reciprocal privileges." Reciprocity privileges were determined by the Department of the Interior, however, so Phillips was to inform Dutch authorities only that "strong public sentiment" in the United States was "leaning toward retaliation" against the Netherlands.[54]

While the initial Dutch response had emphasized the legal equality of United States and Dutch citizens, Washington's implied threat of "retaliation" prompted the Dutch to take another tack. Phillips reported van Karnebeek's complaint that while American capital was "sincerely desired" in the Indies, the Dutch had to be "very careful" regarding the foreign relations of its colonies; "otherwise its colonial possessions might pass under the political control of other Powers." Dutch officials particularly worried that "foreign capital" would be used for "political purposes." Phillips quoted van

Karnebeek as saying, "Of course, we have nothing to fear from America, but that does not mean that we have nothing to fear from others."[55] The cause of Dutch fear was left unnamed, but Japan was the only other country attempting to acquire oil concessions in the Netherlands Indies at that time.

Washington officials were not impressed by the Dutch invocation of impending Japanese aggression, since the possibility of this aggression was one reason why they wanted United States oil companies to have concessions in the Indies. State Department officials encouraged a representative of Sinclair Oil Company of New York to formally apply to participate in the Djambi concession. When he was told that a Dutch company, Bataafsche Petroleum Maatschappij (BPM), had been awarded the contract one year previously and was merely awaiting confirmation by the Dutch Parliament, Phillips cabled the department that he could "do nothing further here" without the threat of "retaliatory measures." One week later Phillips received notification of a decision by the secretary of the interior that Dutch "restrictions are such as to practically exclude Americans" from oil concessions. This decision meant that the Netherlands could be declared a "nonreciprocating country" under the General Leasing Law, and no company with Dutch shareholders would be granted leases on federally owned land in the United States.[56]

Subsidiaries of Royal-Dutch Shell in the United States, notably Roxana Petroleum Corporation and the Shell Company of California, made "several applications for leases" between 1920 and 1923, but "none . . . were granted." The Department of the Interior kept these applications "under consideration," with a presumption of denial if Dutch policy did not change.[57] The parameters of both United States and Dutch policy remained unchanged between 1920 and 1923. Dutch officials offered help, short of oil concessions, in an effort to meet United States reciprocity requirements without changing their policy. The minister of colonies asked BPM, the company which received the Djambi concession, to allow American capital to participate. The BPM director, Colijn, agreed to allow Sinclair Oil to purchase stock in the company, but would not allow "right to possession of the produce."[58] In April 1921 the Dutch government proposed an amendment to the bill then pending to confirm the award of the Djambi concession to BPM. This amendment would have split the Djambi concession between BPM and the NKPM, but it was defeated the same day it was introduced.[59] After that the best the Dutch foreign minister could offer was the possibility for American capital to participate in future concessions offered.[60]

Throughout the 1920s the Dutch also continued to play the Japan card, and United States officials took note, although it had less effect than the communist card did in the same years. In the debate in Parliament on the Djambi bill in June 1921, the Dutch foreign minister, van Karnebeek, pointedly noted that Japan was requesting information on how to acquire oil concessions in the Indies.[61] Two years later, in a meeting between Louis Sussdorf, United States chargé in The Hague, and Six, chief of the Division of Mineral Resources in the Dutch Colonial Ministry, Six also emphasized that while the Dutch government wanted to open planned new oil concessions on a "competitive basis" and that Royal Dutch-Shell "would not now be averse to American companies entering" the Indies, the real issue was how "to exclude Japanese competition without offending the Japanese Government."[62] Sussdorf was highly skeptical about the welcoming attitude of Dutch officials and Royal Dutch-Shell, but he accepted without question the need to devise a way of excluding Japan.[63]

The assertion by Six that Royal-Dutch Shell and the Netherlands government had decided to accept the presence of United States oil companies in the Netherlands Indies is a reminder that oil had a national, strategic importance dwarfing all other commodities as early as the 1920s. All land controlled by a government, in this case the Netherlands, whether in colonies or the metropole, and all explorations by a company, in this case Royal-Dutch, served national purposes. To allow in a competitor, as Royal-Dutch Shell did, in some ways had to serve the national purposes of the government controlling the land. The Dutch had apparently decided that the presence of United States oil companies would better serve Dutch interests. Here the politics of oil subsumed all potential difference within empires, as well as all potential common interests across empires. National security, understood broadly, was most important.

Whether in Washington, The Hague, or Batavia, United States officials believed that the Dutch had a better chance of ultimately resisting Japan by inviting United States capital into the Indies than they did by excluding it. That was not the only reason, of course, that they continued to push for concessions for United States companies. As soon as the Djambi concession was formally awarded to BPM in July 1921, the U.S. Senate requested the Federal Trade Commission to prepare a report on "the whole subject of foreign ownership in the foreign and domestic oil industry."[64] The primary target of this report, completed in February 1923, was Royal Dutch-Shell; the bulk of the report detailed the company's holdings within and outside the United

States. One month later the United States secretary of the interior, Albert Fall, denied the application of Roxana Petroleum Company, a Royal Dutch-Shell subsidiary, for an oil lease on federally owned lands in the United States.[65]

The Dutch foreign minister, van Karnebeek, had said that both the Netherlands and United States deserved to have their own oil policies, implying that each should have an oil policy best suited to its interests.[66] But Dutch officials envisioned an oil policy which precluded the oil policy believed by United States officials to be best suited to United States interests. The concessions that the NKPM had acquired before 1912 began producing commercial quantities of oil in 1926, but United States officials maintained their pressure on the Dutch government to grant new concessions to demonstrate an adherence to an open process. In August 1926 the Volksraad, the consultative legislature of the Indies, voted on whether to grant oil concessions to NKPM, but the proposal failed. The Indies government forwarded the proposal to the Netherlands for approval anyway, where the Staats Generaal eventually acquiesced.[67]

Two changes in the Indies made the United States case more appealing. The new governor general, A. C. D. de Graeff, came directly from the United States, where he had been the Dutch ambassador. Upon hearing that de Graeff would be the Indies governor, the United States minister in The Hague, Richard Tobin, immediately wrote to Washington, urging officials to capitalize on de Graeff's fondness for the United States and push the NKPM case.[68] Perhaps someone did get to de Graeff while he was in Washington, because the British consul general in Batavia reported in March 1927 that de Graeff was the "original author" of the NKPM concessions, and "conceived the idea while he was still Dutch Minister in Washington."[69] De Graeff's sympathy, as well as his previous post as Dutch ambassador to Japan, may have made him more sensitive to shifting power relations in the Pacific, and more amenable to arguments from Washington about the benefits of United States capital in the Indies.

In addition, once the small concessions which the NKPM had acquired began producing commercially viable oil in 1926, the company built a pipeline and refinery in that year to begin marketing its oil. The original reason given by the Dutch for excluding foreign capital had disappeared: the NKPM oil wells in existence would be enticement enough for a Japanese invasion in time of war. The second-best strategy open to the Dutch was, as some United States officials had been urging, to allow more United States capital into the Indies in the hope that the United States would feel compelled to come to the Indies' defense if they were invaded. Although the Dutch foreign minister did worry about the massive power of Standard Oil of New Jersey, because he believed the separation of Standard Oil companies to be more fiction than fact, a concession to the NKPM, in return for a return to reciprocating-nation status, seemed the best policy.[70]

British officials were still less enthusiastic. They realized that both the oil concession itself, and the successful efforts of the United States government to get these concessions for a Standard Oil subsidiary, revealed a changing power balance in the region. In private memos London officials wrote in sarcastic terms of the vast reach and power of Standard Oil. In early 1928, after the NKPM concessions had been approved by one of the two houses in the Dutch parliament, Grindle, of the Foreign Office, commented on the report from the British legation in The Hague, "we should eagerly await the building of a sky-scraper by Standard Oil on Whitehall Gardens!" The reply warned that "we should be more depressed than impressed."[71] Officials in the Foreign Office referred to the large, impressive building that the NKPM had built in The Hague to convince the Dutch government of the company's determination, but they worried that this success, which they attributed to the concerted efforts of the United States minister Tobin, backed by the State Department, and to Dutch desire to regain American good will, would encourage United States oil companies and the United States government to try again in the British Empire. That British officials did not want.

Dutch representatives of Royal Dutch did not want the NKPM to acquire concessions either. Adriaan S. Oppenheim, legal counsel to Royal Dutch, in 1927 turned to the British consul in Batavia, Crosby, in the hope of finding an ally. Oppenheim told Crosby that he had complained to officials in The Hague about the proposed concessions, reminding them that Americans were "bluffers by nature" and that the Dutch had no guarantee that a concession to NKPM would be considered sufficient to have the Netherlands reinstated as a reciprocating country. Oppenheim had also reminded the Dutch colonial minister that granting concessions to United States companies "must almost inevitably be followed by demands for similar favours from Japan." Crosby promised to assist Oppenheim in blocking the concession to NKPM, although he doubted that his assistance would be of much value.

The strategic considerations followed the economic ones closely. When Oppenheim told Crosby that the Dutch government wanted to avoid granting oil concessions to the Japanese, he was reminding Crosby that the British Navy, soon to be occupying its new base in Singapore, depended on Dutch sources of oil in the Pacific.[72] From the British perspective, however, oil concessions which benefited the U.S. Navy were only marginally better than ones which would have benefited Japan. British officials would have preferred that neither country receive concessions in the Indies, but they no longer had the power to prevent them. As Wills, in the British Board of Trade, noted, "if the Americans were at the moment keen on getting into British Crown Lands, their success with the Dutch would encourage them to renew their efforts."[73] Britain's supremacy in colonial Asia had not yet been challenged, but British officials worried that a successful challenge could be launched. The question was whether the United States was refraining because of lack of power or a lack of will.

Oppenheim's comments were not without effect. In October 1927 the Dutch foreign minister instructed van Royen, the Dutch minister in Washington, to inform the United States government that before further progress could be made on the four concessions proposed for the NKPM in the Indies, it needed to be "understood that the Netherlands is considered as a 'reciprocating country.'" The same day, the foreign minister sent the Dutch colonial secretary a note, saying that he thought it "highly desirable" for the NKPM to "bring her influence to bear on Standard Oil in order to promote the Netherlands attainment of the 'reciprocating country' status."[74] In early November van Royen formally asked the U.S. Department of State to reconsider the Netherlands designation, in light of the pending oil concessions. To make clear the importance of this request, the Dutch foreign minister, Beelaerts van Blokland, met with the United States minister in The Hague, Tobin, and also requested reconsideration.[75]

Early in 1928, after the First Chamber of the Dutch Parliament had also approved the concessions, van Royen was informed that Royal Dutch-Shell should submit an application to the secretary of the interior; approval of that application would be a de facto indication of a return to reciprocating status. Tobin reported that he doubted the Dutch government would be "entirely satisfied" with this procedure. The "charges" against the Dutch had been "made publicly," and Tobin predicted that the Dutch would want to "clear the record of the charges of lack of reciprocity." The concession bill, passed by Dutch Parliament, would not be signed until the United States issued a formal statement.[76]

The response from Washington was not all that the Dutch could have hoped. The department wanted to continue "informal" discussions rather than make formal statements, and provided three conditions that the Dutch should meet to be assured "in principle" of reciprocating status. The Netherlands government should "confirm" its policy of not discriminating against Americans in granting rights to oil concessions, should "definitely grant an important concession or concessions to American interests," and should promise in future to "treat responsible American interests on a footing equivalent to that accorded to Dutch interests."[77] After some further disputes about whether either the secretary of the interior or the secretary of state would issue a written declaration that the Netherlands was again a reciprocating country, and whether Royal Dutch-Shell, part British-owned, would be eligible for oil concessions in the United States although Britain had been declared a non-reciprocating country, the bill granting to NKPM its oil concessions was signed in July 1928. Upon learning of this development the United States minister, Tobin, sent a formal letter to the Dutch minister of foreign affairs, Beelaerts van Blokland, informing him that the United States "recognizes" the Netherlands "as a reciprocating State."[78]

The eight-year struggle appeared to be over, and the door to United States investment to be open. But other United States oil companies did not find much welcome in the Indies. NKPM merged with a subsidiary of Standard California to form Socony-Vacuum, but no other United States firms acquired concessions in the Indies. When NKPM requested to be allowed to build oil storage tanks on the island of Bangka, presumably necessary for expanding production in the Indies, the Dutch government denied permission on the grounds the facilities would be a "powerful attraction" for "foreign navies" during wartime and make Dutch neutrality impossible.[79]

Scholars of this period of late imperialism have been fascinated by how claims of a civilizing mission led imperial states to intervene more thoroughly in the lives of colonial subjects, and to extend their controlling power in tandem with the beneficial offerings of the imperial state. The politics of oil, oddly, had a similar effect. Control of oil resources meant not merely the ability to use them for one's own country (its navy and industrial base) but also to deny them to one's competitors and enemies. When oil was located "out" in the colonies, an imperial state like Britain or the Netherlands might be reassured, because the metropole would not have to supply the energy resource. But the location of oil out in the colony also meant that the source of oil was attractive to competitors and needed a higher level of protection. Imperial states did treat oil fields, wherever they were, simply as pieces of land owned by the state, to be disposed of for the good of the state. But when those pieces of land were far from the metropole, in previously undefended colonies, the demands on imperial state resources increased. The struggle over oil described above threw these early-twentieth-century developments into sharp focus, revealing the shifting balance of power in Southeast Asia.

United States Power at Its Peak

The year 1928 could well be considered the height of United States economic power in the region before the Second World War. The buying power of the United States, assisted by the producing power of the Netherlands Indies, had broken the Stevenson rubber restriction plan. The holding hostage of lands in the United States that were rich in oil reserves had forced the Dutch to grant oil concessions to an American company, although Dutch officials believed such concessions to be against Dutch strategic and economic interests. A large proportion of the region's exports went to the United States, meaning that variations in the United States market were among the most significant foreign developments for the colonies.

The United States government, in the guise of Congress, the State Department, the Commerce Department, and occasionally the president, was willing to use the political and economic power of the United States to secure a better position for United States businesses wishing to trade or invest abroad. The combined force of business and government was sufficient to achieve the goals of each. What is striking, however, is how limited these goals were. Lower rubber prices sufficed; rubber producers in the United States did not attempt to control the whole market by acquiring massive rubber plantations. Likewise, an oil concession to one United States company sufficed. Neither the oil companies nor the State Department insisted that the tenets of the Open Door be followed to the letter.

Throughout the 1920s Washington officials did whatever was necessary to assist United States companies in gaining access and fair prices, but they always stopped short of actions which would have required or implied an American commitment to uphold a particular political constellation in the region. It was precisely this lack of commitment that made European officials, particularly those heavily involved in colonial affairs, wary of any United States involvement. They worried that the presence of the United States could change the political situation, either by upsetting the international power balance or by encouraging political action on the part of Southeast Asians. The biggest international concern was Japan, as both the Dutch and the English feared that opening their colonies to United States investment would prevent them from blocking Japanese investment. Without a commitment by the United States to help defend the regional status quo in the event of war—a commitment not forthcoming in the 1920s—Britain, France, and the Netherlands were reluctant to allow Japan to improve its strategic or economic position. But the actions of the United States in support of its own economic agenda gave the Europeans little choice. During the 1930s the dangers of this situation would only grow.

United States policymakers recognized that Japan was a potential threat to the region. They were much less willing to acknowledge that economic involvement by the United States might have what Europeans considered a detrimental effect on domestic political arrangements. One of the reasons why Southeast Asia appealed to United States investors and traders was its relative political stability. Oil companies, for example, had undergone bad experiences in Mexico with radical nationalists and hoped to avoid repeating them in Southeast Asia. Similarly, the United States consul in Batavia argued that one reason why the Indies was a better place for rubber plantation investment was that the labor and political situation was much more favorable than in Liberia, where Firestone eventually established a large plantation. European colonial officials thought that the Americans had a strange way of promoting stability, since an explicit goal of United States investors was an improvement in the standard of living and educational attainment of Southeast Asian workers. Americans, whether in the State Department or private business, promoted this kind of development as a means of moving Southeast Asians from colonized to self-governing status without revolution (potentially within the framework of a commonwealth rather than as independent countries). Better education, a higher standard of living, and greater access to consumer products, they believed, would tie Southeast Asians to the same economic and political order endorsed by liberal Europeans. In retrospect the economic victories of the United States in Southeast Asia during the 1920s look limited. But at the time Washington officials believed them sufficient to provide the space for the American dream to transform the region and the people.

In spreading capital into Southeast Asia, Americans appeared to be at their most anti-imperialistic. They hired indigenous people for jobs previously considered suitable only for Europeans or Chinese; they encouraged the entrepreneurial spirit of Southeast Asians; they worried little or not at all about the disruptions caused to European governance by their relentless pursuit of the best economic interest of their company or country. Yet virtually none of the involved Americans had any quarrel with traditional imperialism. If imperialism could adapt to the changing economic conditions, that was fine with United States officials and businessmen. If imperialism could not adapt, then it would come to be replaced by something else. There was, on the part of these Americans, remarkably little concern either way during the boom years of the 1920s.

|||||||||||||||||||||||||||||||||||||||||||||||||||||||||||||||||||||||||||||||||||||||||||||||||||||||||||||||||||||||||||||||||||||||||||||||||||

An Empire of the Mind

American Culture and Southeast Asia, 1919–1941

In 1921 a Vietnamese student in the United States wrote to his parents and brother back in Vietnam. We do not know whether they ever received his letter because French officials intercepted it, and had their worst suspicions about the growing influence of the United States confirmed. In the letter the student reassured his parents that although he was no longer studying in France, he was doing well. In France, he wrote, he had been treated "with too much scorn and had been accorded no freedom," but in America, the "best civilization in the world," he was learning and prospering. He concluded: "Dear brother, if you have sons, make sure they learn English."[1] For this Vietnamese student, clearly a member of the élite, the United States symbolized a bright future—for him personally, since he could find freedom and respect there, but also for his country, represented by his nephews, whose knowledge of English would enable them to enter the more appealing, modern world that America offered. This vision did not appeal to French officials, who seized the letter, presumably preventing it from reaching its intended destination. The French ambassador in Washington quoted the letter as part of his discussion of the danger to French Indochina should the United States grant more autonomy to the Philippines. He was warning officials in France that the United States did not have to grant independence to the Philippines to be a destabilizing force in the region; the example of increasing self-government and the rhetoric of equality would suffice.

Probably unwittingly, the Vietnamese student effectively reflected the type of relations that the United States wished to have with the colonies of Southeast Asia. Washington officials, whether of the commerce or state department, hoped that the American example as represented in American consumer products, political values, and missionaries, and governance of the Philippines, would persuade Southeast Asians and European colonists alike that following the American example was the best way to organize political, economic, and social relations in the region. Movies, missionaries, and Chevrolets were cultural products, and promotion of them is properly called cultural relations, but both the objects and the promotion were inextricable from American political goals in the region. United States officials wanted to create a new basis for international relations, in which traditional realpolitik could be replaced by a harmony of interests and values. Naturally the new standard would be American; when others accepted American values, disagreements would be minimal and susceptible to solution through compromise, negotiation, and the market. Formal colonial rule would no longer be necessary, replaced by an empire of the mind.

Americans touted the benefits of American cultural products for Southeast Asia. They believed in the potential for Hollywood movies to promote independent thinking and consumerism, for American missionaries to inculcate in Southeast Asians modern, responsible approaches to moral choices, and for consumer goods to encourage capitalistic behavior. In short, they believed that American cultural influence produced modernity. But equally important, many Americans believed that if Southeast Asians did develop along this American path, these Southeast Asians would evolve, perhaps slowly but steadily, into people deserving of self-rule. The American example, represented in all the ways discussed below, would allow this process to occur with a minimum of contention, and to result in harmonious relations among Europeans, Americans, and Southeast Asians. Even while Americans talked about the "routine of freedom" inherent in American culture as presented to Southeast Asians, few of them meant that as a critique of imperialism. They rather meant it as a critique of an approach to imperialism which had perhaps been appropriate for the eighteenth and nineteenth centuries but was no longer viable in the twentieth. American culture, these Americans believed, had the potential to dissolve the differences separating colonized from colonizer.

Europeans and Southeast Asians recognized this policy for what it was: both a good way to involve the government in promoting United States business and a policy reflecting a sincere belief in the need to change political values. For Europeans, the promotion of American culture frequently seemed more threatening to their rule in the region than the more traditional political or economic activities of Americans. But it was also more difficult to know how to prevent these cultural influences from entering their colonies. They tried censorship of movies, discriminatory import duties, and rigid restrictions on American missionaries, but none of these strategies was completely effective. Southeast Asians seemed uncritically enthusiastic about American consumer culture, if often less welcoming of American Protestantism. Across the board, most Southeast Asians from traditionalists to Marxists appeared to welcome American culture. Yet they often consumed American culture in ways which European and American observers found idiosyncratic, unsettling both expectations and fears.

America and the Beginnings of Mass Culture

After the First World War American companies, products, and values had an increasing impact on the transformations of everyday life taking place in Southeast Asia. American companies believed that they were changing working conditions. They hired Indonesians and Burmese to work in auto assembly plants, in the face of assurances from Europeans that "natives" had neither the proper motivation nor the ability to do factory work. The U.S. Rubber Plantation Company boasted that it provided superior housing, adequate health care, and schools for the children of workers, drawing a contrast with Dutch- and British-owned plantations.[2] The companies maintained that all successful companies would follow their business practices in future: treating employees well to get maximum loyalty, performance, and profit from them.

If Southeast Asians could make good workers, they could also make good consumers. Throughout the interwar period the United States exported much less to Southeast Asia than it bought from the region, but American cars, sewing machines, flashlights, and kerosene outsold their European and Japanese competitors.[3] While less accessible to the average Southeast Asian than the textiles and bicycles imported from Europe, Japan, and China, American goods had the potential to transform lifestyles. Flashlights and kerosene both allowed more personal control over time, particularly facilitating nighttime activities. A flashlight or kerosene lamp could be used for reading, or for illuminating a late meeting, political or amorous. Sewing machines and autos, more than in Europe or the United States, were not domestic labor-saving devices as much as foundations for small businesses.

America's most successful consumer product came from Hollywood. Movies were as popular with Europeans, Chinese, and Southeast Asians throughout the region as they were everywhere in the world. The number of theaters in Asia numbered 4,315 in 1931, only about one-fifth the number in the United States, but approximately the same as in Latin America.[4] More than in the United States, however, movies were frequently seen outside permanent movie theaters, whether in the auditoriums of American missionary schools to entice people inside, or projected on a sheet strung between two trees in villages remote from any city. And the movies were American. Even in French Indochina, which limited the importation of non-French movies, Hollywood films generally accounted for half the movies shown. In the other colonies the proportion ranged from 65 percent in the Netherlands Indies to 90 percent or more in the Philippines.[5]

Movies were frequently a consumer product for which one had to pay money before viewing, but they were also an activity which could be chosen from among others. Already in the 1920s some observers complained that young people went to the movies too much, and therefore neglected to learn or appreciate traditional culture.[6] And American observers hoped that the movies could be a learning experience. Many articles and reports cited the slogan "trade follows the film," and argued that purchasing desires could be stimulated when viewers learned about the consumer products seen and used in films.[7] The articles and reports also emphasized that American political and economic values exemplified in the films, such as the rags-to-riches narrative and skepticism toward government, could only appeal to Southeast Asians. The "routine of freedom" in Hollywood films, reinforced by what Washington officials viewed as the obvious superiority of United States policies in the Philippines, were both advertisements for American ideals. And although not as popular with Washington officials as United States business and consumer products, American missionaries had difficulty separating their religious mission from their promotion of American political and cultural values, for which they were often better advocates, particularly in their emphasis on the establishment of schools virtually everywhere they went, on the teaching of English in those schools, and in their commitment to turn churches over to indigenous leadership.

American cultural products, whether consumer goods, movies, or less tangible representations of American political or economic values, were by no means the only products or the most prominent products available in interwar Southeast Asia. But the frequency with which colonial officials expressed concern about American products suggests that American culture was highly influential. Southeast Asians were in no way Americanized;

Mickey Mouse and Coca-Cola were not yet household names, although the latter was available in some colonies.[8] But as we shall see, Southeast Asians had already integrated many aspects of American culture into their everyday lives, often with the meanings hoped for by Washington officials, but at least as often in unexpected ways.

Missionaries and the Promotion of Autonomy

Missionaries had been among the first Americans to go to Southeast Asia. Adoniram Judson, the famous American Baptist missionary, had arrived in Burma in 1813, and Baptists had had a continuous presence there ever since.[9] Hundreds of American Baptists served as missionaries in Burma at any one time during the interwar years, leading churches, making evangelistic tours into non-Christian villages, and running almost one thousand schools.[10] In the other Southeast Asian colonies American missionaries arrived later and came in smaller numbers, but some were present in each colony. The Methodist Episcopal Church had some missionaries in Burma, and more in British Malaya and the Netherlands Indies, while the Christian and Missionary Alliance (CMA) focused its regional effort in French Indochina. There were a few Seventh Day Adventists in each colony as well.[11]

Many Europeans and Southeast Asians alike believed that the missionaries were proselytizers for Americanism as much as for Christianity. Before and during the First World War CMA missionaries were unable to get permission from the French government to establish mission stations in French Indochina. French officials believed that the missionaries were engaged in "political actions."[12] CMA missionaries were more evangelistic than many American Protestant mission groups, meaning more focused solely on conversion, and so could not comprehend the French objections. Part of the problem was that French colonialists did not believe that the American church and state were separated. The French-language Indochinese newspaper *L'Indépendance tonkinoise* complained in 1924 that CMA missionaries, by then legally present, were recruiting Vietnamese children from the best families, with the lure of going to America for religious studies. In the French view these were political actions "sous le masque confessionnel," and the missionaries were "agents of panamericanism," precursors for the "political expansion of America." For proof the editors offered the small number of converts who had already left to study in the United States.[13]

French hostility had many sources, not least the belief of CMA missionaries that French Catholics needed saving as much as Vietnamese Buddhists did. French concern, and the discomfort of many American missionaries, was perhaps reinforced by the insistence of the Vietnamese on interpreting American Protestantism in their own way, and linking the missionary message to American political values. The CMA magazine prepared for supporters in the United States, *The Call of French Indochina*, emphasized the difficulties that this identification caused. Some Vietnamese, for example, promised to come to worship only if they received "money or if the missionaries would take them to America." In 1930, soon after the Yen-Bai uprising and during the Nghe-Tinh rebellion—two of the greatest threats to French colonial rule before the Second World War—the Vietnamese persisted in calling what the CMA preached "the American Doctrine." That same year an entire village asked to convert, but to the missionaries' consternation they found that the villagers' motive was "not the love of Christ" but rather "a strong nationalistic spirit which they thought an American mission would naturally foster."[14] CMA missionaries may have exaggerated the obstacles to their success to gain sympathy, but the Vietnamese may indeed have been attracted to an American mission for its political possibilities. Educated Vietnamese had read about heroes of the American Revolution and may well have believed that they could use their American contacts to promote nationalist causes.[15]

CMA missionaries represented themselves as acting without reference to the nature of the government in Indochina; they were interested only in souls. Yet French fears had some basis. More than other American mission societies, the CMA saw its role as converting Vietnamese and training them as quickly as possible to lead their own churches and missions among their own people. And they did so. By 1931, when the CMA had been in Indochina for less than two decades, approximately half of both districts and churches were fully staffed, supervised, and funded by indigenous peoples.[16] If Vietnamese could run their own churches, it would become more difficult to argue that they were not capable of running their own country. French officials believed that this idea might occur to the Vietnamese, and while willing to recognize churches led by foreign missionaries, were reluctant to recognize the indigenous CMA churches, which they feared would be used by "communistic or nationalistic elements . . . for political purposes."[17]

Baptists and Methodist Episcopal missionaries struggled to see their Southeast Asian converts as capable of leading their own churches, and in this way seemed less threatening to European colonial rule. Baptists had been in Burma before British rule was consolidated, and the Baptist mission schools followed enough of the British curriculum that they received funds from the colonial government, and prepared their students to take the civil service examinations. The Methodists, whether in Burma, British Malaya, or the Netherlands Indies, also opened schools as one of their first priorities, but did not follow the British or Dutch curricula. Dutch officials found this type of education dangerous. One Dutch official complained to the United States consul in Medan, Walter Foote, that the Methodist schools were "educating the natives promiscuously and rendering them unfit for labor in the fields." Students from mission schools were frequently unable to find suitable employment, and became "disillusioned" and "radical in [their] thoughts."[18]

Missionaries saw the situation differently. In 1923 the *International Review of Missions* noted the "great awakening" in the Netherlands Indies, which coincided with rather than resulted from the presence of Methodist missionaries. This awakening was only potentially religious; it stemmed from a growing sense of nationalism. Missionaries could help channel the "movement . . . spreading all over Asia" into moderate forms, using the "thirst for books" to get people to read the Bible, and the "desire" for education to teach Christianity along with the three R's.[19] Frequently the Baptist and Methodist missionaries did, like European colonial officials, see Southeast Asians as needing to be led in the right direction, whether toward Christianity or toward acceptance of European rule. Especially in their reluctance to turn over the leadership of churches to indigenous Christians, and in their easy acceptance of the restrictions levied by colonial governments, Baptist and Methodist missionaries seemed supportive of colonialism.

European fears about the presence of American missionaries were heightened by the unquestioned assumption among the missionaries that American political and social values applied in Southeast Asia as they did in the United States. A paternalism informed by racism surely followed missionaries across the ocean, but so did a strong belief that education should be available to all Southeast Asians, not merely the élite. Tuition at mission schools was low or free, allowing poor students who could not afford colonial government schools to attend the mission schools. In the Netherlands Indies, Methodists had twenty-two elementary schools and one high school, enrolling 1,665 students. American mission schools in Malaya educated more than ten thousand students, mostly at the elementary level. In Burma, American Baptists ran twenty kindergartens, 821 elementary schools, fifteen high schools, two industrial schools, and two teacher training institutes, with a total enrollment of more than 31,000 students.[20] Baptists also ran daily vacation bible schools in the "hot season" in Burma. In 1932 more than 2,500 children, most of them Burmans, attended such schools.[21] Missionaries viewed schooling differently than did colonial officials, for whom the schools served colonialism. In their view, there should be only as many educated Burmese or Malays or Indonesians as were necessary to help the colonial government function. American missionaries, in contrast, believed that education helped to prepare Southeast Asians to make more informed choices about how to lead their lives. The hope was that students would then decide to become Christian, but the conviction was that education was beneficial whether they chose to convert or did not.

American missionaries frequently carried Progressive values and methods overseas, talking about Southeast Asian students and potential converts in much the same language used by settlement house workers to describe immigrants to the United States. Methodist missionaries in British Malaya and the Netherlands Indies taught English in their mission schools, initially out of necessity, since the missionaries had poor grasp of indigenous languages. One missionary, Natalie Means, found that a side benefit of this policy was that Methodist mission schools became true melting pots, where "all nationalities rub shoulders and learn mutual respect." Malays, ethnic Chinese, Indians, even British and Americans were teachers and pupils together in these schools. Traditional barriers between ethnic groups could be broken down in part because, in her view, so many of the people in British Malaya and the Netherlands Indies were migrants. For the migrants, among whom she did not include herself, "the atmosphere of a new place makes it a little easier to accept new ideas."[22]

Means, and the other American missionaries, had no need to accept new ideas, of course. They were the source of those new ideas, and unhesitatingly advocated the universality not only of the Christian message but also of such American values as melting pots, universal education, and democratically run churches. Means was as confident in her sanction to bring about such changes in people's lives in a British colony thousands of miles from the United States as were those Americans who ran settlement houses in Chicago.

Another group of Americans, secular missionaries, also came to Southeast Asia to transform it by spreading American values: the health professionals of the Rockefeller Foundation, which was active in Burma, the

Netherlands Indies, Siam, British Malaya, and the Philippines. The foundation worked to improve health conditions by promoting better sanitation, vaccination programs, and the training of public health officials, especially nurses and health officers. Rockefeller employees believed that modern educational techniques such as movies, slide shows, poster campaigns, and pamphlets could reach even the "childlike" Southeast Asians. An important goal of the Rockefeller programs was to train indigenous nurses and public health workers, allowing the public health benefits to be widely spread with minimal financial investment. Dr. Victor Heiser, in a report on the efficiency of programs for Java, noted with pride that village headmen were being trained, "carefully and painstakingly," to give public health lectures. The benefits of having this local authority promoting the program were numerous, and Heiser recognized that. But as with the religious missionaries, a tension always remained: were these Southeast Asians worthy of being sent to the United States for training, or should standards be adjusted and training kept local? Rockefeller employees debated among themselves, and this issue was never fully resolved. For his part, Heiser believed that the only real solution to the health problems of Southeast Asians was to have sufficient personnel educated to "American standards," whether or not in the United States itself.[23]

That wonderful paradox of Progressivism permeated American missions abroad. The rhetoric, values, and programs had the explicit goal of transplanting American cultural and social values into deserving, capable immigrants, or Southeast Asians. The result was at once imperialistic and liberating, and the tension resulting from this contradiction affected all American mission activities overseas, none more than efforts to turn mission schools and churches over to indigenous groups. The annual report of the Women's American Baptist Foreign Mission Society for 1925 noted: "the day is surely coming when we must turn over many of our dearest projects in education and evangelism into the hands of the indigenous Christian church and the leaders whom we ourselves have trained." The author saw her society's work as something that the missionaries did for the Burmese, in the way that parents do things for children. But she recognized that the Burmese, like growing children, needed to take responsibility for "projects" to fully understand their value, difficult as it would be for the missionaries to "yield the responsibility gracefully."[24]

Gracefully or not, American missionaries did begin to yield. Already in 1923 the Methodist Church had set up a Southeast Asia Central Conference, which offered "practical autonomy for the various indigenous peoples." In 1931 the Methodist Church in Burma had ten ordained Burmese ministers, and approximately the same number with European names. By 1930 three-quarters of American Baptist schools in Burma were self-supporting, which indicated that they were already controlled by indigenous groups or soon would be. Southeast Asians were increasingly responsible for the functioning of the churches, administrative structures, and schools.[25]

Missionaries trained Southeast Asians to run these institutions democratically as well. In 1930 the Burma Baptist Missionary Conference had to decide how it would administer the new Conscience Clause, a law enacted by the Government of Burma stipulating that parents had the right to prevent their children from receiving religious instruction. Part of the context for this decision was that students at three missionary high schools, including Baptist Normal School, had gone on strike to protest mandatory bible class and a ban on their attending Buddhist holy celebrations during school time. These students applied lessons about democracy in ways that missionaries must have regretted. In the end the Baptists decided to inform every parent of the right to refuse religious instruction, although the result was likely to be a decrease in the number of children receiving Christian instruction. What is more interesting is the way the decision was made. Burmese, American, Karen, and Chinese members of the conference debated vociferously, with no apparent differences in participation based on ethnicity, gender, or age. The question was decided by a vote.[26]

As both the decision and the means of making it suggest, American missionaries were less worried about the development of nationalism among Southeast Asians than colonial officials were. They worked to increase indigenous leadership in local churches. Sometimes they moved slowly because of a personal desire to remain in charge or paternalistic sentiment in favor of longer tutelage. Other missionaries had believed for some time that it was objectionable for churches in Southeast Asia to be "governed by foreigners in some far off, and sometimes unsympathetic land."[27] The trend toward greater indigenous leadership in church institutions in Southeast Asia continued from the end of the First World War through the 1920s and accelerated during the 1930s, reinforced by lower levels of American financial support during the Depression.

Although most missionaries advocated such autonomy only within the religious realm, a few became advocates of political nationalism as well. More often, American missionaries demonstrated an easier acceptance of

Southeast Asian nationalist aspirations than their European counterparts did. Baptists, for instance, perceived growing Burmese nationalist sentiment, and advocated taking advantage of that sentiment to improve the standing of Christianity. They recommended translating into Burmese not only more religious literature but also more of the books used in Baptist schools, so that children could be educated in the language of their country.[28] For these missionaries the benefits were numerous: students could better take advantage of their education; Burmese would be more favorably disposed toward Christianity; and nationalist sentiment would be channeled in beneficial directions. But for colonial officials the distinction between the autonomy of churches and the promotion of anticolonial sentiment was often spurious. The rhetoric and example of autonomy, whether in American mission churches or the American colony in the Philippines, threatened the maintenance of colonial order.

The Example of the Philippines

Washington officials to a large extent shared the assumption of American missionaries that Southeast Asians, especially if Christian, could be capable of more self-government. Yet whether in the State, Commerce, or War Department, they were much more likely to point to United States colonialism in the Philippines as the best model for Europeans to follow than to call for more autonomy for the colonies. European colonial officials and many Southeast Asians did watch the American colonial project closely, attentive to the implications that developments in the Philippines might have for their own policies and plans.

United States colonial officials asserted that their colonial method was superior to that of the Europeans, and urged Europeans to adopt colonialism along American lines to improve both the standard of living for Southeast Asians and feelings of amity between ruler and ruled. As with the missionaries, Progressive ideals permeated United States colonial policies, and the way United States officials portrayed their policies to European colonial officials.[29] Public schooling epitomized United States colonialism in the eyes of many Americans, Europeans, and Southeast Asians. One of the first projects of United States colonial officials was to establish as many elementary schools as possible. A shortage of trained indigenous teachers meant that English was the language of instruction in many of these schools from the beginning. The goal was universal literacy, but with restricted access to secondary and tertiary education. Education was not an end in itself but a means of creating a people capable of self-government and prepared to participate in the modern economy.[30]

The European colonial powers were interested in how the United States had organized schools in the Philippines. In 1916 the assistant director of education in the Federated Malay States, R. O. Winstedt, studied schools in the Philippines and Java as he prepared to reform the school system in Malaya. Winstedt was particularly impressed by the vocational training in Philippine schools, but he thought the Dutch emphasis on vernacular education better suited to British needs than the English-language education available in the Philippines.[31] Education policy in the Philippines stressed preparation for involvement in the political life of the colony as well as in industrialization, however. In a lecture to United States foreign service officers in training in 1926, Prentiss Gilbert criticized the Dutch for having kept the "native population" of the Netherlands Indies "subservient from a social point of view," by not allowing them to learn "Dutch or other western European languages." He did note that the Dutch were "now establishing schools," and connected this "change" to "our attitude in the Philippines."[32]

The Dutch would probably have been surprised by Gilbert's assertion of United States influence on their policy, because most Dutch believed that the United States example was powerful but dangerous to Dutch rule. One American visitor to the Netherlands Indies in 1923 reported that Dutch, English, and Americans who lived there agreed that United States governance of the Philippines was "a failure" generally, and that the "intensive education schemes" were a particular problem. The "educated natives" would "not [be] satisfied to perform manual labor," and would become an unemployed, overeducated, discontented mass. A Dutch official affirmed this sentiment in the following year to a visiting United States Army officer: "You only educate them to shoot them. Look at your own Filipinos." The officer thought this sentiment "extreme" but implied that too much education for colonial subjects might be problematic.[33]

The army officer's ambivalence symbolized the complicated position of United States officials. They believed that colonialism was not a viable system over the long term. But they also had little faith in the ability of Filipinos to function at the same level as white Americans. Dwight F. Davis, governor general of the Philippines in 1930, argued that United States methods were superior to those of the British. He noted that "Filipinos are very ready to accept suggestions from anyone in whom they have confidence." Davis helped build this confidence by making sure that Filipinos got "public credit" for decisions. Davis thought that the "British method in the past of wielding the big stick, kicking natives off the sidewalks, etc." set up an antagonistic relationship which angered "natives" and undermined the British ability to lead them.[34] American paternalism was benevolent, sensitive to Filipino feelings; British paternalism was too heavy-handed and undermined its very object. When British officials in Rangoon asked the United States consul there for information about the United States government in the Philippines as a possible model for increasing self-government in Burma, it merely confirmed the sense in Washington that United States colonial policy was the way of the future.[35]

The inauguration of the Philippine Commonwealth was the culmination of United States colonial policy, and United States officials pointed to the way commonwealth leaders both exercised their responsibility and treasured their connection to the United States. By the mid-1930s leading Filipinos were willing to at least consider continuation of the commonwealth, since independence was sure to be accompanied by unfavorable trade agreements and the withdrawal of protection by the United States Navy. Washington officials downplayed the complex reasons behind these discussions, instead emphasizing that Manuel Quezon and other Filipinos valued the light-handed tutelage of Washington.[36] European colonial officials did not see these developments in the same light. The United States consul in Batavia reported that "all classes of the population" in the Netherlands Indies "fervently hope" that the United States would remain in the Philippines as a restraint on Japanese expansionism.[37] And the Singapore newspapers, at the request of the British government, carried little coverage of the inauguration of Quezon as first president of the Philippine Commonwealth. The British worried that such coverage "might encourage subversive sentiment among the native and other Asiatic peoples" in Malaya.[38]

Historians of the United States, especially of United States foreign relations, have often dismissed the notion that possession of the Philippines played any important role in shaping United States foreign policy. They most commonly cite the pulling back by such an ardent expansionist as Theodore Roosevelt, who after 1907 began to advocate pulling the defense perimeter back to Hawaii, essentially acknowledging that the United States was unable to defend the Philippines.[39] The rising power of Japan did change policymakers' perceptions of the costs and benefits of holding the Philippines as a colony, but the United States did not cede the colony to any other power. The continued United States presence meant that whatever policy it did pursue there had important implications for the surrounding countries. Britain, France, and especially the Netherlands had to attempt to predict what the United States might do, and what the effect on their own colonies might be.

During the interwar period Europeans saw United States policy as inconstant but influential. Initially, as noted above, they worried that the rhetoric of self-determination would pervade politics in Southeast Asia as well as Europe, and undermine their authority even if the United States had no firm commitment to overturning colonialism. This fear did not last long, and the Republicans who were in charge of United States foreign policy throughout the 1920s appeared sympathetic to European concerns, at least politically. Even in the Philippines itself the steps in the direction of independence were slight. The onset of the Depression, as will be discussed further in chapters 4 and 5, prompted a rethinking of colonial policies and rule by all the colonial powers. In the early 1930s colonial powers, including the United States, were concerned with minimizing the cost and maximizing the possible financial benefit of ruling over colonies, while by the late 1930s all the colonial powers were taking concrete steps toward granting more political responsibility, though in limited ways, to Southeast Asians.

The example of the United States as a colonial power in the Philippines was never as powerful as Americans hoped, because it represented neither the danger to the colonial order that Europeans often feared nor the path to quick independence for which Southeast Asians longed. Yet for Washington officials the possibilities that the American example offered for reform rather than radical transformation of the colonial order were exactly why they believed it could be a force for change, since a critical component was the idea that there was a way to reconcile the interests of Europeans and Southeast Asians. The reconciliation could be found in what Emily Rosenberg has called liberal developmentalism, or the ability of enlightened corporations to raise the standard of living for workers while making lots of money for the owners. The managers of many United States corporations in colonial Southeast Asia believed that they were demonstrating new ways of doing business to more traditional European companies. The efficiency and scientific management in United States corporations enabled them, in their mind, to have sufficient profit to treat workers humanely and make money.

Where the $5.00-a-Day Worker Costs Only 28 Cents

Colonial Southeast Asia provided the world with a large share of its requirements for sugar, rubber, kapok, copra, quinine, coffee, pepper, leaf tobacco, rice, and tin, and a healthy amount of oil. The combination of rich soil—leading to abundant food—and low population density in much of Southeast Asia meant that European plantation and mine owners had traditionally imported workers from China and India to perform the backbreaking labor necessary for Europeans to earn the maximum profit from these crops and mineral resources.[40] Colonial policies which professed to value traditional Southeast Asian culture also discouraged any industrialization of European colonies which would have required Southeast Asians to become factory workers, and any urbanization. Investors from the United States viewed the situation somewhat differently. As discussed in chapters 2 and 4, the extent of United States investment in the region was minimal if compared with United States investment in Europe or Latin America. But United States companies did invest in key sectors in Southeast Asia, and sometimes stressed that the introduction of American methods might be both profitable and progressive.

Surprisingly, perhaps, United States firms invested at a modest but steady rate throughout the interwar period. Investment efforts did fall off during the Depression, but not precipitously. During the 1920s United States firms were seeking new opportunities to gain more control over important natural resources as well as ways to expand into developing markets. And during the 1930s new investments were often driven by the desire to be behind tariff walls erected to protect local businesses. Almost none of the scholarship on Southeast Asia, even by historians of labor and economic history, notes the presence of United States firms, or indeed of firms other than those of the ruling power. In addition, a persistent image that colonies were sources of raw materials and agricultural products exclusively, rather than of manufactured goods, continues to shape historical research despite some attention to labor conditions.[41] How industrialization was changing the Southeast Asian and European experiences of colonialism is only beginning to be understood.

Southeast Asia was a risky, marginal place for United States capital, and before the mid-1920s United States firms invested in the production only of rubber and oil.[42] The first was attractive because United States companies were attempting to avoid a British-Dutch stranglehold over its supply, the

second for strategic reasons and worries about the finite nature of oil resources. The U.S. Rubber Company, the Goodyear Company, and the Nederlands Koloniale Petroleum Maatschappij (Standard Oil of New Jersey's subsidiary) built homes, hospitals, and recreation facilities for their indigenous
and European and American workforce, both because Dutch and British law
required it and to attract workers to the sparsely populated sites. Each company insisted that it provided a much higher standard of living and more
opportunities for indigenous workers than those workers had had before,
and better than European companies provided.

In hearings before the U.S. Senate in 1945 representatives of Jersey Stan-
dard/NKPM noted the social and educational benefits their company had
brought to the Netherlands East Indies before the war. Traditional "native"
housing had "split bamboo walls" and a "thatched roof," and was "difficult
to keep clean" as well as "devoid of any modern facilities." NKPM provided
"substantial multiple dwellings" for Indonesian workers, all "provided with
electric light, separate kitchens, bathing and toilet facilities with running
water, and separate laundry facilities." Indonesian "foremen and clerks"
often lived in duplexes. The company also built "large, airy, clean markets"
where Indonesians bought food and other items in a sanitary, convenient
environment. The American emphasis on "modern advantages" such as re-
frigeration also improved the general standard of living.

In the field of health NKPM followed the Dutch lead, but company representatives believed that they provided more and better service. The company had a total of 229 hospital beds, and employed four doctors, fifteen
nurses, and thirty-five medical assistants in 1939. The clinic and Indonesian
"graduate first-aid men" were kept busy by more than 100,000 clinic visits
and 8,900 first-aid cases during the same year. The clinic visits were by
employees and their families; first-aid cases were primarily injuries and ill-
nesses suffered on "geographical exploration parties" and at "wildcat wells."
By the late 1930s all new employees were required to have a full medical
examination.

As in company towns in the United States, NKPM also funded schools
and recreational facilities. All children had an opportunity to attend primary school, although Indonesian and European children went to separate
schools and had separate curricula. The company planned to build a high
school to supplement the government high school in Palembang, but was
prevented by the outbreak of war. NKPM also provided soccer fields, and
clubhouses with dance floors and movie theaters. The NKPM did not over-

Body-assembling department of General Motors Assembly Plant, Batavia, Java, 1927. National Archives and Records Administration, 151-FC-78B-1.

turn the social order; it built separate facilities for Europeans and Americans and for Indonesians.[43] Some Dutch employees perceived a challenge. As early as 1926 NKPM received complaints that the similarity of facilities for Dutch and Indonesian workers lowered the prestige of the former in the eyes of the latter.[44]

American observers liked to portray resident American businessmen as unconcerned with prestige or tradition, but rather interested in efficiency and opportunity. In 1929 the United States consul in Batavia, Coert du Bois, compared the "youth and energy" of American businessmen with the "staid old conservative heads of the large Dutch and British business houses."[45] The difference went beyond style. Companies such as General Motors, Goodyear, and Jersey Standard introduced rough versions of Henry Ford's notion of raising workers' standards of living in order to create consumers of them. Jersey Standard had oil wells in Sumatra and also built a refinery to capture the local market. As one oil executive noted, locally refined oil is frequently less expensive to the consumer, which results in "a higher standard of living" and "greater consumption" of automobiles and other equipment.[46] Jersey Standard was so successful at marketing its oil in Asia that its distinctive five-gallon oil cans were ubiquitous throughout the region, reused often for oil but also as cookstoves or to carry water, among other things.[47]

General Motors established an assembly plant in Batavia in 1926 and Goodyear a tire factory in Buitenzorg in 1934. The production of each was destined for the regional market. Both companies also made a point of hiring indigenous workers rather than Chinese or Indians. As du Bois reported, Americans broke "another precedent" by their "attitude toward and success with native labor." In the GM plant "all of the industrial labor is done by natives under American supervision," and "in certain lines their output is higher than in any other foreign assembly plant of the company." He explained that the American managers had awakened the "dormant aptitude" of Indonesians for skilled labor by treating them as "members of a team playing an interesting game" and promoting a "general spirit of fellowship in work." These "American" strategies worked much better than the "drill-sergeant methods" of the Dutch.[48] The factory was a decidedly primitive-looking building (as shown in the photograph), but it is possible also to see modern machinery, operated with pride by the Indonesians pictured.

Buying American

Only a tiny number of Southeast Asians worked in factories, and only some of these earned enough to buy manufactured consumer goods. The growth of the market in Southeast Asia between the wars stemmed from increased demand for agricultural products of the region, particularly rubber. Publications of the U.S. Bureau of Foreign and Domestic Commerce urged American firms to consider marketing to the smallholder rubber growers of Burma, Malaya, Siam, and the Netherlands Indies. They assumed that consumer goods could be as transformative for Southeast Asians as they had been in the United States, creating a mass culture oriented toward a regimen of work and consumption. The result would be a more efficient economy, as Southeast Asians began to specialize in producing export goods. The market for "American foodstuffs" in the Netherlands Indies had grown during the 1920s, for example, as Indonesians "learned" that they could "improve their economic position materially" by purchasing imported food and growing rubber or other products for export.[49]

Sun-Maid Raisins and California fruit provided two of the seemingly unlikely food imports to Southeast Asia. California fruit growers promoted their plums and peaches with a public display of freshly arrived fruit in Batavia in 1927. Their marketing was traditional, as represented by the photo of the United States trade commissioner Donald Renshaw and the Dutch importer P. G. H. Muller marveling over, one assumes, the freshness and beauty of products shipped halfway around the world. Sun-Maid perhaps made more of an impact on Southeast Asians with its imports of raisins, since it pursued an aggressive marketing scheme. A truck painted to mimic the raisin carton traveled throughout Java selling raisins in "every country village." Once there, the raisins were further distributed by "school-boys" who sold them throughout the village, in much the same way that boys in the United States might sell newspapers. In this way Sun-Maid potentially changed eating habits but more importantly provided entrepreneurial opportunities, modest as they were, to young Indonesian boys.[50] United States officials promoted Sun-Maid and California fruit because doing so was their job, but they also believed that for Indonesians to take advantage of these

Freshly imported California fruit, Batavia, Java, 1927. National Archives and Records Administration, 151-FC-77B-1.

new, modern opportunities would be a means of demonstrating their ability to move toward self-rule.

Consumer goods, especially of United States origin, were both the means for and the result of cementing Southeast Asia's position within the interdependent international economy. Some of the ubiquitous United States consumer goods in the region were, as noted, canned fish, fruit, and vegetables. In the long-settled areas Southeast Asians could shift from a subsistence lifestyle of rice production and fishing to producing such export commodities as rubber, pepper, or leaf tobacco while relying on imported canned foods to replace what they had previously grown. Canned foods also enabled Southeast Asians to push out into unsettled areas such as the rich lands of Borneo. Hoover, the United States consul in Batavia, explained that "Chinese traders" took small boats to the inaccessible rubber growing areas, loaded on the trip out with "foodstuffs in tin cans . . . toilet goods . . . and a surprisingly wide range of other goods." These goods were traded for rubber grown on the smallholder plots, such that "the value of the rubber is enjoyed in goods."[51]

The explicit message was that consumer goods enabled Southeast Asians to join the modern international economy, which could only be to their benefit. Eventually too, these goods could help to transform Southeast Asians into modern consumers. That process was far from complete, as United States observers made clear in their descriptions of foolish purchases or inappropriate usage. In January 1926 the United States consul in Soerabaya noted that "natives who cannot read or write . . . and may still do some furtive headhunting have donned dress suits without wearing shoes" and purchased automobiles although frequently there were few roads on which to drive them.[52] Winslow's comment, meant at the time to amuse by evoking the incongruity of a primitive "native" driving an up-to-date automobile, demonstrates that Southeast Asians did not always use their modern consumer products in ways envisioned by United States officials or advertisers. American makes of cars were popular in Southeast Asia precisely because they were rugged enough to complete the off-road tasks for which they were purchased.

Opposite page—top: Trucks painted to resemble the Sun-Maid carton sold raisins throughout villages in Java. National Archives and Records Administration, 151-FC-77B-3.
Bottom: Boys sold Sun-Maid raisins door to door throughout Java. National Archives and Records Administration, 151-FC-77B-4.

Southeast Asians were much more likely to buy a can of grapes or a flashlight and batteries made in the United States than a car, but United States automobiles dominated the roads in the region, providing a highly visible sign of the association between modernity and the United States. The rubber boom made the Chevrolet dealer in Sumatra happy; he reported that "the natives would come to town with their pockets fairly bulging with money," which they used to pay cash at his dealership.[53] In 1928, in fact, the United States provided 79 percent of the 17,588 cars imported into the Netherlands Indies, while the next year more than 1,000 cars and trucks were imported by Burma from the United States.[54] Most cars were owned by Europeans, of course, including the governor general of Netherlands Indies, who purchased two Chryslers in 1926.[55] Southeast Asians who purchased cars were usually large landowners from the traditional élite, or newly rich rubber growers, but some bought sturdy, reliable American trucks and larger cars to begin their own transport businesses.

The rubber price boom of the 1920s was a key factor in providing indigenous Southeast Asians with more money with which to buy American imports of all types. Most of the examples cited above are from that relatively brief period when Southeast Asian products commanded high prices on the world market, and the number of people able to consume grew larger, if it was still modest in size and in amount of United States goods consumed compared to markets in places like Europe and Japan. The arrival of the Depression did not end Southeast Asian demands for manufactured consumer goods. Southeast Asians still wanted to consume these goods and searched for cheaper sources. Some United States firms made efforts to produce in Southeast Asia to reduce costs, but Japanese firms also stepped in with cheaper versions of imported goods. These Japanese imports prompted some European concern about Japan's influence over Southeast Asians.[56] The hopes of United States officials about the influence of consumer purchases, and the fears of European officials about those same purchases, suggest that the spread of manufactured consumer goods was believed to have some impact, but that no one yet agreed on what that impact would be.

Whether automobiles, canned goods, or machine-woven cloth, most goods from the United States were luxuries for Southeast Asians, but luxuries which United States observers predicted would be transformed into necessities as the region became more developed and more enmeshed in the global economy. American culture was transmitted more powerfully by Hollywood than Detroit, then as ever since.

Charlie Chaplin in the Jungle

The culture critic Gilbert Seldes wrote in 1937, in *The Movies Come from America*, that people went to the movies "simply to be at the movies." The experience, he claimed, was made that much more intense by being a "mass entertainment," in which "several hundred other people feel at the same time" the same emotions.[57] In Southeast Asia, although the great majority of movies came from Hollywood, there were few movie palaces. Still movies were a mass event, with an average attendance of two hundred or more in theaters which, at least in the cities, might have four to eight hundred seats. American observers, like the United States vice-consul in Medan, Sumatra, Daniel M. Braddock, noted as well that movie theaters were among the few places where the "heterogenous population" of the colony gathered together, although effectively segregated by ticket price.[58] Observers of all nationalities agreed that movies were a force for both modernization and Americanization, and divided only in whether they judged this trend beneficial or harmful.

Movies Come from America

The movies did come from America to Southeast Asia, as to the rest of the world. After the First World War the dominance of Hollywood worldwide meshed neatly with the growing importance of Southeast Asian exports to encourage both the supply of movies and demand for them. By 1925 the Philippines had more than fifty movie theaters, showing 90 percent or more American movies; Burma had fifty-seven movie theaters in the same year, the Netherlands Indies thirty-four.[59] The number of theaters was small compared to the United States, but much larger per capita than China, which had only 120 theaters by 1928.[60] Southeast Asians living in towns of the most modest size had easy access to a theater. The number of permanent theaters was also supplemented by missionaries who showed movies in their recreation halls, in an effort to bring people through the door, and by traveling movie shows. In 1926 Charles Merz reported that he had watched from the streets of Singapore as "a Ford car head[ed] into virgin jungle with five reels of a great passion jugged in a tin box on its running-board." Later that night the driver would string a white sheet "between two stanchions in a copra shed" and run the projector off "a dizzy little motor" so that "two hundred natives" could see "American life as it is lived, presumably, in our best families."[61] Before 1929 reports by the Bureau of Foreign and Domestic Commerce noted that 90 percent or more of the movies shown in Southeast Asia came from the United States, with the total number of feature films imported ranging from three to five hundred per year per colony.[62]

The advent of sound pictures did cut the percentage of American films shown, but only slightly. French import restrictions meant that Indochina in the 1930s had only approximately 50 percent American films, while the Netherlands Indies had approximately 65 percent, but figures in the British and American colonies were between 80 and 90 percent. The competition did not come from European films primarily but rather from Indian, Chinese, and Japanese films.[63] Thus Hollywood had a virtual monopoly over the most lifelike medium for presenting images of the West to indigenous Southeast Asians. Commentators agreed that "natives" made up "of course the vast majority of motion picture audiences," and disagreed only on the effect of the movies on Southeast Asians.[64]

The United States consul in Rangoon, Winfield H. Scott, argued in 1934 that United States distributors should make sure that the films they sent to Burma were interesting to the "indigenous classes" who made up the "'paying' moving picture public." Europeans, he noted, had more money and therefore a wider range of entertainment options; Burmese faced both income and "class distinction" barriers to joining social clubs. They found movies "a comparatively cheap, interesting, and indiscriminating form of . . . entertainment."[65] A French travel writer stumbled upon "savages" in the mountains of Indochina watching their first Charlie Chaplin film. He reinforced his description of their "primitive" nature by explaining that they found none of Chaplin's antics at all amusing, but laughed uproariously at the "young heroine . . . weeping glycerin tears."[66] The discrepancy between what the writer expected moviegoers to find amusing and what made them laugh demonstrates the difficulties of interpreting the meaning of these films for early-twentieth-century Southeast Asians, but it also demonstrates, forcefully, that Southeast Asian consumers constructed their own meaning as they watched. And they kept watching, with obvious enjoyment.

Chaplin was a favorite among children in Java as well, who abandoned the traditional *wayang* puppet show in one pavilion at a village wedding ceremony, which their parents were watching, to double over with laughter at the movie. Hubert Banner, the American travel writer who was amazed to find movies shown in "the jungle," also lamented the loss of indigenous culture which he believed they foretold, perhaps within the lifetime of those laughing children.[67] If Chaplin's physical comedy and action movies proved as universally popular then as similar films do now, United States officials responsible for advising film distributors had difficulty providing consistent advice about what else would sell. Westerns appealed in some times and places, but they seemed to be falling out of favor by the 1930s; "college dramas" and "good mystery" stories might sell, while "sophisticated" dramas and comedies were both risky. Famous Hollywood stars could always sell a movie, since many observers noted that Southeast Asians were familiar with these stars and with "American slang."[68]

Censoring Dangerous Ideas

What would sell was one major concern; what would pass the censors was another. Each Southeast Asian colony had a board of censors which had to review every movie imported. The law in each colony stipulated clearly the procedure for sending a film through the review process, but provided little guidance about what topics or behavior would trigger cuts of footage or an outright ban. Contrary to what one might expect, United States film distributors lodged more complaints about review procedures than about the criteria for censorship. The themes which would cause problems with the censors were well reported by United States officials in the region: any scenes of plotting against the government, revolution, anything which reflected negatively on royalty or the police, gunplay, and detailed depiction of crimes, particularly if successful. Sex scenes caused some trouble, but already by the 1920s American filmmakers were toning those down for the United States audience.[69]

Most importers believed that they knew which films would pass muster in their own regions, and how to prepare films for the boards of censors. Colonial governments, which levied an import tax on each foot of imported film as well as a fee, also per foot, for the review process, were reluctant to allow film importers to have access to the films first, because they believed that the importers would then submit far fewer feet for review and decrease tax revenues. In the Netherlands Indies this issue arose as early as January 1925. Two weeks after a request from the representative of Universal Pictures in the colony for assistance from the State Department, the newly formed Motion Pictures Producers and Distributors Association (MPPDA) asked for United States consuls throughout the region to send copies of import regulations and censorship laws through the Department of Commerce to the MPPDA. Hoover, in Batavia, was key to this project in Southeast Asia, since he was also a member of the "local Motion Picture Distributors Committee."[70]

State and Commerce Department officials worked for the next two years with film distributors in Batavia to make import and censorship regulations simpler and more predictable. In the process slightly unethical practices were revealed on both sides, such as the practice by some Dutch of forming private clubs where the uncut version of films submitted to censors boards were shown to members only, all of whom were of course European and none of whom paid any money which reached the films' distributors. The United States film distributors were themselves taking advantage of temporary permits which had been issued for some serials to avoid the censorship process, and attempting to avoid import duties by taking films for pre-censorship. Yet throughout the drawn-out negotiations, not once did United States film distributors contend that the content cut from a film had been harmless and should be restored.[71]

The only substantive complaints about the censorship process were from European film distributors and some colonial officials, with both groups finding the censors too lenient about what they allowed to be shown. For example, the agent for the British film *The Only Way* wrote to the secretary of the colonies to complain that his film had been banned while the American film *A Tale of Two Cities*, with the same subject matter, had not been. A flurry of telegrams flew between Singapore and London in an attempt to discover the reason, with the governor general of Singapore initially arguing that the two films were "entirely different," but backpedaling when asked to describe the difference. He blamed the ban on more stringent standards in place when the British film was reviewed, owing to "present conditions," presumably a reference to the recent PKI rebellion in the Netherlands Indies. Officials in the Colonial Office felt that a potential problem had existed, and noted wryly that "after all it is not our policy to discourage British films."[72]

The governor general believed that censorship could not provide a solution to either of the problems he perceived: the small number of British films and the lack of films "ideal" for the Malayan audience. He argued that "to cut out all that might be represented as derogatory to the European, as sensational or unedifying, would be tantamount to banning the cinematograph altogether." That, he acknowledged was unrealistic, and he hoped rather for "the gradual substitution of British for foreign films" as a partial solution. By October 1927 a quota of British films for the Straits Settlements market,

beginning at 7.5 percent and rising gradually to 30 percent, had been proposed in the colony's Legislative Council.[73] Since British films had as much
trouble passing the censors as the American films did, the quota suggested
that markets were a greater government concern than content.

Trade Follows the Film

In November 1925 the *Saturday Evening Post* published a lengthy article
titled "Trade Follows the Film," to indicate that a new type of empire was
being created, since "the sun . . . never sets on the British Empire and the
American motion picture." Trade no longer followed the flag, as during the
period of British expansion when gunpowder was necessary to induce trade.
In the new era the United States was becoming "the best-known and most
widely advertised country to the remotest habitations of man on the globe."
The empire of trade was one which people worldwide would choose to join.
An editorial in the *London Morning Post*, quoted in the article, expressed
the British fear that "if . . . not checked in time," film would "Americanize
the world." The global stretch of Hollywood was demonstrated by the second illustration for the article: a photo of the Empire Theatre in Singapore,
with advertisements for the fourth annual Paramount week prominently
displayed.[74] The accompanying photograph gives a more usual view of this
theater in 1927, then showing *The Love Thief* (John McDermott, 1926). The
crowds outside are examining the movie posters and selling from street
stalls.

Films advertised both American goods and the American way of life. The
U.S. Departments of Commerce and State paid close attention to the possibilities of film advertising for goods. In August 1928 the newly formed
Motion Picture section of the Bureau of Foreign and Domestic Commerce
requested from trade commissioners abroad "specific examples" of movies
helping to sell "American merchandise." The trade commissioner in Batavia
responded that the movies helped to sell American fashion, especially "hats,
shirts, hosiery and the like," in the Netherlands Indies.[75] The trade commissioners were generally careful not to overstate the case, and direct correla-
tions between films viewed and products purchased are difficult to discern
even with today's sophisticated marketing studies. United States representatives abroad did note some suggestive trends, including the apparent
preference of wealthy Southeast Asians for American models of cars and
the tendency of ethnic Chinese and Malays in British Malaya to purchase

Movie theater in Penang, Malaya, 1927. National Archives and Records Administration, 151-FC-14B-3.

more American goods in the midst of a "Buy British" campaign launched by British patriots in the colony during the Depression.[76] The colonies of Southeast Asia also had substantial trade surpluses with the United States, and the movies themselves were an American export helping to bring dollars directly back to the United States rather than following the triangular route which had prevailed, with the United States buying raw materials, the Europeans selling finished goods in the region, and the dollars returning later to the United States through trade with Europe.[77]

The low standard of living of the vast majority of indigenous Southeast Asians meant that the purchase of a movie ticket was an important consumerist act, and as much of one as many could probably make. Going to the movies did begin to change the relationship of Southeast Asians to entertainment but did not transform it. Traditional forms of entertainment, such as the wayang mentioned above, were usually sponsored by wealthy members of the community and cost nothing to attend; they lasted all night, so that people came and went during the performance; they took place outdoors in a party atmosphere of eating, drinking, and some chatting; and they usually featured well-known stories which people could follow with minimal attention. Going to a wayang performance, or partaking in similar forms of entertainment that existed in the other colonies, was more like going to a party at which a play was shown than like going to a modern theater.[78]

Movies, shown indoors with fixed, limited showtimes, seating determined by ticket price paid, and unfamiliar stories requiring the audience to pay attention to the plot, would seem to require a new attitude toward entertainment. At one level they certainly did, and the new attitude was broadly a modern, industrial one. People's lives, both at work and at play, were more likely to be organized by a clock than in the past, for example. But Southeast Asians did not capitulate completely to externally imposed standards for the showing of movies; rather, they attended movies in ways which served their own conceptions of entertainment forms. In French Indochina, for example, the regular program was relatively long by United States standards, consisting of a newsreel, cartoons or other shorts, and then the feature film. On the weekends the theaters remained open all night. Tickets cost a bit more then, but patrons could stay as long as they wished. In Singapore, the United States consul general Addison E. Southard reported, the "practice of the theaters catering to the mixed audiences" was to run one long show each evening, lasting from 7:30 p.m. to 11:30. The first half was programmed to "the native taste," while the second half offered films "of a better type for European patrons." Still, the "native invariably arrives at the beginning and stays through the entire show."[79] These four-hour shows more closely approximated the length of traditional entertainments, and meant that Malayans did not have to completely change their habits to become patrons of the movies.

United States consular officials had the job of reporting back to Washington the movie-viewing habits of Southeast Asians, so that this information could help movie production companies in the United States to better market in the region. From these reports, as well as from references in writings by Southeast Asians, it appears that movies were popular because they were both modern and familiar. Rudolf Mrázek evokes the newness of film, and the wonder of projected light, in his description of the colonial exhibition of 1916 in Batavia. The exhibition featured many traditional entertainments, such as clowns and animal displays, but also an open-air cinema. The crowd, made up of most of the many groups in the Indies, sat on the ground in the darkness, illuminated by a few oil lamps and the flickering beam of the movie projector. The "immense crowd," the "amazing multicolored stilllife," had a look of "placid happiness" as the viewers sat until the end, and then returned peacefully to their villages. The Dutch observer who described this scene imagined that the viewers had been unchanged by their experience, willing to "live again in their *kampongs*, and work again with their primitive tools."[80] In 1916 it was still a rare event, likely only at a festival in a city, for an ordinary Indonesian to see a film. But theaters sprang up quickly, in large cities first but spreading out into small towns as well. Theaters were often the first air-conditioned buildings in the colonies, and were quickly equipped with sound equipment after its invention. Tan Malaka, Indonesian revolutionary, casually mentioned "cinema" as among the "light diversions" available to ordinary people during the flush years of 1926–27. Nguyen Hong's autobiography *Days of Childhood* (1938) just as casually refers to the way that he, a poor child, would often use infrequent allowances or money earned to buy a ticket to the movies. An Indonesian in exile on Boven Digoel in the mid-1930s somewhat ironically evokes the attraction of Tarzan films, among the films shown regularly at the camp, to the local Kaja-Kaja tribe, called "ghosts of the forest" by the exiles.[81] During the 1920s and 1930s attending movies became common enough to require no special explanation.

Routine of Freedom

The movies in Southeast Asia were, as in the United States, also a place for dreaming of adventure and romance. Officials from the Departments of Commerce and State did not discuss the dreams in their reports, but memoirs of politically active Southeast Asians do. Sukarno, a student and budding political activist in the 1920s who in the 1950s became president of independent Indonesia, remembered paying his three cents for a cheap seat at the movies. He was so fond of westerns that he taught himself to read the Dutch subtitles, a particularly impressive feat since the cheap seats were behind the screen and the titles read backward.[82] U Nu, who would be prime minister of Burma in the 1950s, wrote about his attempts to meet girls outside the movie theaters he frequented with his friends. U Nu intimated that some feelings are universal when he recalled that his teenage self lacked the courage to speak to any of the girls lingering outside the theater.[83] The stories of Sukarno and U Nu of the part that movies played in their teenage years resemble those told by immigrants to the United States, or small-town boys dreaming of making it big in the city.[84] Through a medium provided by Hollywood, the whole world had access to similar images and a similar vocabulary to describe what then appeared to be very similar dreams.

Americans writing about the impact of films worldwide did not, in the 1920s and 1930s, comment on the dream of an Indonesian student that he might someday ride the white horse and save the town from the bad guys, but they did note the "routine of freedom" in American life which the movies presented as ordinary. This message, they believed, was pervasive, highly appealing, and therefore potentially transformative. Part of the message was the possibility of material success for the "poor boy," or the existence of a nation "where mechanics possess cars." The high standard of living was not all, though. According to an article in *Foreign Affairs*, the "ordinary unregimented individual" lived a remarkably free life in Hollywood films; he "travels at will, loves whom he pleases, outguesses his boss, and wisecracks the government." The article went on to note that the freedom from coercion by government or capitalist institutions that Hollywood preached might "bring cheer and thought to peoples less fortunate."[85] Most American observers believed that the combination of freedom and material well-being presented in Hollywood films both appealed to a wide range of people worldwide and presented them with a nonrevolutionary means of transforming their own lives to match the Hollywood image.

Many European observers, though, found Hollywood films a positive danger in the colonies. Some of their criticisms turned the virtues extolled by Americans on their heads. An editorial in the Dutch-language newspaper *Java Bode* decried Hollywood's message that "nothing is so sacred or good that it cannot be bought for the Dollar," and its trivializing of beauty. For an example it noted that the Butterfly in the film version (1932) of Puccini's *Madame Butterfly* whispered "Okay." American financial success seemed likely, even in the 1930s, to bring about a homogeneous world culture which at least the editor of the *Java Bode* thought "vulgar, bombastic, and often dangerous."[86]

More dangerous than the materialism in American films was the "degradation" of white men and women that these observers perceived. *Java Bode* presented the problem in a manner familiar to readers of newspapers in the American South: the "white woman" had been "degraded" by being "systematically" presented as someone who "at the first sight of a waiter-faced fellow with patent leather hair who three times raises his eyebrows, starts undressing." The "police-courts," the editorial continued, were feeling the full "effects of the crime films." The British author Sir Hesketh Bell argued more emotionally, if less colorfully, that the "remarks and catcalls" which greeted the "amorous passages" shown on the screen would "make blood boil." The French scholar A. F. Legendre evoked the image of "beautiful women," with their décolletage "down to their navels," who were a bit indiscriminate with their favors. It came as no surprise to him that many Southeast Asians believed Europe and America to be lands of "bandits and prostitutes."[87] Although these authors surely overstated the purity of the regard in which Europeans were held by Southeast Asians, images of sexy Europeans and Americans, with hints of their sexual activities, may have reinforced the diminution in European prestige generally, after the senseless carnage of the First World War.[88] But sex was a concern for censors worldwide, and the implementation of the production code in the United States largely answered this criticism.

The absence of sex seems to have led to the increased use of violence in Hollywood films of the 1930s, and to colonial censors violence—whether in the form of crime, war, or revolution—was not any more popular than sex. European officials, concerned that Southeast Asians might imitate the crimes they saw in the movies, grew increasingly likely to ban films or cut scenes because of "excessive gunplay." In 1939 officials in the Straits Settlements banned Columbia's I Am the Law as likely to "put ideas into the heads of Asiatic hooligans." Americans sometimes defended the films by observing that justice always prevailed; crimes were always punished.[89] The American defense missed the real concern of colonial officials: colonial subjects did not have to read the films the way they were intended to be read. Maybe the Mexican bandit robbing rich white people on trains was gunned down in the end, but he also probably enjoyed the good life for a while, and took some of those white people down with him. Or perhaps Southeast Asians did not identify along the color lines which might seem natural to observers today. Perhaps they equated the British and the Dutch with the bandits, and saw themselves, or anticolonial nationalists, as the forces of justice. It is difficult to say, but all observers agreed that movies provided new windows onto the world, accessible to literate and illiterate alike. Southeast Asians could create their own images of the rest of the world, and of their place in it, with less and less reference to the images provided by colonial governments. That was enough to frighten colonial officials.[90]

The strong association of movies with America, one of two major sources of anticolonial rhetoric though not of anticolonial policy, only increased the fears of Europeans. Southeast Asians might well buy what the Americans were selling, since the images presented were so novel, so forceful, so appealing. What would an empire be worth to the French, the Dutch, or even the British if the inhabitants purchased American goods, spoke American-accented English, went to American mission schools, and viewed the ideal society as pictured by Hollywood? In the movies the empire of the mind which Americans often believed would make formal colonial rule obsolete was most vividly portrayed. This Americanized world might be filled with pliant workers diligently attempting to earn enough to purchase the good life, and therefore unlikely to challenge their government in radical ways, but Europeans found no comfort in that possibility. They understood that Southeast Asians might not read the cultural messages in this way. And even if Southeast Asians did buy into this message from America, the result might just as surely be the demise of European power in a competition taking place in marketplaces and movie theaters rather than battlefields, with the victorious United States gaining profits and converts rather than land and governing responsibilities.

Scratches on (of) the Imperial Mind

In 1958 Harold Isaacs published a revealing book titled *Scratches on our Minds: American Images of China and India*. He wanted to explore the mental images that Americans had of China and India, the "scratches" which education, popular culture, travels, journalism, and sometimes the experience of living in those countries had made on the minds of a few hundred prominent Americans. Throughout his analysis he seemed bemused by the staying power of stereotypes and the sense of estrangement and relative ignorance of most of these Americans, a remarkably well-educated sample, even those with long experience of Asia.[91] What is striking as well is that Isaacs's "Asia" consisted only of China and India: in his book the Philippines receives only two brief mentions, neither noting that a dozen years earlier the Philippines had been ruled by the United States. The other countries of Southeast Asia receive scant mention as well. The scratches of imperialism were apparently faint, and had healed leaving no scars.

It is notable that no one has written a book titled *Scratches on our Minds: Southeast Asian Images of the United States*, especially not for the 1920s and 1930s. The compelling questions for many scholars of Southeast Asia who focus on the late nineteenth century and the early twentieth have revolved around nationalism: how did it develop, what made the nations of Southeast Asia, why nationalism at all, and relatedly, what was the course of the anticolonial struggle? The answers appeared to be found easily within what are now the nations of Southeast Asia, and in the relations of the colonial ruling country and struggling-to-be-free colonized people. The narratives nearly always focus tightly on the dyads of colonized and colonizer. In this way scholarship on the nineteenth century and the early twentieth deviates from the compelling sense present in scholarship on the fourteenth to eighteenth centuries, in which Southeast Asia was a vibrant, polyglot, multiethnic, global trade center.[92] Colonialism probably did result in increased contact between, for example, Indonesians and Dutch, at the expense of contact between those same Indonesians and the rest of the world. But the globalized nature of Southeast Asia was not subsumed. Southeast Asians for centuries had been welcoming to, and resilient in the face of, new cultural influences. As American culture powerfully entered Southeast Asia after the First World War, Southeast Asians were growing increasingly restive with colonial rule, and looking for a variety of ways to resist that rule. Southeast Asians were also somewhat more likely to have a cash income, and to want to spend it on consumer goods.

Thus American culture came into a Southeast Asia which was welcoming. American missionaries and movies and products found an audience, or market, of open-minded, curious people. Were these Southeast Asians curious and welcoming because the cultural products were from America? Despite limited suggestions that the American provenance was appealing, as when the Vietnamese wanted to hear missionaries preach the "American Doctrine," it is more likely that the modern, often technologically superior nature of American culture was what appealed.[93] And was American culture universally appealing to Southeast Asians? It is safe to say that it was assuredly not, but in the 1920s and 1930s American culture was not yet so ubiquitous as to have to be resisted. It could simply be ignored, and those who rejected it therefore left little record of their distaste.

If only some Southeast Asians were "scratched" by American culture, then in what ways did United States cultural relations with Southeast Asia possibly scratch Americans? Harold Isaacs's work suggests that the scratches were so faint as to have been nonexistent. The persistent belief of many Americans, academics as well as the general public, that the United States was not an imperial power at all would tend to reinforce that sense. Recent scholarship suggests that the myth of American non-imperialism may have led to a lack of attention by scholars to ways in which the empire came to

America. But empire did come to America, and Americans were sometimes welcoming and sometimes hostile to the imperial presence. Mae Ngai has explored what happened when the people of the empire really did come to the United States, in the form of Filipino migrants flocking to Hawaii as well as the mainland (primarily California, Oregon, and Washington). Filipinos came for all the usual reasons, but they were not technically immigrants because they were "United States nationals." Although they were Asian, they could not be excluded. But as Asians, they could also not attain citizenship. The tens of thousands of Filipinos who arrived in Hawaii and the additional tens of thousands who arrived on the mainland between 1910 and 1930 brought the fact of United States empire very much to the attention of many Americans. The scratches on American minds from this encounter included extensive public discussion about the proper racial classification of Filipinos, the effects of the United States colonial policy of educating Filipinos widely and in English, and the limits of paternalistic empire in the face of violence against Filipinos by white Americans.[94]

Ngai reminds us that the United States, like European imperial powers, had to accept the empire into the metropole in unexpected and contentious ways, not least in its schools and labor markets. Sometimes these "United States nationals" attracted nearly no attention, saving Americans from having to confront the fact of empire. At other times these United States nationals were welcomed as proof of American benevolence, especially when the Filipinos were educated and ambitious enough to go back to succeed in the Philippines. But as Ngai demonstrates, when the concentration of Filipinos in an area became great enough, white Americans did notice. Indeed they protested, passed discriminatory laws, threatened the farmers and businesses which hired Filipinos, and sometimes attacked and killed Filipinos.[95] The empire made itself felt in the United States.

Other than in the Pacific coastal states, many Americans could live their whole lives without seeing any Filipino migrants, but the literal fruits of empire entered the homes of virtually all middle-class Americans during the late nineteenth century and the early twentieth. Kristin Hoganson has extended the vibrant scholarship on consumption, consumerism, and domestic politics by drawing attention to the imperial sources of many of these new, fashionable goods, especially foods. Magazines and cookbooks promoted an Americanized global cuisine. Women were encouraged to prepare meals with ingredients new to them and originating in all corners of the globe, such as pineapple, curry, and chili peppers. Decorating the home could also be an exercise in global consumption, with Persian rugs, Chinese textiles, and Philippine rattan furniture. Hoganson forthrightly addresses the difficulty of interpreting the meaning of these acts of consumption: Did Americans know or care about the political economy which enabled these goods to reach the United States? She demonstrates that imperialism was part of the narrative woven around these goods in advertisements and magazine stories.[96] Empire touched Americans in their consumption.

Americans encountered empire in one additional place as well: in their Protestant churches. Hoganson notes the propensity of church bazaars to have tables with different national themes, so that one could buy shells and embroidery at the Philippine table, wooden shoes and chocolate at the Dutch table, and so on. These churches were often raising money for mission work.[97] Missionaries who had lived in imperial settings, both United States and European, visited churches to give lectures and slide shows. Sometimes these missionaries were accompanied by converts, allowing Americans to meet them. Pamphlets and magazines reported on the activities of the mission fields. The Sunday school curriculum, for children and adults, emphasized the success and cultural benefits of mission work. By the 1920s and 1930s American missionaries embodied the tension between a powerful tradition of seeing the objects of their missionizing as "uncivilized heathens" and a more progressive, modern tendency to respect elements of indigenous life and culture. Fortunately they could resolve this tension for themselves by promoting a greater American presence in indigenous people's lives. Accompanied or not by the formal structures of empire, American missions could transform without destroying. This method of resolving the tension allowed Americans to focus on what America offered much more than on what it mandated, or on the people who received it. The surface of the American mind proved difficult to scratch.

Thoughts on the Meaning of Culture

Many Americans did, and do, believe that United States cultural power, though so strong as to appear imperialistic, has been a transformative force for good in the world. As the rest of the world accepted American cultural products, which in the mind of many Americans as well as in the policies of the United States government meant products as diverse as Ford cars, Hollywood movies, a particular approach to Christianity, and democratic institutions adhering to the American model, people would become wealthier, freer, and more entertained. American culture did come to colonial South-east Asia during the 1920s and 1930s, and often was perceived to be what was most modern about this modern age, by both Southeast Asians and Europeans. For involved Americans, the march to modernity was inevitable and to be celebrated, even if many believed that Southeast Asians could march only at a slower pace. Southeast Asians quickly incorporated many of the new products into their daily lives and worldviews, but often in ways at variance with how Americans believed they should, or for different pur-poses than Americans had imagined. The cultural empire proved as unruly as the political ones. Europeans often displayed a deep ambivalence, unable or unwilling to resist the advance of American cultural products yet recog-nizing that those products, and the economic power which underlay and promoted them, would profoundly disrupt their imperial project.

4

||||||||||||||||||||||||||||||||||||||||||||||||||||||||||||||||||||||||||||||||||||||||||||||||||||||||||||||||||||||||||||||||||||||||||||||||||||||||

Depression and the Discovery of Limits

The foreign economic policy of the United States during the 1920s had been all about confidence—confidence that an economic foreign policy would suffice as the United States foreign policy, confidence that United States economic power would prevail if given a fair chance, and confidence that the presence of United States institutions, especially its businesses but also its movies and missionaries, would have a beneficial, transformative effect on peoples around the world. As the magnitude of the economic disaster now called the Depression dawned on United States policymakers and business leaders during the early 1930s, this confidence was shaken. But not destroyed. The Depression presented a dilemma. Most Americans who had been involved in international trade and investment during the 1920s continued to believe, through the 1930s, that one of the best ways, if not the best way, out of the Depression for the United States and the rest of the world would be to concentrate on keeping the barriers to trade and investment as low as possible throughout the world. The dilemma, of course, was that few other people, whether in the United States or other countries, agreed. As virtually all countries moved increasingly to autarkic, nationalistic organization of their economies, policymakers and business leaders faced difficult choices.

In the short term they had to preserve the national interest or the existence of their companies. This responsibility meant that they often acquiesced in the raising of tariffs or the establishment of cartel-like arrangements to restrict the production of certain goods in the hope of increasing prices. But in the long term they hoped to return to a relatively open world economy, because they believed that the United States would come out on top in such an economy. So they pushed also for policies designed to re-produce the conditions of the 1920s, when they believed the economy had worked well. By the end of the 1930s, when neither strategy had proved effective at improving economic conditions, some of these men were begin-ning to believe that more systemic changes were needed. Labor conditions, balanced production and consumption, and, in colonial areas, tension be-tween who controlled politics and who controlled sources of wealth were increasingly important in determining the health of the economy. These sys-temic changes received little sustained attention, since the growing interna-tional conflicts leading to the Second World War overshadowed them.

The Depression had contradictory effects on the economics of late high imperialism. The 1920s had prompted colonial officials, willingly or not, to continue to integrate colonial Southeast Asia into the increasingly global economy. Southeast Asian exports went more often to the United States than to the colonial ruling power, imports came also from a greater variety of countries, and regional trade had increased.[1] One effect of the Depres-sion was to prompt a return to traditional economics of imperialism, with attempts to tie colonies tightly to the economies of their ruling power by setting production quotas and tariff policies which mirrored the autarkic trade policies adopted in imperial capitals. At the same time, there was greater regional cooperation among colonial powers, especially the Euro-pean countries but including the United States as well, to attempt to control production and exports for the benefit of all producing countries. Return to the traditional economics of imperialism proved unfeasible, but regional cooperation was challenging to realize as well, not least because of indige-nous resistance. Throughout the 1930s imperial government policies were primarily ad hoc, immediate responses to perceived crises, rather than con-sidered plans appropriate to the new conditions created as colonial South-east Asia's economy became more strongly linked to the global economy.

The Depression years saw United States officials and businessmen accept, however grudgingly, the economic attitudes associated with traditional imperialism. The tension between a visceral desire to turn the collective American back on a world that proved too threatening or complicated, and an equally powerful desire to transform the world, reached a high point dur-ing the 1930s. This tension played out starkly in the politics of imperialism in colonial Southeast Asia. The United States granted commonwealth status to the Philippines in the mid-1930s both to pull back from defense commit-ments and to free United States sugar producers of economic competition from Philippine sugar. Yet the United States also moved away from the tendency prevalent in the 1920s to encourage indigenous rubber producers to undercut the European plantations, and instead began to cooperate with those European planters and governments. United States officials and businessmen might have wanted, all other things being equal, to see an end to imperial rule in Southeast Asia. But during the Depression other priorities came to the fore, and United States economic policy functioned to uphold imperialism in both economic and political guise.

The Depression in Southeast Asia

An Americo-centric narrative of the Depression has its beginning in the last week of October 1929, as signified by the terrifying drop in prices on the New York Stock Exchange. The story is familiar: a headlong rush to the bottom followed, with margin calls leading to a drain of investment dollars throughout the country and of available dollars for the purchase of consumer goods, which left companies unable to sell their products or find new investors, leading in turn to layoffs, high unemployment, and fewer consumers willing or able to spend money. An equally familiar part of the story is the efforts by the U.S. Congress to raise tariffs on imports to protect struggling United States industries and increase revenues for the federal government. In other words, Congress attempted to have other countries pay to help get the United States out of the Depression. For the countries of western Europe the chronology differs, but the basic principle of each government—that raising tariffs would enable it to solve its own national problems—remained, and is central to common understandings of how and why the Depression spread around the world.

Without question the Depression was a worldwide event, and had long-lasting consequences for the organization of national economies. But the familiar story, summarized above, usually neglects the experience of European and United States colonies during the Depression, as well as the role that these colonies played in policies designed to alleviate it for the colonial powers. Scholars of Southeast Asia have long explored the economic factors shaping political movements of the Depression years, and especially since the Southeast Asian economic crisis of the late 1990s have examined concrete developments in economic status and policy for individual countries during the Depression. The meaning of the Depression for the region as a whole has received little attention, and the role of the United States in shaping this experience has received still less.[2] Yet that role was important, as United States officials became increasingly anxious as the decade progressed to participate in establishing international production restriction agreements, with the consequence of moving toward a managed international economy. This relation between the timing and the magnitude of the Depression in colonial Southeast Asia, and the change in the attitude of United States officials about a managed economy, mean that a better understanding of the Depression in colonial Southeast Asia is critical to assessing the impact of these years on United States foreign policies.

Historians of Southeast Asia debate strenuously what the Depression meant for Southeast Asians, and their studies suggest a tremendously varied experience. The Southeast Asian colonies, almost without exception, were exporters of raw materials. Prices of these goods, such as rubber, tin, sugar, and rice, fell early in the Depression, some even before October 1929, and fell far. Rubber, one of the most important export crops, began its tumble in price in 1928 with the end of the Stevenson Plan, falling 50 percent between 1927 and 1929, again from 1929 to 1930, and yet again from 1930 to 1932. The wholesale price of rubber in 1932 was below the cost of production on European-run plantations.[3] Rice in Burma, the country's primary export crop, sold for Rs. 195 per hundred baskets in 1925 (the high price of the interwar years) before dropping steadily until by 1931 the same amount sold for only Rs. 75 (the low price of the Depression). French Indochina, also dependent on exports of rice, saw a similar drop: prices in early 1930 hovered around 11.5–12 piastres for 100 kilos of number 1 grade rice, but then dropped steadily to only 7.08 piastres for 100 kilos by February 1931.[4] Tin, sugar, kapok, copra, coffee, pepper, and the other export crops of Southeast Asia fared no better.

These statistics demonstrate that Southeast Asia was profoundly affected by the Depression, but they only hint at the impact on ordinary Southeast Asians. For some the situation was grimmer than the numbers suggest. For instance, Tharrawady U Pu, a member of the Burmese Legislative Council, reported that Burmese peasants, selling their rice to exporters or middlemen in early 1931, received only 30–40 Rs. per 100 baskets, or approximately half the price for which rice sold in the Rangoon export market. The percentage of markup was probably normal, but the absolute numbers marked the difference between barely meeting and failing to meet basic obligations. Peasants, like peasants everywhere, sold at the bottom of the market to pay taxes and loans they had taken out to see them through until the harvest.

In British Burma in 1931 these demands remained as strict as ever, with the British government refusing to grant wholesale tax relief because the Depression was limiting other sources of revenue. Ethnic Indian moneylenders were also forced to call in debts, because the worldwide money crunch had put pressure on their own outstanding loans. The result was that Burmese peasants sold rice at prices which did not allow them to meet their needs. In Lower Burma's thirteen principal rice-growing districts, the percentage of land owned by the cultivator dropped from 70 in 1925–30 to less than 50 by 1935–39, although this was some of Burma's most fertile land.[5] In these districts as well, 1930–32 were the years of a massive peasant rebellion, which British officials claimed had little relationship to the economic hardship that peasants suffered.[6]

There is some evidence to suggest that those who grew rice for export suffered the worst fate of all Southeast Asian peasants during the Depression. Those who grew other export crops, especially sugar and rubber, often had the option of returning to subsistence agriculture, at least in part. Those Malayans and Indonesians who produced rubber on their small plots, commonly less than a hundred acres, had generally planted rubber trees either interspersed with other crops (like coffee) or on land that they did not need to plant with rice, fruit, and vegetables which they ate. They tapped their trees and entered the rubber market only when the price was right; when it was not, they simply followed their traditional subsistence lifestyle. Still, because the price of exports fell more quickly than the price of imports, smallholder producers often experienced declining living standards.[7] Even those Southeast Asians who lived on plantations, or grew sugar on their small plots because they were forced to do so, often returned to subsistence agriculture during the Depression. Plantation owners expanded the area devoted to garden plots for workers, and on Java and Madura the land devoted to growing rice rose almost 14 percent in the 1930s after decades of decreasing or holding steady.[8] Southeast Asian peasants were accustomed to cycles of good and bad times, and for those able to turn to subsistence agriculture, perhaps the Depression appeared to be merely an unusually bad downturn, but still within an expected range.

This optimistic view reflects a belief that most Southeast Asian peasants had not yet, as one historian argued, "disastrously exposed" themselves to the external export market. They still had sufficient ties to the subsistence economy.[9] For certain groups the optimism is clearly misplaced, though some individuals were able to escape the worst effects of the Depression.

Some peasants had entered the export economy more to pay taxes than to buy consumer goods, and while they often attempted to return to subsistence farming during the Depression, sometimes they could not. Scholars disagree about how many peasants faced this situation. Some, like James Scott, argue that colonial governments were more desperate for revenue during the Depression and therefore stricter about tax collection. His view is bolstered by the two large, protracted rebellions of the early Depression— the Hsaya San in Burma and the Nghe-Tinh in north central Indochina— which were marked by peasants' complaints about taxes, as well as such anti-tax actions as the burning of property and tax records, violence against government officials, and the seizure of government stores of grain.[10] Other scholars find that peasants were able to evade taxes during these lean years because government officials—whether out of paternalistic concern for the peasants' well-being or fear of violent resistance—were lax in collection.[11]

Recent scholarship focuses on the diversity of Southeast Asian experiences of the Depression years. Southeast Asians who had more fully committed to participation in the export economy tended to suffer greater hardship, but even here the experiences vary. Tin miners, for instance, often suffered severe hardship as that industry contracted. Many former miners appear to have moved to urban areas and worked as occasional laborers, never a profitable venture and even less so in the Depression. For similar reasons, many plantation workers lost their jobs or were underemployed during the 1930s. Sometimes plantation owners let workers stay in their housing and tend garden plots even when there was no work, but those plantation workers who had been brought in from elsewhere (i.e. from Java to Sumatra or Borneo, from India and China to plantations throughout the region) were often sent home. Their home villages did not always reabsorb them into a subsistence economy. John Ingleson reported on a survey conducted by the Netherlands Indies government in 1931 to find out what was happening to returned plantation workers. Of approximately 68,000 who returned in 1930–31, only 19,000 were found to have returned to their villages.[12] What happened to the other 49,000? Probably some had returned to their villages and were not counted, but others joined the informal economy of under- and unemployed in towns and cities. Such people existed in cities all over the world during the 1930s.

With unemployed coolies migrating to the cities, one might expect to find urban Southeast Asian workers suffering most. Those few industries in colonial Southeast Asia did lay off workers during the Depression, and many urban workers no longer had the option of returning to subsistence farming. Here again, though, there were opportunities as well as problems. Some firms laid off older, better-educated, more expensive labor but then hired younger, less educated, and less expensive labor, as happened throughout the world. In Southeast Asia this strategy also meant replacing European and ethnic Chinese labor with Southeast Asians. So while wages were low, urban Southeast Asians may have been more likely to find industrial or government jobs than other ethnic groups in the colonies.[13] In addition, as during the First World War, some companies now found it easier and more profitable to manufacture in Southeast Asia. Goodyear Tire opened a bicycle tire factory in the Netherlands Indies in 1934. It employed Indonesians almost exclusively, and sold almost all the factory's production in the colony, behind its tariff walls.[14] During the 1930s cheap Japanese imports—especially textiles and other inexpensive consumer goods, like flashlights and even bicycles—also flooded Southeast Asian markets. The Indies government allowed these imports, despite protests from European manufacturers, because they believed that the availability of cheap goods pacified Indonesians, distracting them from revolutionary activities. So while conditions for many urban Southeast Asians were grim, with some leading a hand-to-mouth existence, those who stayed employed often maintained and sometimes even increased their standard of living.[15]

The ineluctable consequence of imperialism for these Southeast Asians was involvement in a global economy and a permanent change in their economic options. Not that Southeast Asia was isolated from world trade before European imperialism, nor that imperialism was the only means by which to enter the world economy.[16] In the 1930s, though, as Southeast Asians attempted to respond to the swirling forces of the Depression, their choices were structured by the changes that imperialism had wrought: inflexible tax demands from a distant government for taxes which had to be paid in cash, the production of cash crops rather than food for consumption, a growing dependence on manufactured goods. These changes were not inherently detrimental; they were unavoidable.

The circumstances which sometimes meant that Southeast Asians survived the Depression years with minimal or sporadic hardship meant that Europeans in Southeast Asia were fully exposed to the economic devastation. But the Europeans had political power that they could use to mitigate the consequences. Most Europeans in Southeast Asia were government officials, owners and managers of plantations and industries, or merchants.

When revenues of the colonial governments fell, many European officials were laid off (sometimes replaced by Southeast Asians). Of these many returned to Europe, to uncertain economic situations, and some stayed in the colonies. Eking out a living was difficult, especially since ideas about white men's prestige precluded the possibility that they would do manual labor. Some received payments from the colonial governments to prevent the spectacle of destitute white men and, worse, women.[17]

With many plantation crops selling below the cost at which European estates could produce them, plantation owners also laid off European workers in an effort to minimize losses. These workers rarely saw subsistence farming as a viable alternative, and they scrambled to find other work both in the colonies and in Europe.[18] Plantation owners seem rarely to have lost their land or gone bankrupt, but this was primarily—it appears—because the government granted relief of various sorts. Tax relief was sometimes granted (a topic that needs more careful study), but primarily governments encouraged or formed agreements to restrict the production of export commodities in the hope of raising prices. European planters, owners of tin mines, and most merchants lobbied their governments on behalf of commodity restriction. The strategy of commodity restriction had limited success, as will be explored below, but it does demonstrate that Europeans suffering from the Depression had sufficient political power to prompt their governments to act.

Southeast Asia and the Depression in the United States

The situation for Americans involved in the Southeast Asian economy was different from that of Europeans, although the two groups often saw their political interests as coinciding. These differences become glaring when one examines two of the commodities most severely affected by the Depression: rubber and sugar. Sugar is grown in almost every country in the world, but in Southeast Asia cane sugar was grown for export in Java, the most densely populated island in the Indies, and the Philippines, primarily on the island of Luzon. In both places the crop had been introduced by Europeans, and indigenous peoples had only reluctantly turned to cultivating it. By the 1930s both regions depended on sugar exports, but there were differences in the capacity of the colonial ruling country to absorb the quantities of sugar grown. Although the Dutch in the Netherlands certainly did consume Javanese sugar, the tiny Dutch market could not absorb all of Java's production. Javanese sugar had to compete on the open market, and during the 1930s it was difficult to find buyers for cane sugar almost at any price, let alone a profitable price. Javanese sugar exports, growing in volume and price during the late 1920s, dipped slightly in 1929 and in 1930 began plunging. The volume of sugar exports dropped by almost two-thirds from 1929 to 1936, while the value dropped almost 90 percent.

The Philippines, by contrast, had free access to the United States market and sold virtually all its sugar in that market. Even during the Depression, both the volume and the value of sugar exports from the Philippines grew, although the price per ton of sugar did drop. As a result Philippine exports more than doubled between 1926 and 1931, but the value of this sugar increased by only one-third. Surprisingly, volume and value continued to increase slowly until 1935, when Philippine access to the United States market began to be limited in preparation for Philippine independence. Sugar cost more in America than in Europe, but sugar plantation and mill owners in the Philippines (of whom a plurality were American, approximately one-third Filipino, and 10 percent ethnic Chinese) survived the Depression even if they did not all thrive. On Java plantation and mill owners, mostly Europeans and ethnic Chinese, faced gloomy choices. Ian Brown calculates that land planted with sugar on Java fell 86 percent between 1931 and 1935.[19] The traditional economics of imperialism, which link strongly the economies of colony and metropole, were pursued by both the Netherlands and the United States during the early Depression for the commodity sugar. Market size and widely dispersed production explain the different experiences of sugar producers on Java and Luzon.

The case of rubber provides a strong contrast, not because the United States market was smaller but because rubber was not produced in any United States colony. Few United States companies had invested in rubber production, and United States capital in the rubber plantations of British Malaya and the Netherlands Indies formed only about 5–10 percent of the total.[20] Even those United States rubber plantations which did exist, and which were quite extensive, had been established by major rubber companies intending to consume all the rubber they produced. So Americans bought rather than sold rubber, meaning that their interests differed markedly from those of European plantation owners, as is discussed in more detail below. The United States was the world's primary consumer of rubber, purchasing approximately half of each year's sales. In this situation the steep decline in rubber prices was unlikely to concern American purchasers, and they did show great indifference to the plight of European plantation owners, especially early in the Depression. They particularly pointed to the greater efficiencies on United States plantations, where the cost of production was several cents less per pound than on European plantations, and to the ability of smallholders to produce for lower cost as well. United States rubber purchasers argued that these downward pressures on price had nothing to do with the Depression, so attempting to raise prices by government intervention was a subsidy for inefficient producers rather than a form of assistance to deserving farmers. Americans involved in the rubber industry were more likely to denounce the traditional economics of imperialism because they perceived that interventionist measures promoted economic inefficiencies.

The volatility of commodity markets during the 1930s, as well as the restrictive measures that colonial governments began to institute, were the real problems for American purchasers of Southeast Asian products, and by the mid- to late 1930s representatives of American firms began lobbying to have purchasers represented on restriction boards as the best way to protect their interests. By Roosevelt's second term in office United States government officials clearly agreed, but they still had varying degrees of willingness to assist. Their reluctance was partly due to a sense that the Japanese approach to economic issues might bear the most political fruit. Southeast Asians associated affordable consumer goods with Japan, their country of origin, and Japan was making great effort—although with limited success—to establish various types of businesses in Southeast Asian colonies.[21] Some United States companies, like Goodyear Tire and General Motors, followed similar strategies. They assembled products in the colonies, designed for regional sale.[22] Despite Washington's approval of these ventures they remained limited, and to the extent that United States businesses sought government action in Southeast Asia, they were concerned primarily with protecting the interests of United States commodity purchasers as restriction agreements were implemented during the mid-1930s.

Trade with Southeast Asia declined during the Depression, but in relative terms held its own. As table 2 indicates, the value of goods exported from South and Southeast Asia nearly equaled that from East Asia in 1929 and dipped to a similar level in 1932, but only Southeast Asia rebounded to its pre-Depression level by 1937.

Southeast Asia provided approximately 14 percent of total United States imports in 1929 and 1932, and more than 18 percent in 1938. The United States imported raw materials, primarily rubber, tin, and sugar, from the

Table 2

	1929	1932	1937
United States imports from South and Southeast Asia	630	185	610
United States imports from East Asia	614	165	320
United States exports to South and Southeast Asia	209	83	175

All figures in millions of U.S. dollars.

region, and while the quantities imported fluctuated little, the prices varied widely. Exports to Southeast Asia were minimal, however, hovering at just under 5 percent of total United States exports, and only about one-third of this modest amount was destined for the Philippines. Southeast Asia was important primarily for what it provided to United States industry.[23] During the 1920s, as discussed above, many United States companies hoped to narrow the trade deficit with the region by exporting more consumer goods to Southeast Asians who grew products for the export market. But during the 1930s United States goods were too expensive for most Southeast Asians, who generally purchased Japanese goods if they purchased foreign goods at all.

Tobacco and Tariffs

Trade relations between the Netherlands Indies and the United States were smooth, and United States officials often praised Dutch policy as supportive of Open Door principles. At the beginning of the Depression, though, a dispute over a potential tariff on products made by labor working under penal sanctions exposed some of the conflicts at the heart of United States ideas about colonialism, as well as possible sources of disagreement between the Netherlands and the United States. The Dutch were surprised by the proposal of Senator John J. Blaine of Wisconsin in the fall of 1929 that section 307 of the Tariff Bill of 1930 be amended to prohibit not merely the import of produce of convict labor but also of labor working under penal sanction. Van Royen, the Dutch ambassador in Washington, wrote immediately to officials in The Hague, reporting that the amendment had been introduced and had passed easily. If the bill became law, it could affect "a variety of articles originating in our overseas possessions," he wrote, such as "tobacco, coffee, tea, rubber, and tapioca." Van Royen concluded his report by noting that under the law the United States secretary of the treasury would have "a very great power" to decide whether Dutch colonial products could be imported into the United States, but he did not explain why the power would reside there.[24]

Dutch officials in The Hague were perhaps less surprised than van Royen. Agitation within the Netherlands and its colonies to end labor under penal sanction had existed for decades. In June 1929 the International Labour Organization (ILO) in Geneva held an investigation and hearing into the conditions of labor around the world, focusing particularly on indentured and forced labor in the mandates and colonies. E. Kupers, the workers' delegate in the Dutch mission to the ILO, had given a speech which Senator Blaine had read into the Congressional Record in support of his amendment. This speech emphasized that despite the many regulations put into place to protect contract laborers in the Netherlands Indies, serious abuses still occurred. Kupers argued that these abuses resulted from the unfree nature of the contract, noting that the employee was "bound hand and foot to his employer . . . he really lives in a condition of slavery."[25]

Untangling the motives of senators voting to raise tariffs on imported goods made with forced or indentured labor would be challenging. In the debate on this amendment, several freely acknowledged their primary interest in protecting American labor or business. Yet the most emotionally charged language in the debates was about the unfree nature of labor in the tropics and the duty of Americans to combat, through policy and purchasing practices, all labor practices that resembled slavery. Senator Blaine, not surprisingly, was most evocative: "The form of labor inhibited by this proposed amendment is slavery, nothing short of slavery. Are we at this moment to retrace our steps? Are we going to deny that which we have professed in the past? If so, we would better charge the Lincoln Monument with dynamite, tear down the noblest institutions in our country, and destroy the spirit of freedom . . . I understand that we might suffer some economic loss, but we can not afford any economic gain at the sacrifice of the degeneracy and death of the natives amounting to millions of men and women, who should be under the guidance of a civilization that will give them an opportunity to attain the heights that they may attain in the advancement of human progress."[26]

Throughout the debate United States rule and labor policy in the Philippines was not mentioned, but the metaphors of slavery and the realities of contract labor permeated United States imperialism in Southeast Asia. More than 100,000 Filipinos came to Hawaii, California, Oregon, and Washington, often under labor contracts, before 1930, and the effort to end this migration shaped debates in the early 1930s about whether and how to grant commonwealth status to the Philippines. Increased autonomy for the Philippines in 1935 came with the stipulation that Filipinos would become free laborers with no right to enter the labor markets of the United States. As Michael Salman has shown, United States colonial rule was fraught from its beginning with almost anguished debates about the possible existence of slavery within the Philippines, and the meaning of that slavery for Americans and Filipinos.[27] The echoes of that debate resonate in Blaine's assertion that slave labor conditions hindered colonized countries from achieving the "heights . . . of human progress," and that these conditions demonstrated the insufficiency of efforts by the European colonial powers to provide the benefits of civilization to their colonies.

Dutch responses to the proposed amendment did not focus on the ideological contradictions of United States imperial and labor policies. Van Royen's report on the possible exclusion of products from the Netherlands Indies set off a flurry of activity. Informational memos went to the Dutch Ministries of Colonies, of Labor, Commerce, and Industry, and of Domestic Affairs, as well as to the Deli Maatschappij, representing Dutch colonial planter interests. Some action clearly needed to be taken, but Dutch officials were not sure what could be done. Van Royen's letter had stated that Senator Blaine used highly moralistic language in introducing the amendment, saying that Americans "could not support employers in foreign countries who had such inhumane practices and brought the people to 'poverty and degeneration.'"[28] Questions from the Dutch Foreign Ministry to van Royen showed that they understood only some of their options. First, who had proposed the amendment, and did van Royen believe that "interested parties" were behind it? Second, could the president veto only a section of a bill? Third, who in the United States seemed to be paying attention to this issue? Finally, did the British, French, and Belgian embassies in Washington know of the amendment to section 307, and if so what had been their reaction?[29] The Dutch government was trying to figure out whom it should lobby, and who might be its allies in such a campaign.

By the time the bill became law as the Smoot-Hawley tariff in June 1930, section 307 had been modified again, in a way which significantly improved it from the Dutch perspective. A major exception had been added, allowing the import of goods made with labor under penal sanction if insufficient quantities of those goods were produced in the United States. Senator Blaine's colleagues had raised this issue when he proposed the amendment, questioning whether he really intended to prohibit rubber imports, for example, which would cause great hardship to United States industry. Such prohibitions would not help American labor, the intended beneficiaries of the amendment, and would unduly complicate imports. Although these objections were passed over when the amendment was initially accepted, by the time the bill left the conference committee the exception had been added.[30] Thus section 307 of Smoot-Hawley applied only—potentially—to tapioca and Sumatran wrapper tobacco among exports from the Netherlands Indies.

Privately Dutch officials were certainly relieved that more lucrative products—especially tin and rubber—were exempted. But instead of remaining content with that they worked to continue tobacco imports. They had reason to worry that tobacco would be a harder sell. Senator Blaine had specifically mentioned Sumatran tobacco when he introduced the amendment. He had begun a cost comparison for "production of the foreign wrappers and the domestic wrappers" and discovered that penal-sanctions labor, which he believed had an unfair competitive advantage over American labor, was used extensively in the production of Sumatran tobacco as well as other products of "tropical countries."[31] Under Smoot-Hawley the decision about which products should be exempted from section 307 was made by the United States secretary of the treasury. This made the job of Dutch officials easier, and they focused their efforts on U.S. State Department representatives, a strategy which proved successful.

The United States consul in Medan, Sumatra, Walter A. Foote, wrote to his superiors in August 1930, asking whether section 307 would apply to Sumatran tobacco. His long and detailed report emphasized what he believed were the salient facts. Foote reported that penal-sanctions labor was coming to an end of its own accord. Already the proportion of free labor was increasing year by year, and as a result all labor was, in Foote's opinion, treated well. The additional burden of certifying that particular lots of tobacco had been produced by free rather than contract labor would cut into the already slim profit margins of tobacco producers. Foote noted as well that nearly one-third of tobacco labor was free and that the United States imported only 14 percent of the crop, so it was possible that the United States, unknowingly, already imported only free-labor tobacco. But more important than any of the logical or statistical arguments, Foote believed, was the traditional welcome that the Netherlands Indies had provided to goods and investment from the United States. More than $100 million had been invested in plantations in the colony, dwarfing the roughly $4 million spent on Sumatran tobacco in 1928.[32] Foote argued strongly for a "favorable" decision for tobacco planters.

His report found sympathetic readers in Washington. A memo prepared within the Division of Western European Affairs in May 1931, summarizing the main issues in the Sumatran tobacco wrapper dispute for top officials in State, acknowledged that Sumatran wrapper tobacco was produced by labor under penal sanction, but argued that an embargo against imports "would have a seriously adverse effect upon Dutch-American relations." It noted that total United States investments in the Indies were approximately $150 million, and that United States exports to the colony averaged approximately $35 million.[33] William R. Castle, undersecretary of state, had these points in mind when he wrote to Ogden L. Mills, undersecretary of the treasury, a few days later. Mills had expressed "the necessity of talking the matter over" before the Department of Treasury made a decision about Sumatran tobacco imports. Castle replied in writing, and stressed, as Foote had, that the Dutch were slowly ending penal-sanctions labor, and that United States trade and investment were too important to be disrupted by the relatively small value of the Sumatran tobacco trade. To convince Mills that an embargo would have a negative impact, Castle noted that the Dutch saw section 307 "as a cynically utilitarian economic attack, launched under a camouflage of highly moral sentiments." This belief rose out of the exception made for goods not produced in the United States: "[The Dutch] will ask why, if it is perfectly proper for an American to ride in an automobile equipped with tires made of penal sanctions rubber (some of it produced by American companies operating in Sumatra), should it be grossly improper for the same American to smoke a cigar covered with a Sumatran penal sanctions wrapper while riding over the moral penal sanctions rubber tires?"[34]

When Dutch members (Enthoven, Rupert, and Boot) of the Tobacco Bureau visited Washington in May and June 1931, they wasted no energy critiquing the moral consistency of United States law. Rather, they spent time meeting with lawyers and United States government officials to try to determine what the decision was likely to be regarding tobacco, and what legal recourse they had against appeals by United States planters if the decision proved favorable to the Dutch. Their own report noted that "everyone [in

Washington] with whom they spoke about the expected ruling, believed it would be a favorable outcome for Sumatra."[35] Van Royen provided more detail in his assessment of the visit, noting that Enthoven, Rupert, and Bool had met with the undersecretaries of the Departments of State and Treasury, and with Walter Foote, now the former United States consul in Medan, and that the visitors had been told confidentially "that the decision was more likely to be favorable than unfavorable." They were also told that a decision would come by the end of the summer.[36] When no decision was forthcoming by then the Dutch government made a bold move, and announced abolition of penal-sanctions labor on Sumatran wrapper tobacco plantations. Only one year's crop—1931—could technically be subject to the embargo.[37]

Officials in the U.S. State Department renewed their efforts. Foote summarized the arguments again for Castle, who reiterated them to both Mills and President Herbert Hoover on 15 October. In the memo to Mills he argued that it would be "a pretty terrible thing to irritate the Netherlands to such an extent as to injure our own trade with the Netherlands Indies and prevent our own people from smoking good cigars for the next year."[38] The memo to the president was a little more formal, reminding Hoover that he and Castle had talked about this issue some months earlier. At that time Hoover had disapproved of an embargo to such an extent that he had called the treasury secretary, Andrew Mellon, noting with approval that "the agitation on the subject has made the Dutch do away with all contract labor."[39] Treasury decided on 2 November 1931 not to ban Sumatran tobacco imports and immediately informed The Hague. Dutch newspapers praised "the American authorities" for not allowing themselves "to be duped by the Connecticut and Florida planters who had, down to the last moment, even after the system of labor under penal sanctions had been abolished on the Deli plantations, made the most powerful efforts to keep Holland's colonial product out of the country."[40] The outcome of this first major struggle of the Depression era over a Southeast Asian commodity appeared to reaffirm United States notions about the efficacy of market forces, the benefits of treating labor well, and the power of United States purchasing strength.

The Dutch planters should probably have considered themselves lucky that this dispute erupted in 1930–31, before the magnitude of the Depression had become clear. Senator Blaine was perhaps genuinely concerned about labor conditions in colonial Asia, but section 307 was only considered for application to one commodity—tobacco, the one commodity which com-

Socony gas station, Netherlands Indies, 1931. National Archives and Records
Administration, 151-FC-78A-1.

peted directly with an American-grown product. Later in the 1930s United
States tobacco growers might have been able to make more compelling arguments about the need to protect American industry.[41] But at this early stage
State Department officials were the only ones paying sustained attention,
and they were wholeheartedly supporting the Dutch planter interests. Individual United States officers, such as Foote, genuinely liked and approved
of Dutch planters. As for others in the department, they recognized that the
Dutch government had been more open than the British or French to United
States investment in the Netherlands Indies. American companies owned
plantations that grew rubber and other tropical products, oil wells, and factories in the Indies. The State Department wanted to ensure continued good
treatment.

Further, the State Department had little problem with penal-sanctions
labor and did not see the principle as worth any sacrifice of United States
interests. Indeed the issue of forced labor had been raised in conjunction
with the United States colony in the Philippines by the League of Nations.
Several times during the interwar period the league requested information
about slavery, debt peonage, and trafficking in women, and United States

officials were deeply reluctant to provide in-depth information about the continuing existence of such practices in an American colony. As Michael Salman has explained, American ideas about the meaning and purpose of their colonial rule relied on an assumption that one inevitable consequence of the United States presence would be an end to slavery and other forms of coerced labor. The reality was often quite different, and it was not until the mid-1930s that the practice of Filipino laborers emigrating to Hawaii under coercive labor contracts ended.[42] In the discussion within the State Department over penal-sanctions labor in the Netherlands Indies and United States (tax) policy toward it, this Philippine context is notably absent, as is the fact that much of United States tobacco was produced by sharecroppers, many of them just as securely tied to their place as if they had signed a penal-sanctions contract.

As the debates and negotiations about penal-sanctions labor and tobacco demonstrate, many Americans had an extremely strong ideological commitment to free labor and a free market. That the realities of United States policy and practice fell short of those ideals did not prevent United States officials and businessmen from judging the policies of other countries and advocating adherence by others to free-labor and free-market standards. These Americans did not believe that a critique of imperial labor practices necessarily meant a critique of imperialism itself. Indeed, as Senator Blaine's remarks suggest, promoting better labor practices within the imperial system would be the best way to offer the benefits of civilization to colonized peoples.

Regulating Rubber

The struggle over rubber differed markedly from that over tobacco. No rubber was produced in the United States or any United States possession, yet the United States was the largest consumer of rubber in the world. In the 1920s United States official and corporate policy had been to encourage indigenous rubber production in Southeast Asia as a way of undercutting European, especially British, government control of rubber prices. The result was a reliance on free-market forces to ensure a reasonable price, and if for involved Americans that meant encouraging self-reliance and possible independence among Southeast Asians, then that was a potentially positive development, but not of much consequence to them.

As the Depression persisted, however, officials and businessmen throughout Southeast Asia, Europe, and the United States were increasingly likely to believe that market forces alone would not be able to improve prices or consumption. They began to consider a variety of regulatory measures to attempt to match production and consumption in the hope of stabilizing markets. In the United States the Agricultural Adjustment Act and National Industrial Recovery Act reflected this approach to ending the problems of the Depression. In agriculture, farmers would be paid to not grow food; industrial leaders could consult in previously illegal ways to minimize destructive competition. Insofar as these domestic programs worked, they did so because the federal government set the rules and parameters of the programs. The task of getting producers in different countries to agree to limit production for the potential good of all producers would naturally be an even more difficult task. Yet as the Depression deepened, commodity prices dipped so low that producers of wheat, sugar, tin, cotton, and rubber, among other products, were willing to try. The hurdles to successful restriction for each of these commodities were substantial, but perhaps greatest for rubber. As with wheat, sugar, and cotton, rubber was grown both on large plantations, where production was relatively easy to control, and on small plots, where control was almost impossible. As with tin, production was concentrated in a few countries. Tin was mined primarily in British Malaya, Siam, the Netherlands Indies, Bolivia, and Nigeria, while rubber was grown almost exclusively in Southeast Asia outside the Philippines. The only important exception was a Firestone plantation in Liberia. Also as with tin, the United States accounted for approximately half the total consumption of rubber. In addition, rubber restriction had already been attempted, as discussed in chapter 2, and had failed miserably. This failure made British and Dutch government officials reluctant, even when rubber plantation owners asked for government assistance, officially to support restriction plans. But the earlier failure also suggested that rubber's problems were systemic and not merely the result of the Depression. The final complication relates to problems in matching rubber production to consumption, since rubber trees need a minimum of five years between planting and initial production. Mature, untapped rubber trees would always represent a drag on the market price of rubber, but the absence of such trees would mean that surges in demand could not be met by increased production.

The multiplicity of interests in the rubber industry means that the struggle to figure out a way to restrict rubber production reflects better than any other effort to restrict a commodity the complexity of changes in the world economy, as well as the complexity of the United States effort to reconcile its competing desires to both lead the world economy and have the closest possible approximation to an Open Door, laissez-faire economy. When the Stevenson Plan ended in November 1928, international demand for rubber jumped sharply, but as the economic historian John Drabble has noted, consumption held steady. As the owners of rubber plantations understood, this meant that rubber consumers were buying the extra rubber to increase stocks to be able to ride out any subsequent waves of higher prices. Since prices held relatively steady for the next year, plantation owners grumbled but did not protest. But by late 1929 rubber prices began their race to the bottom, as with many other commodities. Plantation owners began trying to figure out ways to regulate rubber. Smallholders complicated the effort, since they could earn a profit at much lower prices than the plantations. United States government officials tended to favor the free market, since the United States primarily consumed rubber. As the Depression continued, though, and restriction looked more likely, the United States government began looking for ways to shape rather than prevent restrictions.

Long Road to Restriction

Britain had called an end to the Stevenson Rubber Restriction plan in November 1928 because the effect of restricting production in British-controlled territories had been merely to hand ever-greater market share to other countries, particularly the Netherlands Indies, and to smallholder producers (usually indigenous Southeast Asians) at the expense of mostly European-owned plantations. Even so, British officials and planters still believed that restriction was the best way to stabilize the market and prices at profitable levels, and they began working immediately to include Dutch planters and officials in devising a new restriction plan which would include Netherlands Indies rubber. In March 1929 representatives of British and Dutch rubber planters met to try to devise a restriction scheme, and conversations about restriction persisted until a plan was finally agreed upon in 1934. Two important groups objected to rubber restriction in 1929: Americans and indigenous rubber growers, especially in the Netherlands Indies. The power of each to advocate for a free market in rubber diminished during the early Depression.

In their discussions with the British, Dutch planters and government offi-cials most often emphasized that while they understood how effective restriction would be beneficial to rubber plantation owners and perhaps the industry as a whole, there was almost no way to achieve effective restriction because of the presence of smallholders. Smallholders were a diverse group, including indigenous peoples and ethnic Chinese. Their land was sometimes planted entirely in rubber and at other times they planted rubber as a supplemental crop, on plots ranging from one to a hundred hectares. The vast majority of smallholders in the Netherlands Indies were characterized by their ability to make a profit on rubber at a much lower price than European-owned plantations were, and their tendency to enter the market only when the price offered was profitable to them. With the failure of the Stevenson Plan clear in their minds, British officials took the warning to heart. In a comment on the new restriction attempts of 1929, G. E. J. Gent of the British Colonial Office noted: "All that has been produced is the no doubt true suspicion that with the price of rubber over a shilling there is virtually no limit to the native production. The Dutch have no control and no statistics."[43] Dutch officials also emphasized that "the native population has not asked for measures of restriction" and that a large number of indigenous producers "will by restriction actually be damaged and will not be much impressed by the possibility of future compensation for such immediate damage."[44] Dutch officials believed that any possible restriction plan would be unfair to indigenous producers and, more importantly, could provoke resistance, whether in the form of smuggling or of political agitation.

Concerns about the possibility that indigenous producers would undermine any restriction plan were serious, but the implacable opposition of all Americans interested in rubber was also a factor in the Dutch reluctance to agree to participate in rubber restriction, despite the growing demands of Dutch planters. De Jonge, governor general of Netherlands Indies, indicated in September 1930 that he believed restriction measures raised "the possibility that countries consuming rubber might make reprisals on products from the Netherlands East Indies."[45] Since the United States consumed between half and two-thirds of the world's rubber, and because in the fall of 1930 the application of section 307 to Sumatran tobacco of the Smoot-Hawley tariff (discussed above) was under consideration, de Jonge's concern seemed to be directed at the United States. Although United States documents contain no such threat of a quid pro quo, Dutch officials acknowledged that part of their continuing objection to rubber restriction was "the probable unsympathetic attitude of the United States Government."[46] Even as a rubber restriction plan was imminent in March 1934, the Dutch prime and colonial minister, Hendrijk Colijn, publicly claimed that in de-termining such details as maximum price and how long restriction would remain in effect, he was "obliged to reckon with the United States."[47]

The Dutch were more sensitive to United States objections than the British were, in part because the United States companies which owned rub-ber plantations in the Netherlands Indies were the most determined oppo-nents of restriction. They consumed all the rubber produced on their plan-tations in their own manufacturing plants, and therefore believed that their rubber—which never entered the world market—should be exempted from restriction measures. U.S. Rubber and Goodyear, the two companies with plantations, lobbied both in Washington and The Hague and were prob-ably a minor factor in the difficulties that Dutch and British officials had in agreeing on rubber restriction.[48] American purchasers of rubber generally also opposed rubber restriction, although not as vehemently as U.S. Rubber and Goodyear. Before the Depression set in, American manufacturers re-acted primarily to their bad memories of the Stevenson Plan's wild fluctua-tions and communicated to the Dutch producers "that American producers are only interested in a stabilized price at an equitable level."[49] Restric-tion would be acceptable if it made the market predictable and provided fair profits to all. The United States manufacturers continued to insist that restriction would be acceptable if consuming interests were fairly repre-sented, and centered their protests not on the fact of restriction but on the mechanisms for it.

In this sense the manufacturers were ahead of the United States govern-ment, but by 1934 Washington's attitudes had also changed. Several fac-tors combined to make restriction finally achievable in 1934. First, the price of rubber had dropped steadily, and by 1933 some plantations were going bankrupt. Desperation made all participants determined to figure out a way to institute restriction. Colijn expressed the sentiment well in a conversation with the United States minister in The Hague, Laurits Swenson: he had "de-cided to have restriction unless it should prove unworkable."[50] Since Dutch skepticism had been the primary impediment, restriction soon proved workable. Second, other international commodity restriction agreements, notably for tin, had been instituted by the early 1930s and had seen some success. Although tin was a very different type of commodity to restrict, the major producing countries (British Malaya and Netherlands Indies) were the same, and their relatively positive experience with restriction helped convince officials to attempt rubber restriction.[51]

The change in administration and attitude in Washington was also important. During 1930–32 United States officials pressed consistently for no restriction and celebrated each time Dutch and British meetings on the subject concluded with statements that rubber restriction plans were "unsound" or that "no international rubber restriction plan has been found to be practical."[52] The Roosevelt administration, more open in general to attempts to regulate the economy, worked harder to get voting representation for the consuming interests in any group which would restrict rubber than to prevent restriction altogether. As the likelihood of rubber restriction grew in late 1933 and early 1934, Washington responded forcefully but differently than in the past. Instructions to the United States minister in The Hague, Laurits Swenson, emphasized that Washington understood how "great fluctuations of rubber production and price" had benefited no one while there were "possible advantages of stable conditions and of stable and equitable price," but the instructions also stated that the proposed restriction "amount[ed] virtually to monopoly agreement" and therefore "should be carefully drawn in principle and guarded in operation." To this end Swenson should insist that the agreement "fulfill thoroughly" that part of the resolutions adopted at the Monetary and Economic Conference of 1933 regarding the representation of consumers on commodity restriction boards. He should also work for a maximum price at which all the rubber demanded would be available, and for public disclosure of the process.[53]

The change demonstrates the new understanding that while the free market might always be best, it might not always be practical. Until late April 1934, when the rubber restriction agreement was signed by countries representing approximately 98 percent of the world's rubber production, the Roosevelt administration concentrated furiously on getting formal representation for consuming interests on the decision-making board and in getting assurances about a maximum price. The Dutch government seemed sympathetic to United States interests. Prime Minister Colijn had appointed a (Dutch) employee of the U.S. Rubber Company to the Dutch board negotiating the issue, which kept Swenson fully informed.[54] Colijn expressed willingness to support, although not propose, the notion that nonvoting representatives of the consuming interests should sit on the international committee. Washington officials wanted voting representation for the consuming interests but in the end did not get even as much as Colijn had supported. The consuming interests had merely an advisory panel of three nonvoting representatives who were not allowed to attend all meetings.[55]

Finally, Colijn also consistently claimed that he believed the price of rubber should be stabilized at four pence per pound, while the British were looking for a price closer to eight pence.[56]

The British resisted on each of these points, a task made easier for them since London officials insisted until days before the agreement was signed that it was a producer agreement, and that while they were "aware" of a draft of the agreement, they had nothing to do with negotiations. They could, however, based on the "hypothetical commentaries" of restriction, answer some of the questions posed by the United States government.[57] The detailed and prescient nature of these answers from the British government confirmed the suspicions of the United States that even if British officials had not actively negotiated rubber restriction, they had been fully informed and providing advice. When the producers finally signed an agreement on 28 April 1934, and the British foreign secretary John Simon prepared to announce it in the House of Commons immediately, these suspicions were only further confirmed.[58] Complaints from Washington centered on the lack of effective representation for consumer representatives and assertions that the process did not meet the standards agreed on at the conference of 1933. These complaints bordered on accusations of hypocrisy, but primarily they reveal the paradoxical nature of United States foreign economic policy during the first half of the 1930s. British officials raised one example themselves, pointing out that when the United States passed legislation severely restricting cotton production, no consultations with the primary foreign consumer of that cotton (Britain) had taken place.[59] In 1934 United States officials had embraced, some reluctantly and others enthusiastically, the regulation of commodity markets to minimize the boom-and-bust cycle exacerbated by the Depression. Yet they still insisted on treating each commodity in isolation and attempted to get the best outcome for United States consumers and producers, rather than acknowledge the interconnected nature of the commodities markets.

This commodity restriction did help European-run plantations and companies in the colonies, but United States officials did not think that helping these imperialistic endeavors was part of the benefit of restriction; they were just as likely to believe that it would have been better to let the markets for these raw materials find their equilibrium, even if doing so was politically disruptive and temporarily disruptive to the economy as well. Europeans were often comfortable with the notion that the economics of imperialism sometimes required governmental assistance. Involved Americans were more skeptical, not necessarily because they disapproved of imperialism but because they believed that imperialism proved its worth in part by being efficient and profitable. The need for commodity restrictions merely demonstrated for them that imperialism was probably not the best way to organize the economy of the region.

Rubber under Restriction

The International Rubber Regulation Committee set the official export quotas for rubber from British Malaya, the Netherlands Indies, Burma, Ceylon, Indochina, Borneo, Sarawak, and Siam during the years 1934–41. These countries provided approximately 98 percent of the world's rubber production, so the scheme had as good a chance of working as any restriction scheme would have done. There are ways in which rubber restriction did work. The price of rubber steadily rose through 1934–37, dipped during the worldwide economic downturn of 1938, and then rose again from late 1938 to the end of restrictions in 1941.[60] Since a price rise was an explicit goal of rubber restriction for Britain and an unstated one for the Netherlands, both countries were pleased with this aspect of the plan. United States consumers complained that prices were allowed to go too high and that quotas were sometimes set too low for them to buy all they wished, but not until 1939 were these major problems. For the first three years of restriction, indigenous production in the Netherlands Indies was regulated by means of an export tax designed to indirectly limit indigenous exports to a quota, rather than a quota at point of sale. The indigenous producers exceeded their "quota" in each of these three years, which had the effect of easing in restriction very slowly.[61] The continued threat that indigenous production would enter the market illicitly if the price rose too high also dampened attempts by the IRRC to raise the price as high as the members might have liked.

From the standpoint of both United States rubber manufacturers and Washington officials, the two major problems with rubber restriction were the ones they had identified during the negotiations of 1934. First, the British seemed interested in using restriction to guarantee a high enough price to ensure the continued existence of European-owned rubber plantations, which United States observers believed were simply inefficient producers. United States manufacturers obviously did not appreciate that these plantations were being propped up, and United States officials seemed to agree. Although the indigenous producers could consistently produce at a lower price, United States observers also noted that plantations which aggressively implemented modern methods, as the American-owned plantations did, also had lower per-pound costs. A. L. Viles, president of the Rubber Manufacturers Association, confirmed that the U.S. Rubber Company and Goodyear estates in the Netherlands Indies had per pound costs of approximately 5.15 pence, while the average European-owned plantations had per pound costs above 6 pence.[62] The second problem was that the IRRC did not really have to listen to its consumer advisory board. The U.S. State Department had declined to appoint the United States representative to this board, instead allowing the rubber industry, through the Rubber Manufacturers Association, to make the appointment. Washington officials argued that by refraining from making this appointment they would preserve a greater freedom to criticize the workings of the IRRC.[63] The Departments of State and Commerce did maintain a close relationship with the Rubber Manufacturers Association, and worked with its members to set both industry and government policy regarding the international rubber market.

For the first few years objections from the United States—whether from industry or the government—were primarily objections of scale, relating to too-high prices or too-low quotas. Restriction itself was reluctantly accepted as inevitable given market conditions. Late in 1937, for example, the price of rubber had risen high enough for United States officials to think that the Dutch might support an end to restriction, especially since they had been so supportive of United States interests and since the IRRC was up for renewal in 1938. But when the slump hit in 1938, and price and demand plummeted, both United States officials and manufacturers understood that the inability of United States industry to accurately predict demand was part of the reason for the quota cuts which they did not want. Viles told State Department officials that he was exploring with United States rubber manufacturers ways to better regulate demand.[64] Thus instead of demanding an end to regulation, Americans involved in the rubber industry were emulating the rubber producers. The United States government position again returned merely to advocating somewhat higher quotas and lower prices.

Until 1937 the rubber market was primarily subject to ordinary market forces and the efforts of producers, consumers, and governments to control those forces. But as tensions rose in Europe and Asia after 1935, discussions began about the need to stockpile rubber as a strategic resource. Interestingly, the passage of the Neutrality Act in May 1937 prompted one of the earliest expressions of concern, by Senator Royal Copeland of New York. He introduced legislation calling for appointment of a commission "to investigate and report to Congress regarding the . . . situation concerning rubber." He worried that if Britain went to war, United States neutrality, required by the Neutrality Acts, might make it difficult to meet the country's rubber requirements if Britain demanded war matériel in exchange for rubber. Reaction in the State Department was mixed. Although the department welcomed attention to the need to stockpile strategic materials, rubber was "merely one of a numerous group of commodities which presents the same problem." Secretary Hull's answer also stressed that negotiations with the IRRC were at a delicate stage, during which "any action which might be construed as an aggressive attack" should be "avoided."[65] Japan's invasion of China in early July 1937 and the expansionistic and violent policies of Hitler's Germany merely reinforced industry and government concerns about quietly stockpiling rubber.

During 1938 Herbert Feis, advisor on international economic affairs in the U.S. Department of State, also began to believe that it would be useful to have what he and Viles called a "buffer stock" of rubber in the event of a "period of emergency when foreign supplies may be interrupted or greatly restricted." The problem was how to achieve such a buffer stock. The problems were numerous. Since there was as yet no "emergency," Feis and Viles had to consider how to pay for the major purchases of rubber, who would actually hold them, and how to avoid having stockpiling look—to both the IRRC and the U.S. Department of Justice—like an attempt by the United States rubber industry, backed by the State Department, to influence the price of rubber. Loans from the Reconstruction Finance Corporation, the easiest way to finance the purchase, would require some "tie-up with employment of labor," but Feis and Viles could claim, they assumed, that the money was either for building up stocks of reclaimed rubber or expanding rubber manufacturing, both of which would employ people. These possibilities would solve another problem, in that individual companies could physically hold the stocks, which were perishable and therefore could be used and replaced more easily than if held physically by the government.

Viles took these ideas with him to the July meeting of the IRRC, where he was the United States representative on the Advisory Committee, but he quickly telephoned Feis to report that the Rubber Manufacturers Association had decided to propose a buffer stock "financed and directed" by the IRRC, with 100,000 tons of the inventory to be held in the United States.

They believed that an "American-controlled" scheme might encourage the IRRC to lower production quotas. Feis found it "likely that their judgment is correct."[66]

Official United States involvement in rubber during 1938 was therefore primarily restricted to attempting to shape the renewal of the Rubber Restriction agreement, signed in August 1938. Although the Rubber Manufacturers Association maintained its official opposition to rubber restriction in principle, in practice both Viles and State Department officials like Feis worked merely to improve the representation for United States consumers and to get agreement to the notion that the IRRC would "make available, at all times, now or in the future, all of the rubber that may be required by the world at a price no greater than that required to be reasonably remunerative to efficient producers."[67] In the view of the IRRC the buffer stock that it planned to create would meet the United States concern about availability of rubber, while increasing United States representation on the Advisory Committee from one member to two amounted to meeting the United States halfway. These measures did not go as far as United States officials or rubber manufacturers wished, but they did represent an improvement.

During 1938 rhetoric about stockpiling strategic material was at times alarmist, but action was minimal. Congress was reluctant to appropriate sufficient funds, and Jonathan Marshall has argued that President Roosevelt remained more concerned with balancing the budget than with stockpiling materials until after the European war had begun.[68] Equally important, as the economy picked up during 1939 rubber manufacturers responded to the demand by purchasing rubber for immediate use rather than stockpiling. Government purchases would have raised the prices at which manufacturers could buy. A compromise position which met with surprisingly little opposition in Washington and London resulted in a rubber-for-cotton exchange agreement, similar in some ways to the later destroyer-for-bases agreement. Washington would provide its stockpiled cotton to London in exchange for rubber, which United States officials believed London could purchase outside the IRRC quota system because neither the cotton nor the rubber would enter the market. Events outstripped the agreement, which was signed in June 1939 but did not go into effect until late August, only one week before war broke out in Europe.[69]

When war did break out United States rubber manufacturers, supported by United States officials, scrambled to purchase all available rubber and to persuade the IRRC to raise rubber quotas. The initial chaos of wartime, with shipping disrupted, British officials changing jobs, and Dutch officials unreachable, meant that it was difficult to buy and then ship sufficient rubber. The IRRC continued to restrict rubber production through late 1939 and early 1940, since no one could predict how long the war would last nor what the impact of the war on consumption would turn out to be. But within a few months the primary work of the IRRC was ensuring that stockpiles in the United States, Britain, and Canada could be built in an orderly fashion at a reasonable price. With United States and Japanese entry into the war in December 1941, the IRRC's work effectively came to an end, although the rubber industry had already been irrevocably changed.[70]

Limits to Power

Two conflicting impulses have long existed side by side in United States foreign economic policy. On the one hand many Americans—including many in the United States government—believe that the United States is strongest when it is most self-sufficient, and they advocate policies which enhance the country's ability to go it alone. On the other hand there is an equally strong impulse to have the United States transform the world through the sheer power of its economic might by being a leader in international trade and investment. These two impulses clashed during the Depression, nowhere more visibly than in Southeast Asia. The region was the source of a large quantity of the raw materials not available in the Western Hemisphere, so the United States had to continue to be involved in international trade there no matter the conditions.

Secretary of State Cordell Hull hoped to break through the conflict between these two American principles by negotiating reciprocal free trade agreements with as many countries as possible, and using most-favored-nation policies to use those agreements to open up the world to trade. Hull believed that free trade would create an economically interdependent world, in which nations would have more reason to remain at peace with one another than to fight. Belief in the benefits of free trade remains a strong component of United States foreign economic policy. But the commodity trade in Southeast Asia during the 1930s demonstrated that free trade could also create conflict among nations. Hull's own State Department officials reluctantly realized that the United States would have to participate—even if only informally—in negotiated, regulated trade, with production, price, and consumption manipulated to guarantee some profit to all. The policies look quite similar to New Deal programs to raise the price of cotton by plowing under part of the crop, as the British sometimes bitterly noted. Neither United States officials nor businessmen liked these regulated markets, but all recognized that they were unavoidable. The next step for them was to figure out how to have sufficient power in the future to shape the agreements so as to advance their own interests.

In Southeast Asia the most profound impact of this change in United States policy toward regulated markets was on the indigenous producers. During the 1920s Americans involved in the region had actively encouraged Southeast Asians to grow for the export market. Indigenous producers usually had lower costs, which United States businesses naturally appreciated. United States officials and businessmen alike also believed that they were promoting economic development and self-sufficiency among the Southeast Asians, an important early step on the way to economic and political independence. In this way Americans did not need to care that they were upsetting the economic and perhaps political basis of European colonialism in Southeast Asia. During the economic boom of the 1920s disruption of the economic order seemed to benefit both Americans and Southeast Asians, and the Europeans who emulated United States businessmen could profit too.

The United States approach rested on the assumption that overwhelming economic power combined with minimal political responsibilities would suffice to protect United States interests in the region. During the 1920s the assumption seemed to hold, since the United States acquired its concession to drill for oil in the Netherlands Indies and broke Britain's Stevenson Plan to restrict rubber production. But the economic crisis of the 1930s prompted European colonial powers to use all the political power at their disposal, and United States economic efforts failed in the face of this united European approach. Southeast Asians might still have been willing and able to produce all the rubber that United States consumers needed at low prices, but the governments in the region made it impossible for this rubber to reach the international market. Although rubber manufacturers in the United States briefly considered encouraging massive smuggling to undermine the IRRC restriction plan, the embarrassed response of the United States government to this proposal—and probably the manufacturers' own good sense—led them quickly to drop the idea.[71] Instead they discontinued their support of Southeast Asian growers in an attempt to bargain with the European governments and get the best deal possible. It was gradually becoming clearer to United States officials that economic power alone would not suffice to protect United States interests.

The crushing economic effects of the Depression had contradictory consequences for United States relations with Southeast Asia. As Paul Kramer has recently argued, during the 1930s a "politics of exclusion" developed in United States relations with its colony in the Philippines. It became United States policy to exclude Filipino migrants and Filipino products because of the burdens that continental Americans believed these people and products brought with them. The politics of exclusion helped lead to independence for the Philippines.[72] For the rest of Southeast Asia, by contrast, Depression-era developments led to greater support for imperialism in the European-ruled parts of Southeast Asia. Free-market forces, encouraged in the 1920s, seemed too disruptive. United States officials and United States businessmen alike worked within the power structures of imperialism in an attempt to make economic relations more predictable. They expressed no concern that an unintended consequence of these actions might be to shore up imperialism.

5

||||||||||||||||||||||||||||||||||||||||||||||||||||||||||||||||||||||||||||||||||||||||||||||||||||||||||||||||||||||||||||||||||||||||

Challenges to the Established Order, 1930–1939

The economic challenges of the 1930s threatened the imperial system in Southeast Asia, but officials in the colonial powers in large measure agreed on the most appropriate responses to those challenges. Cooperation in setting production levels and prices was not easy and not fully efficacious, but it seemed gradually to be making markets operate more rationally by the end of the 1930s. The political situation in colonial Southeast Asia in the 1930s was much less tractable than even the devastating swings of the economy. Early in the decade the region saw two major rebellions, in Burma and Indochina, followed by Japan's invasion and occupation of Manchuria, a forceful demonstration of Japan's dissatisfaction with its global status. Officials from the colonial powers spent the 1930s working to contain these two major threats to the imperial order: insistently growing nationalism on the part of Southeast Asians and increasingly worrisome signs of Japan's expansionist desires. Colonial responses from both the United States and European powers vacillated between reform and oppression. The chaotic and ineffectual policies stemmed from an inability or unwillingness to match commitment levels to the challenges posed by Japanese expansion and Southeast Asian nationalism.

During the 1930s all involved powers came to understand more fully that action by the United States was critical for upholding the imperial system in its existing form. European officials wanted to encourage the United States to act to maintain the system, but were not sure whether they wanted to pay the necessary price to gain American commitment, even if they could figure out how to prompt it. They suspected there was a threat level which would prompt the United States to intervene, but feared that this would be a level of crisis so extreme that restoration of the imperial order would be impossible. United States officials were assessing threats and resources, attempting to balance what appeared to be an escalation of threats in the face of diminishing resources. During these years United States policy appeared contradictory, swinging between isolationist pullback and involved responsibility. Even as officials struggled to determine the direction of United States policy, they consistently supported European imperialism over Southeast Asian nationalism and Japanese expansion. This support was not uncritical, nor offered permanently, but it was firm during the 1930s.

Communists and Buddhists Rebel

Plunging commodity prices in 1930 were not the only problems with which European colonial administrators had to deal. That year saw major rebellions in Burma and Indonesia which involved thousands of people, lasted for nearly two years each, and required massive resources to suppress. The Nghe-Tinh Rebellion in Indochina erupted in May 1930 and was not fully suppressed until the late fall of 1931. The Saya San Rebellion in Burma began in December 1930 and lasted until the spring of 1932. Although neither posed a physical threat to the seat of the colonial government, Europeans found the length and size of both rebellions threatening. Colonial officials across the region did not always agree in their interpretations of the causes of the rebellions, but offered unconditional support for measures taken to suppress them. In assessing both the causes and the scale of these rebellions, officials revealed an incipient sense that Southeast Asian anticolonial activism had taken on a new, worrisome character. Overwhelming that sense was one dominant theme: the rebellions demonstrated that Southeast Asians were still incapable of responsible self-rule, and therefore not deserving of it.

These rebellions occurred in the two Southeast Asian colonies where the United States had the fewest material interests, yet the local United States consuls reported on them extensively. Department of State officials in Washington read the reports and commented on them—rare for reports from the region during these years—and sometimes shared them with officials from other departments. The rebellions attracted attention because of their size and duration and their potential to disrupt the production of commodities such as rice, but most importantly because of what they did, or might, signify. The uncertainties of these years meant that even while many Washington politicians seriously contemplated drawing back into an American shell, the real possibilities of doing so shrank.

The Nghe-Tinh rebellion was a series of uprisings in 1930–31 in three provinces of north central Vietnam: Nghe An, Ha Tinh, and Quang Ngai. It has also been called the Red Soviet uprising, because when the peasants succeeded in seizing power they established soviets, redistributed land, abolished taxes to the central government, and redistributed food stocks when necessary. The Indochinese Communist Party[1] had been organizing in Nghe-Tinh since 1929. The call to prepare for May Day celebrations and protests in 1930 met with a greater response in Nghe-Tinh than ICP cadres had dreamed possible. Armed only with sharpened sticks or nothing at all, peasants staged demonstrations in front of the homes of landowners against whom they had grievances, burnt down such symbols of power as pagodas and *dinh* (village communal temples), and intimidated local officials into relinquishing power.

Officials of the French government, whether local Vietnamese officials and mandarins, soldiers, or French district officials, were afraid to attempt to reassert their authority because rebel leaders had threatened them with death or the wrath of the villagers. The rebels conducted government as they thought proper. They forced local officials to resign and to swear to obey the ICP, imposed taxes on the wealthy, "pillaged and burned" houses of officials and wealthy people who did not cooperate, and according to the inspector, accused those who spoke out against them of being traitors. He reported that these "traitors" were denounced, then "beaten unmercifully." The rebels operated "openly" and had confidence. The inspector concluded by listing "those dangerous zones in which there is no question of venturing without a substantial detachment."[2]

The French government tried all measures to suppress the rebellion. In Annam, the *résident supérieur*, Le Fol, requested and received a squadron of planes to drop bombs on the rebels. Protests from the court at Hué and fears of a public outcry in France put an end to the bombing, but only on the same day that several companies of the Foreign Legion arrived. In spite of these efforts peasants were encouraged by their successes and the rebellion continued to spread. In June 1930, 130 soldiers of the French government faced a crowd of four to five hundred Vietnamese, armed only with knives and sharpened sticks, as the soldiers attempted to arrest village leaders who had helped the rebels. After a twenty-four-hour standoff the French commander ordered his troops to fire, dispersing the crowd while killing sixteen rebels and wounding fifteen. In September 1930 "several indigenous militiamen" attacked a district capital, freed some prisoners, destroyed records relating to the tax on alcohol and salt, and set fire to the homes and offices of local authorities. They dispersed upon the arrival of reinforcements from the Garde Indigène.

By mid-September 1931 Sûreté reports claimed that demonstrations had almost completely ceased, but noted the presence of "many new associations" with strong "nationalist" spirit.[3] Involvement by the Indochinese Communist Party in the rebellion varied, but the most recent scholarship indicates that the ICP followed the peasants to a much greater extent than it led them. Bad harvests, high taxes, corrupt officials, and government apathy toward the needs of peasants contributed to the peasants' willingness to revolt.

The rebels' initial successes brought a swift, harsh French response. Hundreds, perhaps thousands, of peasants died when the Foreign Legion fired on unarmed demonstrators. The Sûreté began also to infiltrate spies into the movement and keep elaborate dossiers on all participants.[4] By the fall of 1931 the French had suppressed almost all remnants of rebellion, and thousands of rebels had been herded into makeshift jails. Those party members who survived fled, when possible, to Thailand, Burma, or China to wait for a more opportune moment.

The Saya San rebellion began on the night of 22 December 1930 with an attack by rebels on the headmen of villages in the Tharrawaddy District of lower Burma. British officials initially responded by sending only a few police in hopes of making arrests and ending the incident. Instead they met fierce fighting. That first night the Burmese deputy superintendent of police, Maung Maung Gale, led a contingent of fifty military police and a handful of civilian police to meet the rebels. His force was overwhelmed and suffered many casualties. Maung Maung Gale was killed. The rebels frequently entered villages in search of guns and food, sometimes leaving peacefully if they received assistance but often killing local officials and burning houses when they met resistance or to settle grievances. By 10 February 1931 the British government reported that the rebels had "murdered" twenty-eight people, most of whom were government officials, and that three police had been killed in action. Property damage was also extensive, with more than fifty villages attacked, including four which had been burnt to the ground. As in the PKI rebellion, rebels attacked means of communication and by 10 February had destroyed two railway stations and one railway bridge. The rebels had suffered greater losses: a fight on 7 January 1931 left forty-seven rebels killed in Pyapon, while approximately five hundred rebels throughout Insein and Tharrawaddy had been killed in the course of the rebellion by 10 February. British officials had arrested more than eleven hundred people to that point, although not all would be tried.[5]

In unfortunate timing for a significant first, a Burmese (although not ethnically Burman), Joseph Maung Gyi, was serving as acting governor of Burma at the time the rebellion broke out.[6] Maung Gyi quickly committed troops to suppress the rebellion but hesitated to make any policy changes. When Governor Innes returned in early February 1931, he declared the Soe Thein General Council of Buddhist Associations (GBCA), a predominantly Buddhist, anticolonial organization which advocated noncooperation, to be an "unlawful association." The official statement explained that the rebellion was a "concerted plan to overthrow the Government by armed force," which amounted to treason. Saya San, the rebellion's leader, was a Soe Thein GBCA member, and the statement claimed that Soe Thein GBCA members knew about the rebellion while it was still in the planning stages, but failed to inform the government.[7]

In addition, Governor Innes decided to delay for three weeks, from 15 February to 7 March, collection of the land revenue tax, one of the taxes against which the rebels protested. Governor Innes acknowledged that this was "not a very long postponement" but claimed that it would "give the agriculturalist longer in which to dispose of his paddy."[8] British officials did not believe that economic conditions were a primary cause of the rebellion, and therefore made almost no attempts to end the rebellion by meeting the widely publicized economic demands of the rebels. They relied instead upon force and beginning in July 1931 on an amnesty program for rebels who surrendered unconditionally.[9]

The rebels never had a remote possibility of succeeding in forcing the British out of Burma, or even of achieving their more limited goal of cancellation of the capitation and *thathameda* taxes. Eight British-led battalions (one British and seven Indian), fully armed, were more than a match for tens of thousands of rebels armed with a couple of hundred guns, homemade bombs, and innumerable *dahs*. But the rebellion did last into April 1932, and spread into twelve of Burma's twenty districts. More than 1,300 rebels were killed in the fighting, and a further 125 were hanged by the British government for their participation. Approximately 9,000 rebels surrendered or were captured or arrested, with 1,389 of those sentenced to prison or transportation. By the first week of October 1931 British-led forces had suffered 160 casualties and government noncombatants 30 casualties.[10] Trials of rebels continued late into 1932, as did reports of the rebellion in the Burmese press.[11]

Understandings of Nghe-Tinh and Saya San Rebellions

These two rebellions share so many characteristics, in their stated motive, the type and number of participants, their length, and the means used to suppress them, that the tendency of scholars to compare them is not surprising.[12] Yet the most striking difference between the rebellions—the presence of the symbols and rhetoric of communism in the Nghe-Tinh rebellion—made all the difference in how the rebellions were interpreted, especially in terms of their long-term significance, by Europeans and Americans, whether colonial or diplomatic officials or newspaper reporters. The initial reports in United States newspapers reflected the tone which officials would also take. The stories were mostly small, provided by wire services, and buried on inside pages. In Nghe-Tinh "rebels led by Communists" had risen up. Stories explained "that the recent troubles in Indo-China were stirred up on direct orders from Moscow." The Saya San rebellion received more prominent placement and more stories in its initial days, perhaps because newspapers were already reporting on political issues in India. The *New York Herald Tribune* had a story nearly every day during the first week of the rebellion, including one front-page story. The Saya San rebellion was also more exotic in these reports, with the leader a "mysterious figure" who had an alluring name which the reports translated as "King Golden Crow."[13] By evoking the traditional and exotic nature of the Saya San rebellion, these reports suggested that suppression would follow soon after the leader was captured or killed. The evocation of the communist inspiration for the Nghe-Tinh rebellion served the opposite purpose: to suggest that the French were facing the difficult task of rooting out the Bolshevik agitators and their ideas. These assessments formed the subtext of the newspaper reports, but similar assessments were bluntly stated in officials' reports on the two rebellions.

British officials in Burma from the earliest days of the Saya San rebellion emphasized its traditional characteristics and steadfastly refused to acknowledge any economic component. Instead they claimed that Saya San hoped to overturn the government and become king, in the sort of takeover that had often occurred in Burma's past, and in January 1931 they decreed that the Saya San rebellion was "mainly an insurrection of the usual Burmese type."[14]

After the rebellion was over the British government published a sixty-page report titled "The Origins and Causes of the Burma Rebellion (1930–1932)." The bulk of the report was devoted to providing examples to back up each of the government's contentions about the rebellion. First, the rebellion was political rather than economic, as demonstrated by the long, detailed planning for it and the rebels' intention to take over the government "by force of arms." Second, this traditional rebellion was founded on the "superstition and credulity" of Burmese peasants, as seen both in Saya San's use of traditional oaths and rituals and in the peasants' belief in tattoos and charms for "invulnerability." Finally, the rebellion was led primarily by members of the non-cooperationist, anticolonial Soe Thein G.C.B.A., demonstrating the treasonous character of that organization.[15] For most British observers the meaning of the rebellion lay right on its surface, visible in the tattoos, charms, oaths, and other colorful components of traditional Burma. Not modern, it posed a threat no greater than its physical presence. Once quelled, it faded from British memories. In 1934 officials deciding whether the report on the rebellion, just published, should be placed in the Parliament Library called it "dull and uninforming," but more importantly, out of date.[16]

French officials were equally quick to form lasting impressions of the Nghe-Tinh rebellion. The earliest reports, from May 1930, already claimed that communist agitators, many of them "strangers," were responsible for stirring up the local population.[17] Within a few months the French launched an elaborate inquiry into the causes of the rebellion, taking déclarations from a variety of French and Vietnamese officials and private citizens, including many of those arrested for participating in the rebellion. Despite the massive effort and thousands of pages of testimony, official French understanding of the rebellion was not shaped or changed by this inquiry. Even when participants explained that promises to abolish the hated salt and alcohol taxes had prompted them to join, French officials said that this only proved the peasants' "credulity," since the peasant "accepts all these promises without worrying himself about whether they are realizable."[18] The report acknowledged that the region most strongly affected by the rebellion did suffer poverty, corrupt local (mostly Vietnamese) officials, insufficient irrigation, and an inadequate educational system. These problems were said to be not the fault of the French government but expected growing pains, as the French helped the Vietnamese adjust to a "new mental milieu."[19] The real problem then was not peasant grievances, though some existed, but rather that "the rulers of the U.S.S.R. have realized the ineffectiveness of their efforts in the European countries, and have dreamed of reaching those countries through their colonies."[20] As in Burma, colonial officials admitted that peasants were suffering economic hardship, but in neither colony would the officials admit a relationship between the poor economy and the rebellion. Still, the apparently communist nature of the Nghe-Tinh rebellion meant that this rebellion was a cause for long-term, regional concern, and even action.

The size and duration of the Saya San and Nghe Tinh rebellions meant that officials from regional colonial powers reported on the events and drew conclusions about their meaning. British claims about the traditional nature of the Saya San rebellion were readily accepted, and the rebellion prompted little concern. Likewise, French assessments about the role of communism in motivating Nghe-Tinh rebels provoked no controversy, and intercolonial cooperation against communist influences intensified. These officials, though occasionally critical of British or French methods, gave no indication that the rebellions suggested any flaws in imperialism itself. The United States consul in Rangoon, George Haering, reported monthly on the course of the Saya San rebellion. In response to standing State Department instructions about communism, he found "no outside influences" on the rebels. Rather, Haering echoed British explanations about the well-known lawlessness of the Tharrawaddy region where the rebellion began, and noted that troubles were common in Burma at tax collection time. Although alternate explanations provided by Burmese authors for English-language publications were available, Haering only consulted British sources, and not surprisingly accepted the British explanations.[21] The Dutch and French were still more reliant on British sources, since they did not maintain consulates in Burma.[22] The French consul general from Calcutta did tour Burma in February 1931, and concluded from interviews during his trip that the Saya San rebellion was "better organized than its predecessors" but ultimately traditional. Dutch reports in the *Koloniaal Tijdblad*, journal of the Netherlands Indies Civil Service, were brief and factual. After the rebellion had lasted approximately one year French and Dutch officials expressed some concern about the ineffectiveness of British suppression efforts, and slight worry that the civil disobedience movement in India was fueling Burmese anticolonial sentiments.[23] But the French and Dutch generally perceived no threat to their own colonial interests. Traditional rebellions, although somewhat influenced by nationalists or helpful to them, were not threatening.

Assessments of Nghe-Tinh by British, Dutch, and United States officials accepted French explanations about the communist nature of the rebellion, but also placed some blame for the appeal of communism on the inadequacies of French colonial rule. Henry Waterman, United States consul in Saigon, filed numerous reports titled "Communistic Activities in French Indo-China," in which he described the activities of communists, identified by their communistic tracts and their use of flags with hammer and sickle.[24] According to the Dutch *Indische Gids*, it had been "clearly demonstrated" that "Moscow had a hand in all the revolutionary disturbances" in Indochina. The British consul general, F. G. Gorton, also accepted the explanation of communism and carefully reported the numerous atrocities during the course of the rebellion, all said to have been committed by communists in his reports, but he also stated that if the Vietnamese had had enough to eat, they would have been less likely to listen to communist propaganda. As the rebellion continued for months, Gorton began to worry that the problem was greater than "merely a wave of communism." Perhaps there was "something radically wrong in Annam."[25]

After the Nghe-Tinh rebellion was finally suppressed in mid-1932 communist activity in the region entered a lull, as most communist parties had been decimated by the repression of the late 1920s and early 1930s. The colonial powers did not relax but instead intensified the cooperation they had revitalized during the Nghe-Tinh rebellion. For example, in spite of declining numbers of raids of communist organizations, and consequent declines in arrests and convictions of communists, in 1934 the Malayan Special Branch reported "close and cordial" liaison that year with secret police in Rangoon, Saigon, Hanoi, Bangkok, Hong Kong, Shanghai, and Batavia. Throughout the 1930s the routing list for the Malayan Bulletin of Political Intelligence included the advocaat generaal and the advisor for Chinese affairs in the Netherlands Indies, the head of the Sûreté in French Indochina, and the head of the secret police in Burma, as well as the British consular officials in Saigon, Batavia, Soerabaya, Medan, Bangkok, and Chiengmai. That the United States did not have a secret police force, not even in the Philippines, meant that information sharing with United States officials was less formal, but it was nonetheless routine.[26]

All the activity, fear-laden rhetoric, and harsh punishment of suspected or proven communists suggest that Europeans and Americans in colonial

Southeast Asia saw communism and communists as the greatest threat to the colonial order. By 1932, though, communism may instead have been the threat they could most easily imagine eradicating. Other growing threats, such as the intractable economic situation already discussed or the uncompromising demands of nationalists, not to mention an increasingly restless Japan, were less easy to arrest or repress out of existence. For colonial officials it may have been easier to imagine that the presence of communism in their colonies inhibited solutions to these other, intractable problems.

Japan to the Forefront

As large and serious as the Nghe-Tinh and Saya San rebellions were, they did not pose an immediate threat to the colonial order in Southeast Asia. But in the early 1930s it became clear that to a large extent the Southeast Asian colonial order rested on contained, channeled Japanese ambitions and a willingness by the United States to participate in the region, especially in containing Japan. When Japan invaded and quickly occupied Manchuria, officials from European colonial powers were hopeful about the effect of Japan's actions on their Southeast Asian interests. Both Britain and France saw the potential for some short-term benefits, while Dutch officials hoped that Japan's attention would be distracted for some period.[27] Growing evidence in the second half of the decade that Japan would not be satisfied by its Manchurian conquest, combined with apparently concrete movement by the United States in granting independence to the Philippines, promised to upset the established order in the region. Continued radical nationalist activities in Europe's Southeast Asian colonies added to the sense of uncertainty in European colonial officials about how they could protect their Southeast Asian interests. None of their options looked particularly appealing in the absence of a strong military commitment by the United States to defend the region.

Yet within the United States government some officials perceived that developments in the region threatened United States interests as well, and they grappled with the possible responses, both feasible and acceptable. During the 1930s, just when some United States officials and politicians were talking openly about pulling back from political, strategic, colonial, and sometimes economic activities in Pacific Asia, European officials were beginning to acknowledge, though it gave them little comfort, how much the existing regional order depended on having the United States participate in it.

These three considerations—Japanese expansionism, the uncertain nature of the United States commitment to the region, and Southeast Asian nationalism—became intertwined in colonial officials' understanding of regional politics. Cheap Japanese imports placated Southeast Asians who were suffering economically and restricted politically, but they meant that Japan also became identified for Southeast Asians with an improved standard of living and anti-European protest. The United States was the only power potentially strong enough to contain or defeat Japan, but the United States was not reliable and sometimes threatened to pull out of the region altogether. The possibility that the United States would grant independence to the Philippines seemed to give a green light to Japan's expansionist hopes, but it also encouraged Southeast Asian nationalists to demand autonomy or independence for themselves. Until 1937 it was not clear which of these developments posed the most serious immediate danger, nor was it clear to anyone how any particular policy could satisfy the interests or goals of any group involved. European, American, and Southeast Asian actions all seem muddled, contradictory, and tentative during these years.

The initial reactions to Japan's invasion of Manchuria by United States and European officials involved in Southeast Asia reveal the extent to which Japan had come to be accepted as one of the great diplomatic and colonial powers of Asia. Even the Dutch, who had the longest-lived and deepest fear of Japanese expansion into their colony, in November 1931 told Laurits Swenson, the United States minister in The Hague, that Japan's takeover of Manchuria might be good for the colonies. The Dutch colonial minister said that the Netherlands Indies had "nothing to fear from Japan." A greater concern was "that China might become a real menace in case the present disintegrating and anarchistic forces were not checked." If the Japanese dominated Manchuria, they would "form a bulwark against Russian bolshevism and have a stabilizing influence in China." Indeed, the minister "admired Japan as a country of law and order and praised the Japanese for their organizing and constructive ability." The meeting's purpose became clear when the Dutch colonial minister told Swenson that "it would have a very demoralizing effect in the different colonial possessions if the United States should withdraw from the Philippines and give them complete independence." A British participant in the conversation, Sir Cecil Hurst, a judge on the Permanent Court of International Justice, must have believed that the colonial minister was being too subtle, since he then chimed in that complete independence for the Philippines would "set the whole East ablaze."

Swenson reported none of his own contributions to the conversation, and provided little comment on it other than that it was "very interesting."[28]

Given that Dutch officials had often expressed concern about Japanese expansionism, and were actively limiting Japanese access to oil exploration in the Netherlands Indies,[29] the relative lack of concern about Japanese expansion into Manchuria could have several explanations: the Dutch were putting on a brave face, or they believed that Japan would have its hands full for some time in consolidating and expanding in northern Asia, or they believed that these Japanese moves would convince Britain and the United States that Japan was a serious problem.[30] United States and British officials also found the French initially unconcerned about Japan's expansion. They believed that the French had their own reasons, the most important of which was France's own sphere of influence in the Yunnan province of China. Yunnan is more easily reached from Indochina than from most other parts of China, and the French may therefore have been pleased to see the beginning of what could have been the formal breakup of China into spheres controlled by others.

French officials understood that their actions were being so interpreted. After Pierre Pasquier, the governor general of Indochina, made a successful visit to the Philippines, the French consul general reported that one beneficial result was the easing of suspicions of a secret pact (*un pacte secret*) between France and Japan.[31] French and Japanese actions were being compared in late 1931: William R. Castle, United States assistant secretary of state, asked about the possible reaction of the League of Nations "if the French soldiers chased bandits in Yunnan." The French were pursuing rebels from the Nghe-Tinh uprising across the border into China, and Castle was suggesting that these actions could appear similar to Japan's in Manchuria. In reply Stanley Hornbeck, of the Far Eastern Division of the United States Department of State, drew the distinction between the French action and Japanese actions in Manchuria: "if French soldiers occupy the whole of the southern half of Yunnan and drive out all Chinese administrative agencies and seize all public utilities, banks and a good many business enterprises, etc., etc.,—*shouldn't* the League of Nations and the United States go into a huddle or two huddles?"[32] Chasing "bandits" into a neighboring sovereign country was one thing for the international community and occupation was another, but Castle rightly perceived that at some level they were simply different points on a continuum. Figuring out the beneficial and correct policy response was difficult.

Back in Washington officials had been thinking about the connections between Japanese expansion and a possible United States grant of independence to the Philippines for many months before the incident in Manchuria in September 1931. In preparation for the debate on what became the Hare-Hawes-Cutting bill, officials in both the War and State Departments began to explore the implications for United States foreign and military policy of possible independence for the Philippines. Most officials in both War and State agreed that independence for the Philippines would encourage Japanese expansion, destabilize the "political equilibrium,"[33] and be unpopular with European colonial officials. The Europeans believed that an independent Philippines would encourage their own colonial subjects to rebel.

Despite broad agreement on these three likely consequences, there was no consensus about the degree of danger to United States interests. When Colonel Stanley Ford of the Military Intelligence Division wrote that Japan was a "nation needing and demanding expansion privileges" and the "logical successor to political and territorial power which the United States would give up in leaving the Philippines," one reader of the memo indicated some skepticism by drawing a large question mark in the margin.[34] Stanley Hornbeck, in a surprisingly cautious statement for the Sinophile that he was, emphasized more strongly that Philippine independence "would probably encourage the intensification of nationalistic activities on the part of the native populations in all neighboring colonial or dependent regions." He acknowledged that expansionistic rhetoric emanated from Japan but "doubted whether the more intelligent and thoughtful of Japan's responsible leaders cherish ambitions for extension of Japan's dominion southward." Still, it would be dangerous for the United States to pull out of the Philippines, since that would leave a "political vacuum," and Japanese politicians might be tempted to intervene either by "disorder" in the Philippines or the desire of "diverting the attention of the Japanese people from other matters." Hornbeck believed that granting independence to the Philippines would not be seen as a sign of the generosity or altruism of the United States, but rather of its weakness, selfishness, or cowardice.[35]

Perhaps because concerns about Japanese expansion had so long been part of United States thinking about the implications of granting independence to the Philippines, Japan's occupation of Manchuria did not have an immediate, dramatic effect on United States thinking in this area. When Secretary of State Henry Stimson finally sent the State Department's formal (but secret) reply to the request from the secretary of war regarding whether United States possession of the Philippines was "an asset or a liability," Japan was mentioned only once. Stimson claimed that for the United States to withdraw from the Philippines would result in "economic chaos and political and social anarchy," into which would step "some foreign power, probably either China or Japan." Since it would have been difficult to imagine an expansionistic China in 1931, when China was barely a coherent political entity, Stimson probably included China merely to avoid appearing to single out Japan. The rest of the memo, which was also sent to Senator Hiram Bingham, chairman of the Senate Committee on Territories and Insular Affairs and in March 1933, at his own request, to President Franklin D. Roosevelt, then newly inaugurated, studiously avoided mention of Japan while referring more than once to the threat to the "political equilibrium" and "world peace" of a United States withdrawal from the Philippines. Stimson concluded by calling the Philippines an "enormous asset." Leaving would lead to "an irreparable loss."[36]

These Washington officials had been among the main architects of the Washington Treaty System and were comfortable with the level of commitment that the system required from the United States politically and militarily. But in the early 1930s they faced mounting dilemmas. There was a growing sentiment in the United States that the government should commit formally to independence for the Philippines, a sentiment prompted by the struggles of United States domestic sugar growers to compete with the vast sugar production of the Philippines, debates about the immigration status of Filipinos, and the return to power of the Democratic Party, which had long promised more concrete steps on independence for the Philippines.[37] Additional dilemmas stemmed from the clear weakness of China in resisting the Japanese invasion and the reluctance of European powers to take any concrete steps to come to China's aid. The carefully constructed orders—both colonial and the integrity of China—of the Washington Treaty System seemed to be crumbling, just slowly enough that United States officials could not declare a crisis requiring extraordinary measures, but quickly enough that they were scrambling to figure out new ways to shore up the system.

British officials observed the dilemmas facing the United States and provided an unsentimental assessment of the likely result of not facing those dilemmas over the next few years. Perhaps because it was the final blow to a policy of attempting to contain Japanese ambitions by treating Japan as one of the great powers, British officials were most pessimistic about the implications of Japan's invasion of Manchuria. As early as February 1932

Pratt in the British Foreign Office wrote: "Ultimately we will be faced with the alternatives of going to war with Japan or retiring from the Far East. A retirement from the Far East might be the prelude to a retirement from India." India was a key British concern in all possible responses to Japan. A possible boycott of Japanese goods, an idea batted around in Washington and appealing to many Chinese, might increase Chinese purchases of British goods but likely would not be observed by India, making the matter "obviously one of great difficulty and delicacy."[38]

British officials seemed to assume in early February that the United States might well follow a policy of "pressure" on Japan, through the severing of economic and diplomatic relations. If so, United States officials would want British support. But from the British perspective, the problem with following the United States in an embargo on Japan was that the United States could not be relied upon. Wellesley, writing on 1 February 1932, agreed with his colleagues in the Foreign Office that Britain alone was not sufficiently strong to fight and defeat Japan, but he also noted that Britain had to consider relations with both Asia and Europe. He made the assessment that Britain needed the United States in Europe more than in Asia. Given these unappealing choices, Wellesley advocated an independent course for Britain on the Manchuria question, since sacrificing good relations with Japan in order to ally with the United States in Asia could impel the United States to leave Britain "in the lurch in Europe," with Britain's "Far Eastern interests sacrificed for nothing."[39]

Maintaining relations with Japan also allowed for a potential short-term gain from the invasion: Chinese who boycotted Japanese goods would buy more British and Indian goods, but Britain would not have to make difficult decisions about boycotting Japan. From Washington the British ambassador Sir Ronald Lindsay wrote to acknowledge that the United States was "never able to take firm commitments" and that United States "support" could "never be relied on without question," but also that United States policy toward Japan had been remarkably consistent, and deserved British support.[40] Despite Britain's rather more prescient view of the situation, the British were no better able than the Dutch or French to come up with a satisfying response, since everyone agreed that only the United States had the power, mostly in the form of economic power as Japan's largest trading partner but also in latent military power, to force Japan to stop expanding.[41] The colonial powers in Southeast Asia had a shared sense that Japan's actions might well change the colonial order in the region, and that only continued involvement by the United States in the region, likely or not, could prevent that change. The problem was that no one, least of all the involved United States officials, perceived a way to get the United States to commit to such continued involvement.

Normalizing Uncertainty

Once it became clear that the height of the world response to the invasion of Manchuria would be Secretary of State Stimson's Non-Recognition Policy, notably not popular with the other colonial powers of Southeast Asia, and the threat by the United States to pull out of the Nine-Power Treaty if Japan did not adhere to the Open Door, colonial and foreign policy officials treated the new status of Japan and Manchuria as simply one more factor to consider when formulating policies for Southeast Asia. Uncertainties about Japan's ultimate intentions, coupled with uncertainties about the future of United States rule in the Philippines, made it virtually impossible to make long-term plans on political, strategic, or military matters. Japan became like a sore tooth—everyone felt compelled to poke at it, and knew that it needed some kind of expert attention, but no one really wanted to know how serious the situation was. Better to take painkillers and forget about the problem until a crisis erupted.

Suspicions continued that the French had a "comparatively uncritical attitude . . . toward Japanese activities in northeast Asia" because of the French desire to dominate Yunnan to a greater degree. A memo prepared for the internal use of the U.S. War Department found France "not unready if China is to be partitioned or if the balance of power in the Far East is to be readjusted as a result of the increase in Japan's authority."[42] This memo may suggest more coherence than French policy had. French officials did worry about Japan's expansion in Asia, and in the fall of 1933 officials from the French Foreign Ministry discussed a possible entente with the Soviet Union, aimed primarily at Japan. The sous-director of Asian affairs protested, saying that the Japanese would surely consider any French assistance to the Soviet Union in a war to be "an act of aggression." Then "our possessions in the Far East would be threatened and it is only too certain that we would be at pains to assure their defense."[43] Japanese ambitions seemed directed more toward other parts of Asia than Indochina in the early and mid-1930s, giving the French a little breathing room.

Dutch views of Japan in the mid-1930s were intimately tied to the important economic role that Japan played in the Netherlands Indies. The decisions that the Dutch needed to make about Japan may have been the most concrete of all those facing the colonial powers. Foremost in everyone's minds was that Japan required foreign sources of oil, for industrial production of course but more importantly for the Japanese navy. Any military expansion by Japan in any direction meant that Japan would need the oil produced in the Netherlands Indies. At times this Japanese need gave the Dutch some comfort, as in early 1934 when the Dutch colonial minister, Colijn, wrote to the Dutch foreign minister, de Graeff, that in case of a war between Japan and the United States, "a *neutral* Netherlands-Indies, from which the necessary oil could be obtained, would for Japan be of great importance."[44] So long as the Japanese could buy their oil, they would not invade the Netherlands Indies. Yet Dutch officials were also prudent, and had already begun to improve the defenses of their oil installations.[45]

If Japan's primary importance to the Netherlands Indies had been merely as a purchaser of oil and other colonial products, Dutch officials might have tried harder to keep Japan at arm's length, but Japan was also a major importer of inexpensive consumer goods to the islands. The importance of these goods in maintaining a decent standard of living for indigenous Indonesians increased as the Depression deepened, and many Dutch officials believed that one price of relative Indonesian quiescence was access to affordable consumer products. Indeed, one high-ranking Dutch official in the Indies government told the United States consul general, K. S. Patton, that "in his opinion, cheap Japanese imports are essential to the welfare of the natives."[46]

Sensing that the Japanese threat was farther away than that from Indonesian nationalists, and could perhaps be contained by means of good trade relations, Dutch civilian officials chose to placate both Japan and the nationalists. Even this policy had potential disadvantages, since Indonesians came to view Japan as interested in their welfare. The Dutch recognized this: the advisor for native affairs told Patton "that in any conflict of interests between the Dutch and the Japanese, no confidence could be placed in the loyalty of the natives to the government."[47] Officials back in Washington compared Dutch worries about Japanese influence in their colony to "the decline of Western prestige in Asia" noted by Edgar Snow in a recent article in the *Saturday Evening Post*. Recognition by the Dutch that none of their feasible policy options promised long-term security, and reluctance by Washington officials to criticize a Dutch choice that worried them, suggest that Southeast Asian colonial powers in the mid-1930s perceived virtually no active steps that they could realistically take.

This perception was obviously most frustrating for the British, who were used to thinking of themselves as the guarantors of security and the balance of power in Asia. But in reading British foreign and colonial policy documents of the mid-1930s, the overwhelming impression received is of a country stretched too thin, aware of inadequate resources, yet unwilling to publicly cede influence or control in any part of the world. British policymakers during the mid-1930s may have been much concerned about economic issues in their Southeast Asian colonies (as discussed in chapter 4), but strategically and militarily they were completely distracted by developments in Europe and to some extent in China and India.

In August 1933 the Foreign Office circulated a memo stating: "The time has come to take stock of the position in the Far East." Although myriad problems were raised for all the colonies, they boiled down to two key questions. First, what can and should Britain defend if Japan continues to expand? Second, what might rouse the United States to take strong steps or even fight against Japan? There was no possibility of providing an honest answer to the first question, because all studies showed that the only hope of providing the most minimal defense to Hong Kong, Malaysia, Singapore, India, Burma, New Zealand, and Australia (and possibly South Africa) lay in making an immediate commitment to finishing the barely started base at Singapore, providing it with sufficient weapons and men, and stationing part of the Royal Navy at that base. Although successive British governments made promises about the base at Singapore to the colonies and dominions, most of these governments had greater fears of spending money during the tight Depression years, as well as a desire to promote worldwide disarmament by setting a good example.[48]

They also, as the 1930s progressed, came to see developments in Europe as more immediately threatening to British interests than Japan's actions in Asia. A minute by Wellesley on a report in 1934 from the British ambassador in Japan expressed the hope, sometimes belief, which allowed British policymakers to move so slowly to fortify Singapore: "The key note of Japan's policy is always the fear of political isolation & however much we may quarrel with her in the end she will always come back to her first love [Britain], not because she really likes us but because on the whole we are the best of the bunch."[49]

The other British hope which shaped policy was that despite protests to the contrary, support from the United States for the existing order would somehow materialize if a serious crisis developed. British expectations were minimal, but in August 1933 a Foreign Office memo did suggest that the "United States would never go to war for any Far Eastern issue less than armed aggression by Japan against Hawaii, Philippines, Guam, Singapore or the Dutch Indies."[50] In other words, the United States would go to war if its own territories were attacked (Hawaii, Philippines, Guam) or if its access to the important raw materials of British Malaya or the Netherlands Indies was threatened. Although nowhere in the United States documents does such a concern with access to these raw materials appear as early as 1933, the British memo does imply an understanding that those raw materials of Southeast Asia were the reason for Japan's interest in the region, and that a Japanese attack there would likely indicate broader Japanese goals. Still, as the basis for a British policy, the memo was not merely tentative but also demonstrated Britain's military weakness and consequent inability to actively shape regional politics.

Given the stated United States policy for Southeast Asia, the British view may have been optimistic. The best that United States officials who wanted to remain involved in the region could offer during the mid-1930s was the possibility of a neutralization treaty for the Philippines, to take effect when the United States granted independence to the islands. The proposed treaty would be an agreement by all regional powers to respect the sovereignty of the Philippines and to refrain from attacking it. Stanley Hornbeck suggested in January 1932 that since "the granting of Philippine independence by action of the Congress of the United States is inevitable," the "Administration" should propose an amendment or separate bill which would require both a bilateral treaty between the United States and Philippines and a multilateral treaty to guarantee Philippine "independence and integrity."[51]

The official position of the State Department, expressed in the memo of October 1931 discussed above, recommended retaining the Philippines. Hornbeck's proposal was both a contingency plan, intended to maintain American influence and interest in the region if the colony itself was lost, and perhaps more importantly a vote of continued confidence in the principles of the Washington Treaty System. Hornbeck recommended that the neutralization treaty for the Philippines be "similar to the Nine-Power Treaty" by providing for the "maintenance of the territorial and administrative integrity" and protect the "principles of the open door and the settlement by normal processes of peaceful negotiation of all disputes" arising over the Philippines.[52] The guarantees that China received in 1922 would be extended to the Philippines upon its independence. For a Congress supposedly isolationist in its determination to grant independence to the Philippines, this proposal received remarkably little debate when submitted as an amendment to the Hare-Hawes-Cutting bill. A less restrictive version, which "requested" rather than required the president to sign the proposed treaties before independence, easily passed.[53] Congressional attention was primarily on the tariff question, especially during the ten-year period of transition to independence.

The Hare-Hawes-Cutting Act took effect under a different name (Tydings-McDuffie) early in Roosevelt's administration, with minor revisions regarding retention by the United States of bases in the Philippines but the same wording on neutralization. Roosevelt was not immediately inclined to open treaty negotiations, however. Ten years, the transition period to independence, was a long time, Filipino leaders were divided on the utility of a neutralization treaty, Roosevelt had other, more pressing matters, and his own State Department split on the issue. One draft memo produced in State suggested that even there some people advocated pulling back into the Western Hemisphere. This memo argued that the three guiding principles of United States policy in Asia since the First World War had been the Open Door, respect for the sovereignty of China, and "mutual respect for the possessions and dominions in the region of the Pacific."[54]

With the end of United States rule in the Philippines, the memo argued, there was "no longer . . . any weighty reason" to be "greatly concerned" with the third principle, and upon Philippine independence it should "be eliminated from our future policy in and toward the Far East." With that principle gone the United States should recognize that while there was "sentimental interest in China," the United States would never fight for Chinese interests. It would be better to acknowledge this fact but not actively work to dismantle the Nine-Power Treaty. Rather, the United States should "let this subject sleep and refrain as far as possible from making mention of it," while letting the "most concerned" countries (France, Great Britain, and Russia) take the lead. The Open Door should still be defended, but since "the tendency today is toward economic nationalism," the United States should be looking to replace Asian imports with sources in the Western Hemisphere.[55] Although intended merely to spark discussion within State about the possibilities for the future, the memo is a remarkably isolationist statement and reveals the extent of confusion among foreign policy officials about what they could and should accomplish. When Hornbeck wrote a cautionary memo in March 1935 which warned that United States policy was "drifting" into greater conflict with Japan, while lacking a guiding principle, he was right, but the drift continued.[56]

Hornbeck's caution should not be seen as a warning against conflict with Japan as much as a plea for principles to guide policies. Indeed, Hornbeck's insistence on standing firm on the ratios for Japanese warships (vis-à-vis United States, British, French, and Italian warships) in the face of Japanese demands to increase them was a key reason for the dismantling of the Five-Power Treaty in 1935. Whatever the implications for United States–Japanese relations, the end of the Five-Power Treaty refocused Roosevelt's mind on security arrangements in the Pacific, and he revived the idea of a neutralization treaty during 1936. Still intended to embody the principles of the Washington Treaties, the new proposal was nominally tied to Philippine independence and the need to guarantee Philippine security, but Roosevelt suggested discussing neutralization as one issue among many at a general conference on Far East issues.[57]

Again Hornbeck wrote the influential analysis of neutralization, but he had changed sides since 1932, now recommending against it. Hornbeck had a number of objections, some of which might have occurred to him in 1932 had he been arguing against the neutralization treaty then: Europeans did not want Philippine independence and so would be unlikely to enter into a new treaty to guarantee it; the newly independent Philippines was likely to join the League of Nations, which should act to guarantee its sovereignty from aggression; the United States would have to give up its bases in the Philippines under a neutralization treaty. The most important objection was that "one of the principal signatory powers" was not likely to observe it in times of crisis, especially since that power had substantial and growing economic interests in the Philippines which it would want to defend if attacked by Philippine or foreign forces.[58]

In other words Japan—the primary object of the treaty—had shown no great respect for international treaties in recent years, and had as many economic interests in the Philippines as the United States had in Central America, a comparison the Japanese had made explicitly in early 1932 when they declared an analogue to the Monroe Doctrine for Asia. Hornbeck's internal memo was quite forthright in its language and reasoning. The State Department memo sent to the president in response to his request for analysis of the neutralization possibility made a similar point, with exhaustive attention to the "cons" of four slightly different neutralization proposals, and minimal attention to the "pros." Then, in what was supposed to be the bureaucratic death knell, it recommended further study and private consultations with Britain, Japan, and France.[59]

Roosevelt could play that game, of course. He complained that the State memo presented "an argument of defeatism" and did "not fire one's imagination in favor of neutralization of the islands of the Pacific." And he saw that the thinking in State had changed about the viability of agreements along the lines of the Washington Treaty System, in that neutralization was presented as "merely idealistic and that an agreement would not be lived up to anyway." Concluding by calling himself a "realist," Roosevelt asked to meet with the memo's author,[60] presumably in an attempt to charm him into believing in Roosevelt's style of realism. Whether or not that happened, Roosevelt was president and saw to it that the private consultations with allies took place. British officials were notably cool, and offered an analysis remarkably similar to that coming out of State. The British foreign secretary, Anthony Eden, asked in particular about the "removal of fortifications" and the possibility that Japan would participate. Roosevelt's emissary to Eden, Norman Davis, reported that both were part of Roosevelt's plan, and Eden replied that he would wait to hear Japan's response before offering a formal British response.[61]

European officials, especially from countries with interests in Asia, faced a dilemma in discussing neutralization. On the one hand Roosevelt's neutralization proposal implied a dismantling of nearly all fortifications in the Pacific, leaving Britain and Japan as the only substantial military (naval) powers in the region. Since only Japan worried anyone at this point, neutralization meant in fact that Britain had to be ready to defend all of the Pacific basin against Japanese attack. The British knew that they no longer had the capability to provide such defense. On the other hand, if the United States really did grant independence to the Philippines without concluding a neutralization treaty, then it would have no formal obligation of any type to a particular order in the region. No choice was good from the British perspective, and Eden counseled inaction on the part of the British ambassador in Washington.[62]

Inaction became impossible in mid-May 1937, when the Australian premier, Joseph Lyons, floated a neutralization proposal in a public speech. China and the Soviet Union quickly announced their support for the idea; from Japan came initial expressions of "no objection to participation," which soon changed to a more "reticent" stance. The United States ambassador in Japan, Joseph Grew, reported that in the view of Japanese officials the treaty negotiations would involve unwanted scrutiny of their actions in Manchuria and that Soviet participation might be contrary to Japanese interests. British officials called an imperial conference for the late spring of 1937 in part to discuss the idea, and managed the situation well enough that there was no formal vote on the neutralization idea, while there was general agreement to allow Britain to take the lead in the future. Neutralization was again stalled after the conference and remained so until the Japanese attack on China in July, an event which ended all discussion of neutralization.[63]

Neutralization had been a code word, in a sense, for the European and American desire to figure out how to keep Japan from expanding into the Philippines, and from there potentially into other Pacific islands. The rationale behind neutralization makes clear what might otherwise be puzzling: discussions about the possibilities for achieving neutralization virtually never included mention of the needs or capabilities of the islands to be protected by the treaty. One could read all the diplomatic correspondence on Philippine neutralization, for example, without ever learning that the Filipinos were making some effort to create a self-defense force.[64] Of the other Southeast Asian colonies, the only one mentioned occasionally is Singapore and its naval base. Even European colonial officials were rarely asked their opinions about need or feasibility; no one considered asking Southeast Asians. Part of the reason clearly was the long-standing fear of Japanese expansion, which dated at the latest to the First World War, and an assumption therefore that the identity of the enemy and of the potential victim were understood and agreed by all. Another key reason was the assumption, shared by most officials of the colonial powers, that their colonies had neither ideas about their relations with other countries nor a say in the matter. This assumption faced challenges already in the 1930s, as discussed below, but officials were often slow to perceive the change. Yet the key reason for the restricted terms of discussion lay in the shaky foundations of the colonial order in Southeast Asia by the 1930s. Since the turn of the century peace and security had rested on assumptions that the interests of all involved powers could be satisfied within the existing order, and because of that, no credible defense against external aggression existed for any power. Most obviously, neither France nor the Netherlands had sufficient troops or naval resources to defend its colonies. Britain could count on troops from India, New Zealand, or Australia in a crisis, but transport would be painfully slow, and the reliability of at least some of these troops was questionable. Most importantly, no port in the region could accommodate any significant part of the Royal Navy. The United States, with the greatest latent power of all colonial powers, not only was engaged in an internal debate about its role in the world but also had only a small army and navy during the 1920s and 1930s. As it became clearer that one power, Japan, might not be able to be satisfied within the system, the inadequacies of the defense of Southeast Asia became starkly clear. Few wanted to discuss these inadequacies openly, though, since no one intended to resolve them.

The Changing Face of Southeast Asian Nationalism

Japanese expansion and economic depression were newly threatening to colonial interests in Southeast Asia, but did not mitigate the ongoing official worry about Southeast Asians' continued struggle for independence. After the Nghe-Tinh and Saya San rebellions were suppressed in 1932 the region saw few violent outbursts of political demands. Colonial officials knew that Southeast Asians had changed tactics, not goals, and continued a mix of repression, negotiation, and reform. European officials hoped that their policies would enable imperial rule to continue, although possibly in altered form. The increasingly concrete steps by the United States to grant independence to the Philippines threatened to disrupt European plans. United States officials pursued the apparently contradictory policy of advocating that Europeans follow the American lead while at the same time working to minimize Southeast Asian exposure to the Philippines in order not to upset colonial relationships. Involved Americans may have been more likely than Europeans to believe that Southeast Asians could develop the capacity for self-rule, but these same Americans saw little proof that most Southeast Asians had done what was necessary to deserve independence.

Across the region Southeast Asian nationalists pursued two primary strategies from the early 1930s to the outbreak of the Second World War: political education of their followers, and efforts within the existing system to push reforms as far as possible. European officials were inclined to see these tactics as less immediately threatening than rebellion was, but they worried that they were seeing only the tip of the iceberg. United States observers, by contrast, were likely to see the tactics of Southeast Asians, so long as they stayed within certain bounds, as a demonstration that Southeast Asians could be schooled into wanting an independence which continued to offer many benefits to the former ruling power. They interpreted developments in United States–Philippine relations in much that light, and believed that United States policy provided a model for the rest of the region.

In the Netherlands Indies the line between political education and political organizing was faint. Two well-known Indonesian nationalists, Mohammed Hatta and Soetan Sjahrir, emphasized education as the best means to promote nationalism in the mid-1930s. Under their leadership the Pendidikan, a political organization but not a formal political party, produced a set of "150 Questions and Answers" on such topics as nationalism, Indonesian history, capitalism, and the history of independence movements elsewhere, such as in Turkey and the Philippines. Followers were expected to attend courses to learn this material. Some members, particularly if they were educated, protested. They wanted to work for independence rather than "be pushed back into classroom benches." Hatta did not see the distinction but claimed, "Politics in a colonial period may only mean education." Sjahrir made clear that education was both end and means: "the first aim of the Pendidikan [should be] the education and teaching of members—thus no direct political action."[65]

The Dutch government perceived that education was being used for political purposes. In September 1932 the government issued the Wild School Ordinance, designed to curtail the number and activities of private, mostly Islamic, schools. The ordinance provided that teachers in the private schools had to have government permission to teach. Among other requirements, local officials were to stipulate that the teacher posed no threat to "tranquillity and order." The government hoped to control private schools supported solely by Indonesian private donations. Indonesian political and educational organizations quickly organized protest meetings.[66] The degree to which Indonesian groups unified to protest the Wild Schools Ordinance made Dutch officials anxious. They especially worried that moderate and cooperating groups might become radicalized through the protest organizing. The government took two steps to end the protest. First, it instituted the usual repression, by declaring a ban on public ("open air") meetings organized to protest the ordinance. The second step demonstrated the extent of official fear. The conservative governor general, de Jonge, authorized talks with Indonesian leaders, leading to a compromise under which the government "suspended the enforcement of the ordinance."[67]

The Dutch government had backed down; Indonesian nationalists had won a victory. But the very nature of that victory tended to reinforce the sense of both Dutch and Indonesians that their political goals were incompatible. The victory proved a hollow one as well. Dutch repression of almost all political protest organizations increased throughout the 1930s. Nationalist leaders such as Sukarno, Mohammed Hatta, and Soetan Sjahrir were summarily arrested and exiled.[68] Many nationalists came to believe that only cooperation with the Dutch government could bear any fruit, and even so their expectations were modest. Many organizations turned to social and especially economic issues. Others worked to maintain seats in the Volksraad and to influence the government. The height of this effort was the petition by the Volksraad member Soetjardjo Kartohadikoesoemo in 1936 for Indonesian autonomy within a Dutch-Indonesian union. Soetjardjo was inspired in part by the example of the Philippines. This effort at cooperation failed, and the petition was rejected by the Dutch in 1938.[69] By then international developments were taking priority, but both Indonesians and Dutch understood that their visions for the future of the Indies were irreconcilable.

As the Dutch government relied increasingly on repression, official United States observers predicted that the strategy would not be effective. The United States consul general, K. S. Patton, observed that in late 1932 and 1933 Indonesian nationalists had been calling more "public meetings" and that there was "growing opposition of the native members of the Volksraad to all Government measures." In response the Dutch planned to require opposition political parties to obtain a permit to hold public meetings, and to prohibit indigenous members of the civil service from belonging to parties that the government deemed radical. Patton noted as well the arrest in August 1933 of Sukarno "on the charge of revolutionary action." Patton at no time disputed the right of the Dutch government to engage in its repressive actions, and noted the argument of Dutch officials that strictly controlling public meetings might irritate Indonesians less than shutting them down outright because of seditious comments. The thrust of Patton's analysis, however, was that these measures would both cut off Dutch officials from knowledge about the course of Indonesian political movements, since those movements would necessarily be thrust underground, and that they would "unify and strengthen the nationalist forces."[70] Patton's assessment seemed confirmed in the next few weeks, when he reported "no visible reaction from native political leaders." But, he hastened to add, this "can not be taken as indicative that their desire for independence has, in any way, been diminished . . . but rather as indicative that political action has been forced under cover with a consequent loss of contact by the government with native political movements."[71]

In a State Department generally much more sympathetic to the avowed interests of European colonial governments than the independence aspirations of colonial subjects, Patton was sanguine about nationalists' goals. He could talk about the "natural desire" of Indonesians to become independent.[72] This analysis was common in the 1930s. Walter Foote, who replaced Patton in 1935 when he was promoted to consul general in Singapore, also suggested that the Dutch would do better to accommodate the reasonable demands of Indonesians. Foote noted, for example, the dilemma posed by Soetjardjo's petition for dominion status for Indonesia. The Dutch did not want to grant the petition, but denial could revitalize the independence movement. In later reports on the dominion petition, Foote reported Soetjardjo's reference to the successful transition to dominion status by other colonies, notably the Philippines. If the Dutch denied well-educated and responsible Indonesians this status, why should they not become sworn foes of the colonial system? Foote refrained from criticizing Dutch decisions, but like Patton he believed that suppression was not a long-term solution.[73]

Given the harshness with which the French had suppressed the Nghe-Tinh rebellion, and continuing international concerns about communist influence on Southeast Asian anticolonial movements, the relative openness of politics in Indochina after 1932 comes as somewhat of a surprise. In the aftermath of Nghe-Tinh the most popular mass organizations were Cao Dai and later Hoa Hao, primarily syncretic religious movements with somewhat traditional political goals.[74] Educated Vietnamese élites poured a great deal of energy into education and publishing, especially in promoting *quoc ngu* as a means of enhancing Vietnamese culture and literacy. Political parties were banned except in Cochin China, so political organizing occurred underground in Annam and Tonkin. The French arrested and imprisoned or exiled those considered radical, but they also issued periodic amnesties. Vietnamese anticolonialists often found some room to maneuver.

The situation for Vietnamese nationalists improved markedly in 1936, with the election in France of a Popular Front government. Restrictions on political expression in Vietnam eased, and the ICP, still strong, resurfaced. It followed Popular Front mandates from Moscow and worked to appeal to a broad range of Vietnamese. Vietnamese hopes were high that this French government would move quickly toward autonomy. In response to a promise from the new French government of a formal investigation commission, Vietnamese organized rallies, commissions, and entities to collect and convey information. This outpouring of Vietnamese political action, much of it organized by the ICP, threatened French colonial officials, who pressured the French government to back down. Beyond the initial lifting of restrictions on publishing and political parties, and the reform of labor laws, the Popular Front government acceded to French colonial rather than Vietnamese nationalist demands. Even the modest reforms were reversed in 1939, with the start of the war in Europe. The Popular Front era had offered Vietnamese nationalists little more than a large space in which to continue organizing. That opportunity was granted across the political spectrum, in ways which allowed the Vietnamese left to build on earlier successes to a much greater degree than in other Southeast Asian colonies.[75]

United States officials in Saigon offered criticisms of French colonial policy markedly similar to those lobbed at the Dutch. The United States consul in Saigon, Quincy F. Roberts, suggested that repression of "formal communism" had simply prompted Vietnamese communists to pitch their appeal to the "love of [each Vietnamese for] his country and his desire for independence for support in the fight against French colonialism."[76] Roberts quoted with some disapproval the speech of the newly appointed minister of colonies Marius Moutet: "the yellow men of the rice fields and rubber plantations are united with our workmen of the factories and the cultivators of French farms. We place all of them on the same level of moral equality, social justice, and brotherhood."[77] Such language encouraged Vietnamese activism, as Roberts suggested later in the same report: "The 'yellow men of the rice fields and rubber plantations' called a meeting on 13 August 1936 to draw up a list of their grievances against the French administration." United States officials had criticized the Dutch for repression which drove organizing underground. American observers of the French saw a slightly different problem: alternative tolerance and repression of communists, combined with the inability of French colonial officials "to quiet the masses with promises to improve their political, moral, and economic welfare," increased Vietnamese dissatisfaction.[78]

Like his counterpart in the Netherlands Indies, the United States consul in Saigon was quick to note that moderate Vietnamese, notably Le Quang Liem, elected member of the Colonial Council of Cochin China, requested that the French give to Vietnam what the United States had given the Philippines: "[the right to] govern ourselves; that France shall fix a time during which we shall work and merit this independence."[79] American observers continued to believe that the gradual model of the Philippines promoted collaboration rather than resistance.

The British in Burma came closest to following that United States model. They moved gradually during the 1930s to grant the Burmese control over many aspects of domestic policy. The Burmese pushed to expand the scope of their control using largely the same tactics as other Southeast Asians: working cooperatively within the system as well as focusing on social and educational development. In Burma the new efforts at incremental steps toward more self-rule came as a result of the decision to separate India from Burma when India achieved dominion status. The Burmese had mixed feelings about separation, not because many Burmese saw a future for themselves as part of India, but rather because they wanted whichever status would mean the most progress toward self-rule. In fact in 1935, in the first elections following the formal decision for separation, more anti-separationists than separationists were elected to the Burma Legislative Council, but people's positions were complicated. Ba Maw, leader of the largest anti-separation faction, immediately announced that he (like most Burmese, in his view) opposed separation only because the new constitution that was promised after separation was insufficient. He and his followers saw separation with proper guarantees as desirable.[80]

The Constitution for Burma of 1935, which formally went into effect in April 1937, provided for separation from India, an enlarged electorate, increased responsibility for internal affairs, a House of Representatives from which the governor was required to select his cabinet, and a Senate, likely to be more conservative than the House because of income qualifications. The British governor still controlled defense, foreign policy (including tariffs), monetary policy, matters relating to the Anglican Church, and the Scheduled Areas.[81] Important though the exceptions were, by 1937 the Burmese appeared to have a greater degree of control over their own affairs than any other Southeast Asians except the Thai and Filipinos. The policy of working primarily within the system apparently worked.

The constitution of 1935 demonstrated to the Burmese, and to any other Southeast Asians observing the situation, that the outer limits of European compromise, which the new constitution seemed to represent, fell far short of the goals of Southeast Asian nationalists. A conference in 1936 of the nationalist group Dobama Asiayone ("We Burmans") resolved that the "New Constitution will perpetuate slavery and impoverish the people." Dobama members had little faith that the British government would fulfill its promise, as made by Prime Minister MacDonald, that the constitution represented a "potentiality" capable of being improved by the Burmese. Their skepticism was reinforced when five of their members were arrested on the last day of the conference for having given "seditious speeches" several days earlier.[82]

Burmese politicians who participated in the government also became disillusioned with the degree of control that the new Constitution granted. Although many reforms of interest to the Burmese people were introduced, including abolition of the capitation and *thathameda* taxes, other issues of concern remained outside Burmese control.[83] As early as the 1937 session of the House of Representatives, it was clear that Burmese and British had incompatible hopes about the Constitution of 1935—hopes which demonstrated the limits of cooperation. The Burmese saw the new constitution as one means to the end of independence. The British had planned for the constitution to be the final step which would satisfy Burmese demands for greater participation in governing, while reserving ultimate control to Britain.

Like other observers in the U.S. Department of State, the United States consul in Rangoon, Austin Brady, watched the increase in Burmese self-government with a mixture of paternalism and acceptance. For some months after the new constitution was promulgated, his political reporting consisted primarily of descriptions of the composition, rise, and fall of governments. Brady did tend to favor those Burmese politicians whom he believed to be culturally more British or American. He also noted how they had a fair amount of political power. In a report in October 1937, for instance, Brady called the home minister, U Paw Tun, "one of the foremost practical politicians among the Burmans" and reported that he had had "much to do with the formation of the Coalition Government." Then, as if to support his assertion about U Paw Tun's effectiveness, he noted that U Paw Tun had an American wife, whom he had met and married in London, and who helped him with his political career.[84]

The steps toward an American- or British-influenced independent Burma did not disturb Brady or, presumably, his readers back in Washington, who rarely commented on the reports in these years. But in 1938 political and economic disturbances began again in Burma, with a strike in the oilfields supported by the young nationalists known as the Thakins, many of whom were members of Dobama Asiayone. The tone of Brady's reports changed little. British officials may have been "unnecessarily severe" in suppressing the students striking in support of oil workers, and Burmese politicians may have exploited the situation for their own personal political advantage. But Brady was understanding of both tendencies, since the British would be equally criticized for failing to maintain "law and order" and the Burmese politicians had "political considerations which did not exist for the British."[85] Brady seems to have viewed the British and the Burmese as simply representatives of different, but equal, political parties in these reports. Each had their interests arising from the needs and wants of their constituents, and struggles about how to fulfill their needs was to be expected. Brady never advocated either maintaining or ending British colonial rule over Burma, but his matter-of-fact acceptance of these political disputes suggests that he saw the Burmese as equal political actors.

ııııııı

In the late 1930s this United States attitude prevailed. For most Americans, of course, Southeast Asia was a far-off place about which they rarely thought. For those few United States officials who followed the situation there, the small but real steps toward increased self-rule for Southeast Asians were far from alarming so long as the Southeast Asians demonstrated their continued willingness to work within the systems set up by the Europeans. But in 1939 anxiety about the coming war pervaded United States reports. Everywhere in Southeast Asia it was evident that European colonial rule was at risk from Japan. There was the obvious increase in Japanese military ambition and ability, but this was matched by propaganda from Japan. Such propaganda prompted Ba Maw, former premier of Burma, to assert in the Burmese Legislature that the Japanese were going to "promote the liberation of the brown and yellow peoples."[86] Again, as when communism seemed set to promote self-rule in ways unacceptable to the United States, American officials would choose to side firmly with European colonial rulers, showing little concern that such an alliance was at the expense of continued movement toward self-rule for the peoples of Southeast Asia.

The United States attempted to project its power into Southeast Asia during the 1930s in much the same ways as it had done during the 1920s. United States officials were willing to entertain the possibility of increased Southeast Asian autonomy, but only if Southeast Asians asked for the proper kind of autonomy in the proper way. If they did so the United States would not stand in their way, and might provide rhetorical support. If the demands were too radical or too violent, however, United States officials were quick to condemn, and to offer more tangible means of support to European colonial governments. The United States position had changed little since 1918; some Southeast Asians had been learning better how to succeed with incremental demands. Maintenance of the colonial order, unless it could change without damage to United States interests, had been a key goal of the United States since at least 1918. It became more difficult to achieve during the 1930s, but it was valued as much.

Another key goal of United States foreign policy had been to contain Japanese expansion. This goal was shared by the other colonial powers in the region, and they worked in concert to achieve it even when disagreeing on other issues of politics or economics. The goal was so powerfully held that they attempted to accommodate rather than challenge Japan's expansion into Manchuria, in hopes that Manchuria would satisfy Japan. Yet Japan refused to be contained by the methods that the United States and other colonial powers were willing to use in the 1930s.

The coming of the Second World War was long expected, and in some ways anticolonial politics stalled after 1937. Southeast Asians and Europeans alike understood that the impasse was caused only partially by international developments. The two groups had incompatible, nonnegotiable goals which neither could achieve by force or by politics. Involved Americans pointed to the Philippines as a model, but to the Europeans that model was abhorrent and to Southeast Asians it was only a minimum. As would become clearer, these Americans also believed that the model was not a mere guide but rather a recipe which had to be followed exactly to produce a desirable outcome. Any deviation by Southeast Asians prompted the United States to swing its support back to the imperial order.

Conclusion

*The United States and Imperialism
in Twentieth-Century Southeast Asia*

The nearly five decades of United States colonial rule over the Philippines coincided with a period of European imperialism in Southeast Asia which scholars have found intrusive and transformative. Mechanisms of state and industrial power grew in scope and size. Southeast Asians and Europeans alike contended with modernity and national identity.[1] That the United States was present during a time of European and Southeast Asian struggles to define themselves and their place in the world was not coincidence. United States investment, United States purchases, United States policies, United States cultural products, and Americans themselves shaped Southeast Asia during 1919–41. The ways they did so suggest that twentieth-century imperialism in the region needs to be rethought.

Southeast Asia as a Region

The notion persists that Southeast Asia was not a coherent political region until the designation was imposed on it by the rubric of the Southeast Asia Command (SEAC) created by the Allied nations. It is true that the phrase "Southeast Asia" came into common use as a way of referring to the countries bounded by China, India, and Australia during and after the Second World War. But as we have seen, similar experiences with European and American rule and influence, and with struggles against that influence, helped Southeast Asians to see themselves as linked in important ways. The commonalities that scholars today identify as characterizing Southeast Asia—rice growing, syncretic religion, the relatively high status of women, to name only a few—also began to be commented upon during the interwar years. Southeast Asia as a region with intellectual, cultural, historical, and political validity is obviously constructed, but it was not constructed on so flimsy a foundation as might be expected of a command structure in the Second World War. The many actors in this book, as well as others, contributed to that edifice.[2]

European and United States colonial officials in Southeast Asia created political and economic structures which built Southeast Asian institutions during the 1920s and 1930s, even if the phrase "Southeast Asia" was rarely used as a descriptor. The exchanges of information about communism among secret police personnel, for instance, included officials of all countries now considered part of Southeast Asia and rarely those from East or South Asia. Economic agreements during the Depression regarding the production and price of commodities such as rubber and tin had a similar composition and provided an ongoing opportunity for officials and businessmen from the region to meet and figure out ways to advance common interests.[3]

The colonial officials who created these budding regional institutions usually constructed them primarily to suit colonial purposes (as with the economic ones) or were explicitly attempting to control Southeast Asian choices and activities. Southeast Asians did not have to interact with these institutions in the prescribed ways, however, and took some advantage of the other opportunities they provided. Perhaps more important to Southeast Asian observers, the meetings, disputes, and agreements of regional officials, like cross-colonial trade and cultural imports, encouraged Southeast Asians to think beyond the dyad of, for example, Burma and Britain, and conceive of a broader range of options for the future. The developing regional institutions provided a mechanism by which to imagine "Southeast Asia" as one of those options.

Imperialism, American Style?

After 1898 the United States was a colonial power in Southeast Asia, just as France, Britain, and the Netherlands were. Twentieth-century imperialism, especially in Southeast Asia, is inexplicable without attention to the nature and effects of the United States exercise of imperial power. Involved Americans were confident imperialists, certain that their rule could transform the Philippines for the better and provide a model for European colonial powers. Most Americans did believe that formal colonial rule should at some point come to an end, but only after a colonial power had created an empire of the mind. Southeast Asians would prove their worthiness for self-rule by adopting patterns of work, leisure, consumption, and political behavior which approximated modern European and especially American ones. When Southeast Asians had internalized these modern ways of living, formal colonial rule could fade away because it would no longer be necessary.[4]

Until Southeast Asians did become modern in these ways, most Americans believed that colonial rule was not merely justified but positively beneficial. The behavioral standard also allowed Americans to judge both Southeast Asians and Europeans. A protracted rebellion could, and did, prompt United States officials to work with European counterparts on the tracking, surveillance, and detention of Southeast Asian revolutionaries. It also allowed United States officials to criticize European rule for doing too little to develop Southeast Asians into educated, productive, and content subjects. Similarly, interested Americans viewed Southeast Asian rebellions as potentially both outbursts borne of frustrated ambitions and signs of political immaturity. Those Americans involved in Southeast Asia nearly were never anti-imperialist; they saw imperialism as a developmental project of indefinite duration.

Few Americans were knowledgeable about and active in promoting imperialism, but when the resources of both the United States government and United States capital were deployed in Southeast Asia, they consistently worked to shore up the imperial system, at least for the immediate future, although long-term effects were often more ambiguous. During the 1920s and 1930s these resources appear to have been small in absolute terms (in contrast with later years), but given the challenges facing the European powers in the region, they were crucial. During the 1920s, when imperial economies appeared robust, United States investors and purchasers were willing to undercut European interests. But when the Depression threatened the viability of the system, these same Americans collaborated with Europeans to ensure the survival of that system, even at some cost to American interests. Similarly, United States officials may have hoped that Hollywood movies would promote distinctively American values even if Europeans believed that those movies cost them some prestige, but the officials always cooperated fully in censoring anything in an American film which Europeans believed threatening to the colonial order. Americans in Southeast Asia, whether as officials, businessmen, or missionaries, may have believed that an American model for the region was superior to a European one, but in disputes between Europe and Southeast Asia they sided with Europeans in nearly all cases. The United States, in both official policy and the private acts of its citizens, supported the imperial order in Southeast Asia.

Yet the manner in which this support was given did not reassure Europeans that it would be consistent, and it allowed many Southeast Asians to see the United States as a potential source of change. Looking back, United States actions appear weighted in support of European rule in the region. But during the 1920s and 1930s the apparent dissonance between rhetoric and action often reverberated. European officials noted the possibly deleterious effects of the Philippine Commonwealth, lamented when Southeast Asians preferred Hollywood movies to indigenous entertainment, and wondered how to attract guarantees of protection from the wealthy, powerful United States. United States officials were sensitive to these European concerns and took steps to address some of them, but during the 1920s and 1930s they could make no promises. Southeast Asians did find the Hollywood movies and degree of self-rule in the Philippines appealing, but wished for the "routine of freedom" that each implicitly promised.[5] By the end of the 1920s the imperial order in Southeast Asia depended on the purchases and potential protection of the United States.

Continuities and Change in United States Foreign Policy of the Twentieth Century

European colonial and foreign relations officials knew how dependent their continued rule in the colonies was on the latent political power and evident economic power of the United States. They often lamented both the fact of their dependence as well as the unreliability of United States assistance. Many United States officials also regretted their modest ability to commit United States resources in the absence of an imminent threat to the United States. During and especially after the Second World War, the United States commitment increased sharply. The sea change in both dollars expended and assurances given has prompted scholars to see the period 1941–45 as representing a fundamental shift in United States foreign policy. Before, they argue, United States interests were defined as limited, both geographically and in scope. After, United States interests were more global and expansive.[6] In looking from the 1930s to the late 1940s, the dominant theme is change.

The Second World War era did prompt enormous change in many aspects of American life, but my exploration of United States involvement in Southeast Asia during the 1920s and 1930s suggests some important continuities as well. Attention to these continuities illuminates some of the bedeviling contradictions of United States foreign policy during the cold war.

Most obviously, United States foreign policy during nearly the whole of the twentieth century was shaped by an American obsession with a perceived threat from communism. The effects of this perception rippled beyond crackdowns on leftist immigrants in the United States and an initial refusal to establish diplomatic relations with the Soviet Union. Already in these early years, United States officials routinely authorized or approved of secret policy information exchanges, some types of spying, and the denial of rights to suspected communists. After 1945 whole institutions would develop to carry out more systematic and elaborate versions of these policies, but the instinctive reaction of government officials to perceived threats of communism was present in this earlier time. Knowing of these policies helps to explain their explosive growth after 1945. Perhaps more importantly, it demonstrates that United States officials had been willing to sacrifice stated United States values when confronting certain kinds of threats, especially ideological ones, well before the cold war began.

The deep and broad ties among officials of all Southeast Asian colonial powers, including United States officials, helps to explain a second continuity. A consistent rhetoric advocating self-rule coincided with a consistent support for the imperial system during the 1920s and 1930s. It comes as little surprise that United States officials continued to deploy both the rhetoric of self-rule and the policy of support for empire after 1945. Indeed, the degree to which the United States was involved in the imperial system before 1945 suggests that support for independence, rather than support for continued European rule, is what needs to be explained. Historical developments of the 1940s and 1950s pushed all colonial powers to accommodate nationalist demands, and a wave of decolonization did sweep the globe. Often United States officials were as skeptical of these demands as Europeans were, and scholars have noted the influence of racism, paternalism, and fear of leftist politics in shaping United States reluctance to support nationalist movements.[7] These factors played a role, but so too did historic and ongoing United States imperial policies.

The underdeveloped character of United States imperial institutions may have contributed to the influence of imperial practices on United States foreign policy. The lack of an elaborate colonial bureaucracy in which bureaucrats could plan a career meant that United States colonial officials came from the ranks of the military, or were politicians or foreign relations officials. A stint in the Philippines or Guam or Puerto Rico was often preceded or followed by a career in one of these other institutions. The officials' colonial experiences then shaped their understandings and choices in domestic and foreign politics.

Continuities of personnel, whether across the chronological divide of the Second World War or the bureaucratic divide of the Departments of State and War (the latter also housing the Bureau of Insular Affairs), provide a reminder that Southeast Asia was not a truly blank slate for United States officials in 1945, and certainly that the United States was not a blank slate for either Southeast Asians or European colonial officials. The knowledge that each group had of the others shaped expectations after 1945. The information at the disposal of United States officials emphasized the economic possibilities and resources of the region and colonial understandings of indigenous political movements. This type of information may not have provided a sound basis for making effective policy, but that policy rested on knowledge that had been deemed important to gather.

After 1945 the United States significantly increased both spending and assurances in an effort to uphold a particular political order. As a result, both the United States and the world did fundamentally change in many ways. But it is striking, as this examination of how the United States projected its power into Southeast Asia during the 1920s and 1930s illuminates, how similar the motivations and goals remained from early to late in the twentieth century. The United States prioritized combating communism, promoting American business, spreading American culture, and taking concrete steps to prevent types of political development unacceptable to the United States. The legacies of United States involvement in imperialism in Southeast Asia resonated through the twentieth century: the United States favored policies to encourage evolutionary rather than revolutionary change in governments, yet pushed for radical change in economic practices and consumer culture. In the context of the cold war, the combination of these policies often increased conflict as countries in this region struggled for their independence.

Abbreviations

BFDC	Bureau of Foreign and Domestic Commerce
c.	carton
CAOM	Centre des Archives d'Outre-Mer
CF	Central Files
CO	Colonial Office, Great Britain
d.	dossier
DBBPN	*Documenten betreffende de buitenlandse politiek van Nederland, 1919–1945*
DBFP	*Documents on British Foreign Policy*
FO	Foreign Office, Great Britain
FRUS	*Foreign Relations of the United States*
GGI	Gouvernement Général de l'Indochine
INF	Indochine Nouveau Fonds
inv.	inventaris
MR	Mailrapport
MRL	Missionary Research Library, Union Theological Seminary, New York
NNA	National Archives of the Netherlands, The Hague
RG	Record Group
UKNA	National Archives of the United Kingdom, Kew
USDOS	U.S. Department of State
USNA	National Archives of the United States, College Park, Md.

Notes

Introduction

1. European colonial settlers in the Americas had the outlook both of colonized peoples and of imperialists themselves. Arguably the geographical entities which became the United States have been imperial since those Europeans first arrived.

2. For a recent overview of the field by one of its most dedicated and influential practioners see Bailyn, *Atlantic History*.

3. For example see Fieldhouse, *The Colonial Empires*, and Doyle, *Empires*. The Netherlands, Belgium, and Germany are usually included but receive fewer pages of attention because they controlled less territory. Like the United States, Japan's empire is usually ignored, also to the detriment of understanding the nature of imperialism in the late nineteenth and twentieth centuries. For a corrective see Barclay, "'They Have for the Coast Dwellers a Traditional Hatred.'" United States empire, especially in the Philippines, has a rich historiography, and histories of anti-imperialism usually include consideration of anti-imperial rhetoric and action emanating from the United States.

4. For an example of the scholarship on European imperialism see Wilson, ed., *A New Imperial History*. Many of the scholars of United States imperialism who take this approach are represented in McCoy and Scarano, eds., *Colonial Crucible*.

5. Roosevelt, "The Colonial Policy of the United States," *African and European Addresses*.

6. As perhaps has become clear already, I use imperialism and colonialism to refer to different but related constructs. Colonialism, or colonial rule, refers to the situation in which one nation has taken over basic governmental functions of another nation, both setting public policy and administering it. Imperialism is a broader term, referring to a wide array of systems of control. It encompasses colonialism, but includes also situations in which control is exerted less directly, or in which two nations have split control over governmental functions in one nation's territory. For instance, British rule over the Straits Settlements was colonialism. Britain's relationship to the Unfederated Malay States was more imperial than colonial. Similarly, United States rule in the Philippines before 1935 was colonial, but United States rela-

tions with Cuba after 1903 were imperial. I usually use the term "imperial" in refer-ring to the relationship of Europe and the United States to Southeast Asia from 1919 to 1941 because of the wide range of types of control in the region, and because some political arrangements changed during this time.

7. As discussed in more detail below, studies of world imperialism rarely include serious study of the United States. Equally, studies of United States imperialism gen-erally treat it as an American phenomenon, rather than as part of the imperial sys-tem. Stoler's work hints at some possible comparative approaches, especially her "Tense and Tender Ties."

8. The notion persists, despite numerous studies to the contrary, that the United States, if it is imperialist at all, only just embarked on a strategy of imperialism after the end of the cold war. This notion is prominently on display in two books with otherwise contradictory theses: Ferguson, *Empire*, and, Hardt and Negri, *Empire*. In a desire to respond to some of the simplistic assumptions and comparisons in these new works on the American empire, a group of scholars published *Lessons of Empire*, edited by Calhoun, Cooper, and Moore. Tyrrell provides an insightful discussion of the reasons behind this persistent "amnesia" about empire in the United States in "Empire in American History," *Colonial Crucible*, ed. McCoy and Scarano, 541–56.

9. They neither suspected nor would have approved of the transitions to inde-pendence which occurred in Southeast Asia during the late 1940s.

10. Booth's definitive study makes this point clearly. See Booth, *Colonial Legacies*, esp. chapters 2 and 5.

11. Ronald Specter's recent book is an exemplar of this scholarship, with its close look at East and Southeast Asia in the aftermath of the Second World War. See Specter, *In the Ruins of Empire*. See also McMahon, *The Limits of Empire*. McMahon has also written the classic treatment of relations between the United States and Indo-nesia in the early cold war, *Colonialism and Cold War*. For Vietnam see, among many fine examples, Rotter's *The Path to Vietnam* and Lawrence's *Assuming the Burden*.

12. Many treatments of the United States war in Vietnam open with this story. Marilyn Young perhaps uses the story most effectively. See Young, *The Vietnam Wars*, 2–5.

13. Gouda, *American Visions of the Netherlands East Indies/Indonesia*.

14. Bradley, *Imagining Vietnam and America*.

15. David Thelen reported on how these efforts were going to be institutionalized by the *Journal of American History* in his article "Of Audiences, Borderlands and Comparisons." The *JAH* embarked on an ambitious project to provide greater voice to scholars of the United States who lived in countries other than the United States, as well as to publish more scholarship about the United States from international and comparative perspectives. In 1999 it published a special issue on transnational and comparative approaches to United States history, to explore what had and had not changed as a result of new efforts. See especially Thelen's introduction to the issue, "The Nation and Beyond," and Tyrrell, "Making Nations / Making States."

16. Impressive examples abound. For example see Logevall, *Choosing War*; Chen Jian, "The Myth of America's 'Lost Chance' in China"; and Goncharov, Lewis, and Xue, *Uncertain Partners*. McMahon provides a useful overview of the trend in "Towards a Pluralist Vision."

17. Stoler used this phrase in her article "Tense and Tender Ties," 844.

18. The count of twenty-four essays does not include the two which introduce the volume. The two which explicitly discuss United States colonial rule are Rafael's "White Love," 185–218, and Diaz's "Pious Sites," 312–39, in Kaplan and Pease, eds., *Cultures of United States Imperialism*.

19. Kramer, *The Blood of Government*.

20. Abinales, "Progressive-Machine Conflict"; Go, *American Empire and the Politics of Meaning*; Anderson, *Colonial Pathologies*.

21. Stoler's article "Tense and Tender Ties" represents an effort to create a manifesto for such comparative work. Her highly regarded work in Southeast Asian studies positioned her well to prompt this conversation, but she primarily explored cultures of imperialism as manifested wherever the United States governed, rather than paying attention to the consequences of United States colonial rule.

22. Scholars of European empire recognize the dilemma. Their primary solution has been to collect essays about a range of colonizer-colonized dyads and place them alongside each other in a book, tied together by an introductory essay. The conferences preceding these volumes and their publication do promote comparative conversations, which one hopes will lead to comparative scholarship. For example, see the now classic Cooper and Stoler, eds., *Tensions of Empire*, as well as Burton, ed., *After the Imperial Turn*.

23. Stoler, "Tense and Tender Ties"; de Grazia, *Irresistible Empire*.

24. To give an initial example, scholars rarely know, let alone consider the implications of, the fact that from about 1910 the United States was the key recipient of exports from British Malaya, and in most years from the Netherlands Indies.

Chapter 1: New Threats and New Opportunities

1. Erez Manela's interesting study of the reactions of Koreans, Egyptians, Chinese, and Indians to Wilson's message suggests that it did inspire. See Manela, *The Wilsonian Moment*.

2. Arnold Toynbee, "Memorandum on the Formula of 'the Self-Determination of Peoples' and the Moslem World," in papers prepared by the Political Intelligence Department for the Paris Peace Conference, 18 November 1918, file 4353, FO 371, UKNA. This is the same Toynbee perhaps better known to historians as the author of *A Study of History*. Toynbee's service to the British government during the First World War consisted of serving in British intelligence and then as a delegate to the Peace Conference. From there he began his long involvement with the Royal Institute of International Affairs.

3. French vice-consul at Manila (Maurice E. A. Paillard) to French Foreign Ministry, 10 October 1918, d. 1041, c. 110, INF, CAOM.

4. The text of the *Revendications* is in Ruscio, ed., *Ho Chi Minh*, 22–23. For background see Hemery, *Ho Chi Minh*, 42–45, and Bradley, "Imagining America."

5. Levin, *Woodrow Wilson and World Politics*, 1.

6. U Nu quote from his remarks to the U.S. Senate, 30 June 1955, repr. in Nu, *An Asian Speaks*, 9. His speech to the Overseas Press Club, in the same publication at p. 21, makes a similar point.

7. French Ambassador to the United States (Jules Jusserand) to French Foreign Ministry, 25 June 1921, d. 1041, c. 110, INF, CAOM.

8. Not least because of the paradigm shift described in Beisner, *From the Old Diplomacy to the New*.

9. The four powers were the United States, Japan, Britain, and France.

10. Iriye, *After Imperialism*, 15–19. In retrospect it is clear that Iriye identified an important shift, but European colonial officials, and many from the foreign ministries as well, wanted to maintain both imperialism and the diplomacy of imperialism. They were sometimes slow to grasp the importance of the change that the Washington Conference signaled.

11. "Moscow and the Washington Conference," *Papers Relating to Pacific and Far Eastern Affairs Prepared for the Use of the American Delegation to the Conference on the Limitation of Armament, Washington, 1921–1922*, no. 79, series D Far East, entry 648, Records of the Division of Current Information, RG 59, Records of the USDOS, USNA. Although Iriye sees Japanese policy as having different intentions, he notes that these perceptions of Japanese policy pervaded the State Department in Washington. See *After Imperialism*, 13–15.

12. Brimmel, *Communism in South East Asia*, 48; Blumberger, *De communistische beweging in Nederlandsch-Indië*, 30–31.

13. "American Cultural Interests in the Far East," *Papers Relating to the Pacific and Far Eastern Affairs*, no. 79, series D Far East, entry 648, RG 59, USNA, 1023.

14. This subject will be discussed in chapters 2 and 4.

15. "De Philippijnen," *De Standaard*, 22 April 1919.

16. Perhaps ironically, the Philippines represents an exception.

17. How, when, and why particular nationalisms developed out of anticolonial struggle has been of consistent interest to Southeast Asianists for decades. Among the many scholars who have noted the importance of the changes which occurred in the first two decades of the twentieth century are Roff, *The Origins of Malay Nationalism*, esp. chapters 3–4; Anderson, *Imagined Communities*, chapter 7; Shiraishi, *An Age in Motion*; Marr, *Vietnamese Anticolonialism*. Even as scholars of Southeast Asia have become more sophisticated in thinking about various ways of expressing political will and desire, this early twentieth century continues to be identified as a critical period in the development of anticolonial movements. For instance, see McHale, *Print and Power*.

18. Netherlands Indies (1916), Burma (1922), increased Vietnamese representation (1922), slightly increased Malaysian representation in Federated Malay States (1923).

19. Corpus, "Western Colonization and the Philippine Response," 21.

20. Colonial officials at the time, like scholars in the years since, sometimes concerned themselves with whether these Southeast Asian communists were "really" communist, and if so what communism meant to them. This issue is discussed briefly in the context of the PKI rebellion later in this chapter, but in fact communist or Bolshevist doctrines did not play an important part for most Southeast Asians of the 1920s and 1930s, or for most colonial observers of them. The idea of communism was a sufficient threat to prompt the regional cooperation discussed here. Benedict Anderson notes also the global sources of the "first fantasies of liberation" in Java and elsewhere in Southeast Asia, suggesting the need to think outside the dyad of colonized and colonizer. See Anderson, "Language, Fantasy, Revolution," 33–34.

21. U.S. undersecretary of state William Phillips, as quoted in Bootsma, *Buren in de koloniale tijd*, 50.

22. U.S. secretary of state (Charles E. Hughes) to U.S. secretary of war (John W. Weeks), 27 July 1923; U.S. consul in Batavia (Charles Hoover) to USDOS, 18 July 1923, both in 18868-8, entry 5, Records Relating to the Philippines, RG 350, Records of the Bureau of Insular Affairs, USNA.

23. U.S. vice-consul at Soerabaya (Winslow) to USDOS, 14 December 1923, 18868-15A, and U.S. consul at Batavia (Hoover) to USDOS, 22 December 1923, 18868-15B, both in entry 5, RG 350, USNA.

24. Bootsma, *Buren in de koloniale tijd*, 51–52.

25. Bootsma, *Buren in de koloniale tijd*, 52.

26. Department of Political Affairs, Government of French Indochina to governor general of the Netherlands Indies (D. Fock), 11 April 1925, MR 407x/25, NNA.

27. U.S. military attaché in The Hague to Military Intelligence Division, U.S. Department of War, 9 January 1920, file 856–58, box 126, entry 535, Records of the Office of the Counselor, RG 59, USNA.

28. Dutch minister of foreign affairs (van Karnebeek) to Dutch minister of colonies (S. de Graaf), 21 July 1923, in *DBBPN*, period A, 1919–30, vol. 4, 543–44.

29. Attorney general of the Netherlands Indies (H. G. P. Duyfjes) to Fock, 15 July 1926, MR 754x/26; Fock to viceroy of India (Sir Daniel Rufus Isaacs), MR 773x/25; viceroy of India to Fock, 26 September 1925, MR 70x/26; Department of Political Affairs, French Indochina, to Fock, 11 April 1925, MR 407x/25, all in NNA.

30. Cheah, *From PKI to the Comintern*, 6–8.

31. For Britain see director of military intelligence (M. Churchill) to USDOS (L. L. Winslow), 1 October 1919, file 841-59, box 104, entry 535; for France see assistant to undersecretary of state (Alexander C. Kirk) to U.S. Embassy in Paris (Elbridge D. Rand), 18 November 1925, file 151, box 8, entry 538, Confidential Files of the Chief Special Agent, Office of the Counselor, both in RG 59, USNA.

32. Note pour Monsieur, 7 August 1925, vol. 34, sous-série Affaires Communes, série E, Asie-Océanie, Archives de Ministère des Affaires Étrangères, Paris.

33. U.S. legation in Riga (F. W. B. Coleman) to USDOS, 17 September 1925, 812.00B/97, CF, RG 59, USNA. Those familiar with the State Department decimal filing system will note that this document was filed in the Mexico country files, quite probably because United States officials in the mid-1920s believed Mexico to be the focal point of Bolshevist organizing. See Rosenberg, *Financial Missionaries to the World*, 141–44.

34. U.S. consul in Batavia (Kuykendall) to USDOS, 24 September 1926, 856d.00B/6, CF, RG 59, USNA.

35. Dutch consul general in Singapore (B. Kleyn Molecamp) to governor general of the Netherlands Indies (A. D. C. de Graeff), 8 November 1926, MR 12x/27; viceroy of India (Frederick L. Wood) to de Graeff, 28 December 1926, MR 70x/27; Department of Political Affairs, French Indochina, to governor general of the Netherlands Indies (Fock), 11 April 1925, MR 407x/27, all in NNA.

36. Most notably the Netherlands Indies was allowed to send two Indonesian police agents to Singapore in July 1926, where they were able to infiltrate the PKI briefly before being discovered.

37. The Dutch used a two-tier system to administer the Netherlands Indies. The upper bureaucracy, staffed completely by the Dutch, was composed of residents, assistant residents, and controllers. Above them were provincial governors and the central government officials in Batavia. The lower "native" bureaucracy was headed by *bupati* (regents or regency chiefs), then *wedana* (district chiefs), and below them assistant *wedana* (subdistrict chiefs). The native bureaucracy ruled over day-to-day matters, while policymaking and ultimate control remained in the hands of the Dutch. For a discussion of Dutch administrative policy see Furnivall's classic study *Netherlands India*, 257–301.

38. The Veldpolitie, loosely translatable as rural police, had been created in 1920 in response to what the Dutch perceived as an increase in crime in rural areas. The police force was indigenous but had Dutch officers and was under control of the central government in Batavia. The regular local police had indigenous officers. For an explanation of the structure of the police in the Indies from the Dutch point of view, see Wilde, "De Nederlandsche-Indische politie"; the Veldpolitie are discussed on pages 131–37.

39. McVey's classic *The Rise of Indonesian Communism* is still the most comprehensive study of early Indonesian communism. See also Williams, *Communism, Religion, and Revolt in Banten*; Larson, *Prelude to Revolution*; and the introduction to Benda and McVey, eds., *The Communist Uprisings of 1926–1927 in Indonesia*. The United States consul in Batavia observed that Indonesians avoided going out at night in "Insurrection in Java," 23 November 1926, 856e.00/14, CF, RG 59, USNA.

40. McVey, *The Rise of Indonesian Communism*, 320–46; quote at 345–46. The phrase "central committee" implies some hierarchical organization; while the PKI

headquarters and supposedly the national leaders were in Bandung, the PKI had been so harassed by the Dutch government that all but one member of the PKI central committee was in jail or exile. A revolt ordered by the central committee was therefore almost impossible.

41. Larson, *Prelude to Revolution*, 130–32; Williams, *Communism, Religion, and Revolt*, 220–29, 237–48.

42. Resident in Soerakarta (Nieuwenhuys) to governor general of the Netherlands Indies, 23 December 1926, MR 20x/27; resident in Preanger (Mühlenfeld) to governor, West Java (Hillen), 27 December 1926, MR 7x/27, both in NNA.

43. The phrase "little people" may be a literal translation of the Indonesian phrase "wong cilik," meaning people without power, or ordinary people. I am indebted to Takashi Shiraishi for pointing out this possibility. Assistant resident in Pati (Ranneft) to resident in Semarang, 30 November 1926, MR 1229x/26, NNA.

44. Benda and McVey, eds., *The Communist Uprisings of 1926–1927 in Indonesia*, xxii.

45. "Political Note concerning the Indonesian Communist Party: Report Summing Up the Actions of the Indonesian Communist Party, Section of the 3rd International, from July 1925 to December 1926," as trans. in Benda and McVey, eds., *The Communist Uprisings of 1926–1927 in Indonesia*; quote from page 1.

46. For the agreement see attorney general (Duyfjes) to governor general, 24 February 1927, MR 380x/27, NNA.

47. Note sur la propagande révolutionnaire intéressant les pays d'Outre-mer, 30 November 1926, vol. 34, sous-série Affaires Communes; French consul in Manila (Antoine Valentini) to French foreign minister (Briand), 15 January 1927; Note sur la propagande, 31 January 1927, both in vol. 35, sous-série Affaires Communes; French ambassador in Moscow (Jean Herbette) to Briand, 22 November 1926, vol. 5, sous-série Indes Néerlandaises, all in série E Asie-Océanie, Archives de Ministère des Affaires Étrangères, Paris.

48. British acting consul general in Batavia (Fitzmaurice) to British FO, 27 November 1926, W50/50/29; British minister at The Hague (Granville G. L. Gower) to FO, 14 February 1927, W1318, both in file 12696, FO 371; *Malayan Bulletin of Political Intelligence*, November 1926, as found in file 535-28030, CO 273, all in UKNA.

49. U.S. consul general in Batavia (Charles Hoover) to USDOS, 15 November 1926, (telegram), file 800B, vol. 282-1926, Batavia part 8, RG 84, Records of Foreign Service Posts; Hoover to USDOS, 15 November 1926, 856e.00/13 CF; U.S. legation in The Hague (Richard M. Tobin) to USDOS, 17 November 1926, 856d.00B/17 CF, both in RG 59, all in USNA.

50. French consul general in Batavia (Albert Bodard) to Briand, 29 January 1927, vol. 5, sous-série Indes Néerlandaises, série E, Archives de Ministère des Affaires Étrangères, Paris; U.S. consul general in Batavia (Hoover) to USDOS, 26 February 1927, 856d.00/9 CF, RG 59, USNA; British consul general in Batavia (J. Crosby) to FO, 30 May 1927, W6199, file 12697, FO 371, UKNA.

51. First government's secretary of the Netherlands Indies (H. A. Helb) to Dutch consul general in Singapore (Kleyn Molecamp), with enclosures, 25 October 1926, Verbaal 1-7-27-S10, inv. 298, NNA. Alimin and Moeso had gone to Moscow to try to get Comintern support for an uprising by the PKI. Tan Malaka did not believe that the PKI was ready to lead a rebellion.

52. Dutch consul general in Singapore (Kleyn Molecamp) to de Graeff, 25 November 1926, MR 12x/27, as quoted in Shiraishi, "A New Regime of Order," 68.

53. Assistant police commissioner of the Netherlands Indies (Visbeen) to director, General Intelligence Service (van der Lely), 22 December 1926, MR 9x/27, NNA.

54. Kleintjes, *Staatsinstellingen van Nederlandsch-Indië*, vol. 1, 124–32.

55. Attorney general of the Netherlands Indies (Duyfjes) to de Graeff, 27 December 1926, MR 9x/27, NNA.

56. G. Grindle to Home Office, 8 June 1927; governor general of Singapore (L. N. Guillemard) to CO (L. C. M. S. Amery), 30 April 1927 both in W5243, file 12697, FO 371, UKNA.

57. Home Office (Harold Sate) to FO, 15 July 1927; Home Office (John Pedder) to CO, 15 June 1927, both in W6702, file 12697, FO 371, UKNA.

58. Duyfjes to de Graeff, 22 March 1927; Visbeen to van der Lely, 19 March 1927; Visbeen to van der Lely, 16 March 1927, all in MR 405x/27; Visbeen to van der Lely, 21 March 1927; Visbeen to van der Lely, 24 March 1927, both in MR 433x/27, all in NNA.

59. U.S. consul general in Singapore (Addison E. Southard) to USDOS, 31 January 1927, 856d.00B/8 CF, RG 59, USNA.

60. Duyfjes to Dutch consul general in Manila (Bremer), 7 February 1927, MR 200x/27, NNA.

61. Bremer to Duyfjes, 18 February 1927, MR 329x/27, NNA; Southard to USDOS, 23 March 1927; secretary to the governor general of the Philippines (C. W. Franks) to Southard, 10 March 1927, both in 856d.00B/12 CF, RG 59, USNA.

62. The Bureau of Insular Affairs, which administered the colonial possessions of the United States, was housed in the Department of War. Dutch minister in Washington (J. H. van Royen) to U.S. secretary of state (Frank B. Kellogg), 7 June 1927, 811.00B/706 CF, RG 59; U.S. assistant secretary of state (William R. Castle) to U.S. secretary of war (Dwight B. Davis), 9 May 1927, file 18868-25, entry 5, RG 350; Davis to Kellogg, 24 June 1927, 811.00B/717 CF, RG 59, all in USNA.

63. Kellogg to Davis, 14 October 1927, entry 5, RG 350, USNA. Despite Davis's claim of no surveillance during peacetime, the United States government had by the mid-1920s an elaborate if sometimes still ad hoc intelligence system, especially for tracking suspected communists. The contradictions of the United States position in Southeast Asia are discussed below. The broader context is discussed in Kornweibel, *"Investigate Everything,"* 10–36.

64. Malaka, *From Jail to Jail*, vol. 1, 143–49; acting governor general of the Philippines (Eugene A. Gilmore) to de Graeff, 9 September 1927, 811.00B/816 CF, RG 59, USNA.

65. Duyfjes to de Graeff, 24 August 1927, with copies of telegrams, MR 1053x/27; Dutch consul general for South China to de Graeff, 21 September 1927, MR 1216x/27, both in NNA. See also Oshikawa, "*Patjar Merah Indonesia* and Tan Malaka."

66. Kellogg to Davis, 14 October 1927, file 18868-25, entry 5, RG 350; secretary to governor general of the Philippines (Franks) to Southard, 6 September 1927, file 800S-Singapore-1927, RG 84, USNA.

67. From a somewhat different vantage point, Julian Go's work addresses this same issue. See especially his introduction to Go and Foster, eds., *The American Colonial State in the Philippines*, 14–16.

68. The quote is referenced in Quirk, *An Affair of Honor*, 2.

69. British consul general in Batavia (J. Crosby) to FO (Arthur Henderson), 17 June 1929, file 558/62137, CO 273, UKNA.

70. As an example he explained that according to this last requirement regular, full exchanges with Japanese authorities were less desirable than with officials from other countries. Duyfjes to de Graeff, 11 November 1927, MR 1356x/27, NNA.

71. The author found these reports in the archives of the government of French Indochina in Aix-en-Provence.

72. U.S. consul general in Batavia (Coert du Bois) to USDOS, 23 September 1929, 893.00B/655 CF, RG 59, USNA.

73. Dutch consul general in Shanghai to de Graeff, 14 November 1928, MR 1142x/28, NNA.

74. Attorney general in the Netherlands Indies (J. K. Onnen) to heads of local governments in Java and Madura, 9 October 1928, MR 997x/28, NNA.

75. DuBois to USDOS, 20 August 1928, 856d.00B/28 CF; U.S. minister in The Hague (Norweb) to USDOS, 20 February 1929, 856d.00/54 CF; U.S. consul in Rangoon (H. H. Dick) to U.S. consul general in Calcutta (Robert Frazier), 8 January 1929, file Rangoon 1929, Division of Commercial Affairs, all in RG 59, USNA. Onnen to de Graeff, 13 November 1928, MR 1179x/28; Onnen to de Graeff, February 9, 1929, MR 153x/29, both in NNA. "La situation politique aux Indes Néerlandaises," 1929, d. 3018, c. 372, INF, CAOM.

76. The mysteriousness of life in the colonies was not new. Couperus's famous novel *De stille kracht* (best translated as *The Hidden Force*), published in 1900, had this mysteriousness as its central theme. Couperus, *The Hidden Force*.

77. Marshal (Union Coloniale Française) to Georges Leygues (minister of the navy), 15 November 1928, d. 1032, c. 107, INF, CAOM. Marshal was reporting on the visit that the governor general of Indochina had just made to the governor general of the Netherlands Indies.

78. There is welcome and increasing attention to how race played out in the United States colonial vision and project, demonstrating conclusively that United States colonialism was, not surprisingly, conceived through racialist lenses. See especially Kramer, *The Blood of Government*.

79. DuBois to USDOS, 29 April 1929; internal departmental memorandum by As-

sistant Secretary of State Nelson T. Johnson, 10 September 1929, both in 856d.001/16 CF, RG 59, USNA.

Chapter 2: "The Highways of Trade . . ."

The title of this chapter is taken from W. R. Castle (assistant secretary of state) to Republican Club of Massachusetts, 6 March 1928, press release, vol. 25, Division of Current Information, RG 59, USNA.

1. United States exports to Japan exceeded those to Southeast Asia in the 1920s, but not in the 1930s. United States exports to China were always less than to Southeast Asia. United States imports from Southeast Asia nearly equaled those from all of Eastern Asia (China, Hong Kong, Japan) during the 1920s and early 1930s, and surpassed them by far in the late 1930s. See Witherow, *Foreign Trade of the United States, Calendar Year 1938*, part II, *Trade by Regions and Countries*, table on p. 103.

2. Furnivall, *Netherlands India*, 247.

3. "American Invasion," *Straits Times*, 22 August 1922, in U.S. consul general in Singapore (Ernest K. Harris) to USDOS, 23 August 1922, 846d.6176 CF, RG 59 USNA.

4. Hoff-Wilson, *Herbert Hoover*, 67, for self-sufficiency and Open Door; "civilizing influence," Calvin Coolidge, as quoted in Smith, "Republican Policy and Pax Americana," 276.

5. Hoff-Wilson, *Herbert Hoover*, 65–68, 95; Hoover, *Memoirs*, vol. 2, 79–84.

6. Duggan, ed., *The League of Nations*, 3, 17. Duggan considered the people of Persia and China "backward" and the people of Central Africa a step below, as "uncivilized." He does not specify the place of Southeast Asians in his hierarchy, but it is likely to have been between "backward" and "uncivilized."

7. Many observers in the United States argued that economic success and capacity for self-rule were linked. For example, see the letter from W. Cameron Forbes (governor general of the Philippines) to resident commissioner, 28 November 1910, 355; "Report of the Special Mission on Investigation to the Philippine Islands," 8 October 1921, 520–44, esp. 521, both in Forbes, *The Philippine Islands*, vol. 2.

8. For example see "Holland and the Dutch East Indies," lecture for the Foreign Service School by Prentiss B. Gilbert (Division of Western European Affairs), 2 March 1926, entry 623, Records of the Foreign Service School, RG 59, USNA.

9. French vice-consul in Manila (Paillard) to GGI, 6 April 1918, d. 1041, c. 110, INF, CAOM.

10. As I will discuss later in this chapter, the extreme reactions in Singapore to attempts by American capital to participate in development of new rubber plantations demonstrate British concern about United States economic power.

11. U.S. consul general in Singapore (Edwin N. Gunsaulus) to USDOS, 7 May 1919, 846d.00/2 CF, RG 59, USNA.

12. Figures in this table are from U.S. Department of Commerce, *Commerce Yearbook*. See 1925, pp. 142, 585; 1926 vol. 1, pp. 153, 157; 1926 vol. 2, pp. 369, 400, 580;

1929 vol. 1, pp. 171, 697; 1929 vol. 2, pp. 360, 435, 470. I have not included figures for Burma, which until 1937 was a province of India, not governed as a separate colony. There are therefore few statistics for Burma's foreign trade.

13. Kral, *U.S. Commerce Reports*, 26. See also *Commerce Yearbook*, 1925, pp. 142, 585, and 1929 vol. 2, pp. 435, 470.

14. The term is from Wilkins's description of United States rubber manufacturers' policy, as found in *The Maturing of Multinational Enterprise*, 8–9. Direct investment will be discussed below.

15. Hoover, *Memoirs*, vol. 2, 42, 82.

16. U.S. consul in Soerabaya (Rollin R. Winslow) to USDOS, 28 November 1925, 756d.94/4 CF, RG 59, USNA.

17. Hoover, *Memoirs*, vol. 2, 79–81.

18. Memorandum from the Office of the Economic Advisor (Stanley K. Hornbeck), USDOS, 4 November 1922, 856d.51/39 CF, RG 59, USNA.

19. U.S. consul in Batavia (Charles L. Hoover) to USDOS, 26 April 1923, 856d.51/48 CF, RG 59, USNA.

20. "Holland and the Dutch East Indies," 2 March 1926, entry 623, RG 59, USNA.

21. *British Documents on Foreign Affairs*, part II, series C, vol. 17, *Latin America and the Philippines*, 24.

22. See Government of Netherlands Indies, *Handbook of the Netherlands East Indies*, 1930, 289; U.S. consul in Surabaya (Rollin Winslow) to USDOS, February 1926, entry 593, Inspection Reports, RG 59, USNA.

23. *Commerce Yearbook*, 1925, 146–49.

24. This summary does not include the complicated situation which developed in Liberia, arguably a United States protectorate by 1921 at the latest. The story in this chapter is only incidentally influenced by developments in Liberia, since Firestone did not begin planting there until 1927, meaning that no substantial rubber was produced until the early 1930s. For the narrative of rubber development in Liberia see Chalk, "The United States and the International Struggle for Rubber," esp. 77–95, 130–50. For the United States protectorate see Rosenberg, *Financial Missionaries to the World*, 120–22, 226–32. Stockpiling rubber also was a possible solution, and one pursued late in the 1930s, as global tensions which eventually led to the Second World War approached. Effective stockpiling usually depends on government willingness to participate, especially in the case of a perishable commodity like rubber. The United States government did not consider stockpiling until the mid-1930s.

25. Lawrence, *The World's Struggle with Rubber*, 20, 67. In 1918 prices were steady at around $0.55 a pound. The low in 1920 was $0.20 a pound, although the average in these years was closer to $0.40 a pound. The price in June 1922 was only $0.125 a pound.

26. Lawrence, *The World's Struggle with Rubber*, 20, 23, 67.

27. Winston Churchill quoted by Drabble, *Malayan Rubber*, 13.

28. Churchill quoted by Lawrence, *The World's Struggle with Rubber*, 37.

29. Drabble, *Malayan Rubber*, 13–14, 306–7. In 1924 prices reached $0.237 a pound; by early 1925 the per-pound price was just over $0.48. Hoover, *Memoirs*, vol. 2, 84; slogans in Brandes, "Product Diplomacy," 187.

30. Chief, Rubber Division, BFDC (E. G. Holt), to U.S. secretary of commerce, 21 February 1928, RG 151, Records of the BFDC, USNA.

31. Murray, *The Development of Capitalism in Colonial Indochina*, 262; Drabble, *Malayan Rubber*, 3, 13, 17.

32. British ambassador in Washington (Sir E. Howard) to British foreign minister (Sir A. Chamberlain), 12 April 1928, document 44 in *British Documents on Foreign Affairs*, part II, series C, vol. 16.

33. Lewis, *America's Stake in International Investments*, 284.

34. See Babcock, *History of the United States Rubber Company*, 82–89.

35. Percentage computed from figures in Whitford, "The Crude Rubber Supply," 614.

36. Babcock, *History of the United States Rubber Company*, 181–83.

37. Marcosson, "The Crisis in Rubber," 140.

38. As reported in U.S. consul general in Singapore (Ernest L. Harris) to USDOS, 22 August 1924, 856d.6176/13 CF, RG 59, USNA.

39. Growers had to have a coupon to sell rubber to the trading houses, but coupons were usually exchanged near where the rubber was grown. Once the rubber was on ship, the coupons were no longer necessary. So smugglers merely had to get their rubber "under cover of darkness" into Penang or Singapore. The British soon began keeping stricter control over the rubber in Penang and Singapore, which increased the importance of Sumatra for smugglers. See U.S. consul Penang (Renwick S. McNiece) to USDOS, 12 June 1923, 846d.6176/19 CF, RG 59, USNA.

40. Chalk, "The United States and the International Struggle for Rubber," 128.

41. Chalk, "The United States and the International Struggle for Rubber," 128–29.

42. "The Petroleum Policy of the Netherlands Government," *Nieuws van den dag*, 27–28 December 1922, as copied in Naval Attaché Reports, file C-10-l, #14017, RG 38, Records of the Office of Naval Intelligence, USNA.

43. Henry P. Starrett to Phillips, 12 May 1923, folder Starrett, Henry P., box 399, Stanley K. Hornbeck Papers.

44. Internal Memorandum, "Informal and Provisional Memorandum on the General Petroleum Situation," 19 February 1921, 800.6363/325 CF; Office of Naval Intelligence (R. E. Ingersoll to Military Intelligence, 18 November 1921, file 856-129, entry 535, both in RG 59; "British and American Oil Resources and Policies," memo from Office of Naval Intelligence, 28 April 1926, file 18194, O-1-l, RG 38, USNA.

45. Chester, *United States Oil Policy and Diplomacy*, 52, 308–9. The main British company in Burma was Burmah Oil, which in 1909 launched its "all but fully owned subsidiary" Anglo-Persian Oil Co., now better known as British Petroleum. Corley, *A History of the Burmah Oil Company*, vol. 1, *1886–1924*, 2–3.

46. FO, Petroleum Department, *Memorandum on the Petroleum Situation for H.M. Ambassador in Washington, D.C.*

47. Leasing law quoted in U.S. Federal Trade Commission, *Report of the Federal Trade Commission on Foreign Ownership in the Petroleum Industry*, 37; FO, Petroleum Department, *Memorandum on the Petroleum Situation for H.M. Ambassador in Washington, D.C.*

48. "Informal and Provisional Memorandum on the General Petroleum Situation," 19 February 1921, 800.6363/325 CF, RG 59, USNA.

49. During the 1920s Southeast Asia was sometimes called the Middle East, and the countries between the Mediterranean and the Arabian Seas were variously called the Near East and Western Asia. By the 1930s the Near East had become the Middle East, and Southeast Asia had become Southeastern Asia. These shifts suggest a change in the "center" reference point, from which near, middle, and west were measured, from Britain to the United States.

50. The controversy can be followed in documents published in *FRUS* for 1921, 1922, and 1923. See particularly the following: British ambassador in Washington to U.S. secretary of state, 20 April 1921, 841.6363/142; British ambassador to U.S. secretary of state, 15 November 1921, 845.6363/11; U.S. secretary of state to British ambassador, 10 December 1921, 845.66363/11, in *FRUS* 1921; Standard Oil Co. of New York to U.S. secretary of state, 24 February 1922, 845.6363/15; U.S. secretary of state to British ambassador, 10 June 1922, 845.6363/15, in *FRUS* 1922; U.S. secretary of state to British ambassador, 24 March 1923, 811.6363/94 in *FRUS* 1923.

51. USDOS to Dutch legation in Washington, 2 November 1920, 800.6363/183 CF, RG 59, USNA.

52. U.S. legation at The Hague (William Phillips) to Dutch minister for foreign affairs (H. A. van Karnebeek), 5 June 1920, no. 11638, inv. 313, 2.05.37, ARA.

53. U.S. minister in The Hague (Phillips) to USDOS, 5 June 1920, 856d.6363/3: telegram in *FRUS* 1920, vol. 3, 267.

54. Dutch chargé in Washington (de Beaufort) to U.S. secretary of state, 30 June 1920, 800.6363/146; U.S. minister in the Netherlands (Phillips) to U.S. secretary of state, 7 July 1920, 856d.6363/6: telegram; U.S. secretary of state to Phillips, 17 July 1920, 856d.6363/6: telegram in *FRUS*, vol. 3, 1920, 268–72.

55. Phillips to U.S. secretary of state, 22 July 1920, 856d.6363/9, *FRUS*, vol. 3, 1920, 272–74.

56. Phillips to U.S. secretary of state, 27 August 1920, 856d.6363/12: telegram; Phillips to U.S. secretary of state, 15 September 1920, 856d.6363/13: telegram; U.S. secretary of state to Phillips, 22 September 1920, 856d.6363/13: telegram in *FRUS*, vol. 3, 1920, 275–79.

57. Federal Trade Commission, *Report of the Federal Trade Commission on Foreign Ownership in the Petroleum Industry*, 37–38.

58. Phillips to USDOS, 23 March 1921, 856d.6363/45: telegram, *FRUS*, vol. 2, 1921, 533.

59. Phillips to USDOS, 29 April 1921, 856d.6363/83: telegram, *FRUS*, vol. 2, 1921, 540–41.

60. Phillips to USDOS, 11 May 1921, 856d.6363/88: telegram, *FRUS*, vol. 2, 541–42; H. A. van Karnebeek (Dutch foreign minister), "Dagboek van Karnebeek," 22 April 1921, document 308, *DBBPN*, period A, part II.

61. Van Karnebeek's remarks are reported in U.S. chargé in the Netherlands (Armour) to USDOS, 13 July 1921, 856d.6363/130, *FRUS*, vol. 2, 1921, 546–47. For the Japanese request see Dutch minister in Japan (A. C. D. de Graeff) to Dutch foreign minister (van Karnebeek), 13 June 1921, document 372, *DBBPN*, period A, vol. 2, 491–92.

62. U.S. minister in The Hague (Louis Sussdorf) to USDOS, 19 April 1923; U.S. naval attaché in The Hague (D. McD. LeBreton) to Office of Naval Intelligence, 24 April 1923, file 12865-A, O-1-l, RG 38, USNA.

63. U.S. consul in Batavia (Hoover) to USDOS, 26 April 1923, 856d.51/48 CF, RG 59, USNA. He advocated a visit by the United States fleet to the Indies to show that Washington was committed to defending the Indies from Japan.

64. U.S. Senate, *American Petroleum Interests in Foreign Countries, 1945*, 307.

65. U.S. Senate, *American Petroleum Interests in Foreign Countries 1945*, 307.

66. U.S. chargé in the Netherlands (Armour) to USDOS, 1 July 1921, 856d.6363/110: telegram, *FRUS*, vol. 2, 1921, 545–46.

67. The rejection is noted in Government of the Netherlands Indies, *Tien jaar volksraad arbeid*, 79. The United States consul in Batavia made a fuller report; see U.S. consul in Batavia (Charles L. Hoover) to USDOS, 21 August 1926, folder Batavia-1926, Consular Political Reports, Division of Commercial Affairs, RG 59, USNA.

68. U.S. minister at The Hague (Richard Tobin) to USDOS, 27 March 1926, 856d.001/7 CF, RG 59, USNA.

69. British consul general in Batavia (J. Crosby) to FO (Austen Chamberlain), 4 March 1927, W2987, FO 371-12699, FO 371, UKNA.

70. Dutch minister in Washington (J. H. van Royen) to Dutch foreign minister, 4 February 1928; Office of Economic Affairs in Dutch Foreign Ministry to Dutch Colonial Ministry, 23 February 1928, both in Verbaal 16-3-28-A5, NNA.

71. British legation at The Hague (Grumble) to FO, 15 November 1927, with minutes by Grindle, 30 December 1927; ERD, 12 January 1928, and Andrews, 12 January 1928, file 52011-542, CO 273, UKNA.

72. British consul general in Batavia (J. Crosby) to FO, 4 March 1927, W2987, file 12699, FO 371, UKNA.

73. British Board of Trade (J. J. Wills) to CO (Gilbert Grindle), 30 December 1927, CO 273-542/52-11, CO 273, UKNA.

74. Dutch foreign minister to Dutch colonial minister, 10 October 1927; Dutch foreign minister to Dutch minister in Washington (van Royen), 10 October 1927, both in Verbaal 18-10-27-F16, NNA.

75. Dutch minister in Washington (van Royen) to USDOS, 14 November 1927,

856d.6363/494; U.S. minister in The Hague (Tobin) to USDOS, 7 January 1928, 856d.6363/502, both in *FRUS*, vol. 3, 1928, 375–77.

76. U.S. chargé in The Hague (Norweb) to USDOS, 18 February 1928, 856d.6363/511; Norweb to USDOS, 24 February 1928, 856d.6363/512: telegram, both in *FRUS*, vol. 3, 1928, 379–81.

77. U.S. secretary of state to Norweb, 2 March 1928, 856d.6363/512: telegram, *FRUS*, vol. 3, 1928, 381–83.

78. Norweb to USDOS, 5 March 1928, 856d.6363/514: telegram; secretary of state to Norweb, 10 March 1928, 856d.6363/514: telegram; Norweb to USDOS, 14 March 1928, 856d.6363/517: telegram; USDOS to Norweb, 28 March 1928, 856d.6363/523; U.S. minister in the Netherlands (Tobin) to USDOS, 14 May 1928, 856d.6363/531: telegram; Tobin to USDOS, 14 May 1928, 856d.6363/533; Tobin to USDOS, 26 May 1928, 856d.6363/536, all in *FRUS*, vol. 3, 1928, 384–94. For the history of Britain's status as a reciprocating country see solicitor to the Department of the Interior (Nathan R. Margold) to secretary of the department (Harold L. Ickes), 2 April 1936, 845.6363/92 CF, RG 59, USNA.

79. Governor general of the Netherlands Indies (A. C. D. de Graeff) to Dutch minister of colonies, 4 September 1928, Kabinett letter U15, inv. 336, 2.10.36, 051, NNA.

Chapter 3: An Empire of the Mind

1. French ambassador in Washington to French foreign minister, 25 June 1921, d. 1041, c. 110, INF, CAOM.

2. U.S. consul in Medan (Walter A. Foote) to U.S. consul general in Batavia (Coert duBois), 25 April 1929, 856 f.504/6, roll 51; duBois to USDOS, 23 August 1929, 856d.401/5, roll 33, both in microcopy 682, RG 59, USNA.

3. For examples see U.S. legation at The Hague (Henry Norweb) to USDOS, 25 August 1925, 856d.00/5 CF; U.S. consul at Surabaya (Rollin Winslow) to USDOS, February 1926, "Trade Promotion Work at Surabaya Consulate," entry 593, Inspection Reports, both in RG 59, USNA; U.S. Department of Commerce, *Commerce Yearbook 1929*, vol. 2, 467.

4. BFDC, U.S. Department of Commerce. *Motion Pictures Abroad*, April 1931.

5. For a general discussion see Golden, *Short-Subject Film Market in Latin America, Canada, the Far East, Africa, and the Near East*. European films composed a negligible percentage of films imported; the bulk of the remaining films came from China and India.

6. For example see Banner, "The Enchantment of Mountainous Java." People could see movies for free, some sponsored by missionaries. Projects of the Rockefeller Foundation also featured open-air screenings, but primarily of educational films about the benefits of improved hygiene or vaccination. See "Program for 1932 in Java," folder 655 L, Public Health Education 1928–1929, box 2, series 655 Java, RG 1.1 Projects, Rockefeller Foundation Archives.

7. Lowry, "Trade Follows the Film."

8. For instance the Indonesian artist Salim, upon his return to Java after education in the Netherlands, reportedly found work in the early 1930s in the Indies creating advertisements (including neon signs) for Coca-Cola, Tiger Balm, and Heineken Beer. Mrázek, *Sjahrir*, 82.

9. Brumberg, *Mission for Life*.

10. Wiatt, *Burma*. The Baptists in Burma had a strong presence, but they had little success in converting ethnic Burmans to Christianity. Most converts came from the ethnic minority Karens, with smaller numbers of Kachin and Chin. The educational impact of mission schools was broader, since 20 to 50 percent of the students were Burman.

11. Beach and Bartholomew, *World Missionary Atlas*, 84–85; Means, *Malaysia Mosaic*. Initially the Methodist Episcopals viewed their missions throughout Southeast Asia as extensions of the missions in China and India. At first the Southeast Asia missions served the overseas Chinese and Indians in Burma, Malaya, and the Indies. Once established, however, the missions quickly began reaching out to indigenous groups. In the Philippines, Methodists, Episcopalians, and Congregationalists dominated among Protestant missions. See Clymer, *Protestant Missionaries in the Philippines*.

12. U.S. Consul in Saigon (Leland L. Smith) to USDOS, 28 August 1924, 851g.00/16, roll 150, M560, RG 59, USNA; "Conseil de gouvernement: compte-rendu de la commission permanente du 22 mai 1924," *Indépendance tonkinoise*, 28 May 1924.

13. "Conseil de gouvernement," *Indépendance tonkinoise*, 28 May 1924.

14. M. Tiêp, "Extracts from Report to Native Conference by Annamese Worker," *Call of French-Indochina* 7 (April–June 1924), 9–10; Report of N. Curwen Smith, eastern Tonkin district, *Call of French-Indochina* 29 (April–June 1930), 28; "Communism and Superstition," *Call of French-Indochina* 30 (July–December 1930), 15.

15. Bradley, "Imagining America."

16. "A Survey of the Foreign Work of the Christian and Missionary Alliance" (1931), MRL.

17. "Annual Report of the French Indochina and East Siam Mission" (1929), Christian and Missionary Alliance, MRL.

18. U.S. consul in Medan (Walter A. Foote) to USDOS, "Education in Sumatra," 22 December 1927, 856 f.42/1 CF, RG 59, USNA. For Baptist education see Howard, *Baptists in Burma*.

19. "Survey of Ten Years in Moslem Lands."

20. These figures are from Beach and Bartholomew, *World Missionary Atlas*, 126, 128. By 1935 the number of students in Methodist schools in Malaya had grown to eighteen thousand. Means, *Malaysia Mosaic*, 136–37. European-language education was available to only a very few Southeast Asians in the colonies (with the exception of the Philippines). For instance, in 1937 the population of French Indochina was 23 million, and only 500,000 students were enrolled in government schools. Nearly all of these were in the first two grades of elementary school. In the Netherlands Indies, with a population of 68 million, only 93,000 Indonesians were enrolled in Dutch-

language schools, again almost all in elementary schools. These figures are from Steinberg, ed., *In Search of Southeast Asia*, 265.

21. George D. Josif, "Daily Vacation Bible Schools in Burma: Report for 1932," MR. The vacation bible schools explicitly attempted to reach children who did not attend school during the rest of the year, with the hope of providing them with a taste for learning, both in general and specifically about Christianity. Josif reported 47 schools enrolling 2,585 students; 25 schools served the Burman children, of whom 1,315 attended.

22. Means, *Malaysia Mosaic*, 5. The Methodist missions in Singapore and Malaya ran multiethnic schools, but church congregations remained segregated along ethnic lines, with separate churches for ethnic Chinese, ethnic Tamils, etc.

23. A. Carter, "Preliminary Report on Medical Education" (1923), folder 655 A, Medical Education in Java, box 1, series 655 Java; Victor Heiser to general director, International Health Division, 26 February 1928, folder 655 L, Public Health Education 1928–1929, box 2, series 655 Java; Victor Heiser, "Memorandum on Medical Education in Malaya," 1915, folder 473 A, box 1, series 473 A Malaya, all in RG 1.1 Projects, Rockefeller Archives.

24. Foreword by the vice-president (Isabel Warwick Wood), 54th Annual Report of the Woman's American Baptist Foreign Mission Society (1925), MRL, 553.

25. Charles E. Locke, speech for the Central Conference of Southeast Asia of the Methodist Episcopal Church (1923), 26; Burma Annual Conference, Methodist Episcopal Church, *Annual Report* (1928–33), both in MRL; Wiatt, *Burma*.

26. For the strike see von der Mehden, *Religion and Nationalism in Southeast Asia*, 181; *Proceedings of the Burma Baptist Missionary Conference* (3–8 October 1930), MRL, 26–30.

27. Locke, speech to Central Conference of Southeast Asia of the Methodist Episcopal Church (1923), MRL, 26.

28. *Report of the Committee on Policy and Program*, American Baptist Mission, Burma, 1933, MRL.

29. The connection between Progressivism and United States colonial rule in the Philippines is frequently suggested in the literature. My focus is on representations of United States colonial policy to other colonial powers, and so this book will not survey United States policies generally. For contrasting views of the role of progressivism see Stanley, *A Nation in the Making*, and Abinales, "State Authority and Local Power in Southern Philippines."

30. See May's discussion in *Social Engineering in the Philippines*, 77–126; Lardizabal, *Pioneer American Teachers and Philippine Education*, esp. 35–57, for detailed information on early American educational efforts. Julian Go has recently suggested that even within the United States empire the Philippines and Puerto Rico were showcase colonies, receiving substantially more funding for education than did colonies such as Guam and Samoa. Go, "The Provinciality of American Empire," 79–84. For a discussion of political education see Go, "Chains of Empire, Projects of State."

31. As reported in Roff, *The Origins of Malay Nationalism*, 137–40. For an in-depth

examination of this industrial education program, and suggestions that it was not the success claimed by United States officials, see May, "The Business of Education in the Colonial Philippines."

32. Prentiss B. Gilbert (Division of Western European Affairs), lecture to Foreign Service School, "Holland and the Dutch East Indies," 2 March 1926, entry 623, RG 59, USNA.

33. Naval intelligence officer (R. E. Jennings) to Office of Naval Intelligence, 12 March 1923; Naval intelligence officer (R. H. Grayson) to Office of Naval Intelligence, 7 July 1924, #15047-A, file C-9-a, both in RG 38, USNA.

34. Governor general of the Philippines (Dwight F. Davis) to U.S. secretary of war (Patrick J. Hurley), 7 August 1930, Davis's personal file, entry 5, RG 350, USNA.

35. U.S. consul in Rangoon (George J. Haering) to USDOS, 20 August 1930, 811b.01/138 CF, RG 59, USNA. See also Stanley K. Hornbeck's statement that Washington officials were "pioneers" in "preparing dependent peoples of other races for self-government," and his assertion that the British were "working out a similar plan" for India. Stanley K. Hornbeck, draft memorandum for secretary of state, 16 June 1930, box 491, Hornbeck Papers.

36. This brief sentence masks a complex and often astute political game played by both Filipino and United States politicians. Virtually all politically aware Filipinos desired independence, but hoped to retain access to United States markets and protection of the U.S. Navy as well, if possible. Golay covers the debates and maneuvers well in *Face of Empire*, chapters 10–11, esp. 308–11, 370–79.

37. U.S. consul general in Batavia (Walter A. Foote) to USDOS, 23 July 1935, 856d.00/91 CF, RG 59, USNA. Despite Foote's claims Indonesians probably hoped more that the Dutch would leave than they feared that the Japanese would expand.

38. U.S. consul general in Singapore (Monnett B. Davis) to USDOS, 18 March 1936, 846d.00 P.R./55 CF, RG 59, USNA.

39. From quite different perspectives, and with different understandings of the implications, both Walter LaFeber and John Milton Cooper Jr. note Theodore Roosevelt's change of heart. See Cooper, *The Warrior and the Priest*, 280–81, and LaFeber, *The American Search for Opportunity*, 207–8. Only Cooper, however, sees the colonial experience as unimportant.

40. The figures in the heading are based on a report by the United States consul general in Batavia (Coert DuBois) in his report "The European Population of Netherland India," 25 August 1929, 856d.401/5 CF, roll 33, M682, RG 59, USNA. He made a similar point in his report "The Native Population of Netherland India, part 2," 2 October 1928, 856d.401/3 CF, RG 59, USNA. The generalization regarding imported Chinese and Indian labor overlooks much variation by industry and region. For a more detailed discussion see Elson's chapter "International Commerce, the State and Society," esp. 160–77.

41. This inattention by scholars is interesting, given that in the 1920s and 1930s officials in the United States and European colonial capitals were interested in these

issues. The very first publication by the U.S. Council on Foreign Relations, for instance, was Bain's *Ores and Industries of the Far East*, which focused on East Asia's and Southeast Asia's growing importance for industrial production. Some scholars have paid attention to these issues, of course, as discussed further in chapter 4.

42. With the exception of rubber and oil, direct United States investment in Southeast Asia—not including the Philippines—was minuscule before 1925.

43. All details about NKPM facilities are from U.S. Senate, *American Petroleum Interests in Foreign Countries, 1945*, 282–85.

44. Governor general, Netherlands Indies, to Algemeene Secretarie (Fock), 23 July 1926, MR 796x/26, inv. 44, 2.10.36.06, NNA.

45. DuBois to USDOS, 23 August 1929, 956d.401/5, roll 33, M682, RG 59, USNA.

46. Statement of Walter L. Faust, vice-president and director, Socony-Vacuum Oil Co., in U.S. Senate, *American Petroleum Interests in Foreign Countries, 1945*, 107.

47. Yergin, *The Prize*, 68, 70.

48. DuBois to USDOS, 23 August 1929, 856d.401/5 CF, RG 59, USNA.

49. U.S. trade commissioner in Netherlands Indies (Don C. Bliss), "Market for Foodstuffs in the Netherland East Indies," *Trade Information Bulletin* no. 620, BFDC, U.S. Department of Commerce (Washington, 1929), 1.

50. Quotations from captions on photos found in Netherlands East Indies foodstuffs, folder 77B, box 77, RG 151-FC, Photographic Division, USNA.

51. U.S. consul in Batavia (Charles L. Hoover) to USDOS, 29 April 1925, despatch #597, file 861.71, RG 84, USNA.

52. U.S. consul in Soerabaya (Rollin R. Winslow) to USDOS, 25 January 1926, 856d.6176/22, RG 59, USNA.

53. U.S. consul in Batavia (C. Porter Kuykendall) to USDOS, 7 August 1925, 856 f.6176/9, RG 59, USNA.

54. U.S. Department of Commerce, *Commerce Yearbook*, 1929, vol. 2, 467. The Dutch government included in their import figures automobile parts imported for assembly at the General Motors plant in Batavia, which had been established in 1927. The plant provided cars primarily for the domestic market, with some exports to Malaya and China. See Government of the Netherlands Indies, *Handbook of the Netherlands East Indies*, 1930, 379. For Burma see "Burma: A Promising Market for American Goods," *Commerce Reports*, 3 August 1931, 260–61.

55. Kuykendall to USDOS, 8 August 1926, 856d.607/-CF, RG 59, USNA.

56. See the discussion in chapter 5.

57. Seldes, *The Movies Come from America*, 9.

58. U.S. vice-consul in Medan (Daniel M. Braddock) to USDOS, 27 March 1930, 856 f.4061 Motion Pictures/1, and 18 June 1930, 856 f.4061 Motion Pictures/2, both in CF, RG 59, USNA.

59. *Film Daily Yearbook*, 1925, 643–45, 655, 660, 663, 675, 690; "Motion Pictures in India," *Trade Information Bulletin* no. 614, BFDC, U.S. Department of Commerce (Washington, 1929), 15.

60. Golden, *Short-Subject Film Market in Latin America, Canada, the Far East, Africa, and the Near East*, 22.

61. Merz, "When the Movies Go Abroad."

62. Golden, *Short-Subject Film Market in Latin America, Canada, the Far East, Africa, and the Near East*.

63. The Motion Picture Division of the BFDC published a periodic report, *Motion Pictures Abroad*, to assist the United States film industry in maintaining and expanding distribution of United States films. Statistics are from *Motion Pictures Abroad*, 13 April 1932, November 1932, 11 November 1932, 31 March 1931, 14 April 1933, 19 April 1933, 12 May 1933, 25 May 1933, 30 July 1934, 30 October 1934, and 1 June 1936. Sound films, despite their use of English, a language that few Southeast Asians spoke, may actually have been easier for the primarily illiterate indigenous populations to understand than the silent films had been.

64. *Motion Pictures Abroad*, 1 June 1936.

65. *Motion Pictures Abroad*, 25 May 1934.

66. Dorgelès, "Twentieth-Century 'Savages,'" 539, 541–42.

67. Banner, "The Enchantment of Mountainous Java."

68. For example see *Motion Pictures Abroad*, 31 March 1933, 25 May 1934, 1 June 1936.

69. Golden, *Short-Subject Film Market in Latin America, Canada, the Far East, Africa, and the Near East*, discusses censorship generally at the end of the 1920s. Most issues of *Motion Pictures Abroad* in the 1930s reported on censorship.

70. U.S. trade commissioner in Batavia (J. F. van Wickel) to all consulates in Netherlands India and British Malaya, 22 January 1925, file 840.6, Batavia, RG 84, USNA. Most of the other members were from film companies or theaters, including Australasian Films Ltd., Fox Film Corporation, Famous Lasky Film Service, Middle East Films, Universal Pictures Corporation, N. V. Pathé Theaters, and Filmland Theater. This listing from "Report of the Meeting of Film Importers," 5 October 1925, file 840.6, RG 84, USNA.

71. The consular post files contain numerous documents tracing these controversies through 1925 and 1926 in file 840.6, Batavia, RG 84, USNA.

72. See the telegrams dated 2 December 1926, 13 December 1926, and 22 December 1926 in F22273, file CO 273/534/23, CO 273, UKNA.

73. Governor general, Straits Settlements, to Rt. Honourable L. C. M. A. Amery (CO), 8 August 1927; "British Films Banned," *Morning Post*, 10 October 1927, in CO 273/541/28194, CO 273, UKNA. The quota must not have been imposed in the end, because in 1929 the annual report by the police noted that of the films reviewed by the censor, 71 percent were supplied by the United States, 24 percent by China, and only 3 percent by Britain. Inspector-general of police, Straits Settlements (H. Fairburn), "Annual Report on the Police Force and on the State of Crime for the Year 1929," 7 F 74, GGI, CAOM.

74. Lowry, "Trade Follows the Film."

75. Chief, Motion Picture Division, BFDC (C. J. North), to U.S. trade commissioner, Batavia (Thomas C. Barringer), 30 August 1928; North to U.S. trade commissioner, Batavia (Don Bliss), 8 December 1928, both in 400.2 Motion Picture Propaganda, Dutch East Indies, entry 1, RG 151, USNA.

76. Discussion of the "buy British" campaign is from U.S. consul general in Singapore (Lester Maynard) to USDOS, 5 July 1932, 846d P.R./33; discussion of cars in U.S. consul in Batavia (C. Porter Kuykendall) to USDOS, 7 August 1925, 856 f.6176/9, both in CF, RG 59, USNA.

77. This triangular trade would become a critical issue after the Second World War, as Rotter explains convincingly in *The Path to Vietnam*. The pattern, however, stems from the second decade of the twentieth century at the latest.

78. Brandon, *Theatre in Southeast Asia*, 202, 265–66.

79. *Motion Pictures Abroad*, 11 November 1932; "Short-subject Film Market," 1928, 28.

80. Mrázek, *Engineers of Happy Land*, 111–12. Mrázek's study is wonderfully evocative on the multifaceted changes that technology brought in the late nineteenth century and the early twentieth, but it is somewhat odd that a study so much concerned with nationalism has nearly no consideration of the national origin of much of this technology, and the possible implications of different nationalist stories which might accompany the technology.

81. Malaka, *From Jail to Jail*, vol. 1, 140; Hong, "Days of Childhood," 181, 204, 209–10; Mrázek, "Sjahrir at Boven Digoel," 48.

82. Sukarno, *Sukarno*, 36.

83. Nu, *U Nu*, 37, 40.

84. Sklar, *Movie-Made America*, 195–215; Fuller, *At the Picture Show*, esp. chapter 9, "Coming of Age at the Picture Show," 169–93.

85. Wanger, "120,000 American Ambassadors," 45–46; car-owning mechanics quote from Lowry, "Trade Follows the Film."

86. "Americanism," *Java Bode*, 6 November 1933, as trans. by U.S. consul general in Batavia (K. S. Patten) in report to USDOS, 14 November 1933, 856e.911/4 CF, RG 59, USNA.

87. Bell and Legendre both quoted by Harloff, "The Influence of the Cinema on Oriental Peoples." Harloff's article prompted a response from the film industry. See Weait, "The Orient and the Cinema."

88. Clancy-Smith and Gouda, eds., *Domesticating the Empire*. See especially the introduction, 1–20.

89. Harley, *World Wide Influences of the Cinema*, 183–84, for quotes, 3 for defense of United States films. See also chapters 2 ("National Official Censorship of Motion Pictures") and 4 ("Around the World with the Censors").

90. Too little, meaning nearly nothing, is known about how Southeast Asians interpreted the films they viewed, or even about which films Southeast Asians really went to see, how often, and whether people viewed the same movie more than once.

Such research is beyond the scope of this book, but it is an important project waiting for exploration.

91. Isaacs, *Scratches on Our Minds*. See the introduction for a description of the interviewees.

92. Two of the many classics which typify this characterization are Wolters, *History, Culture, and Region in Southeast Asian Perspectives*, and Reid, *Southeast Asia in the Age of Commerce*.

93. Mrázek's *Engineers of Happy Land* demonstrates convincingly the eagerness with which Southeast Asian adopted new technology. For a fascinating look at the appeal in Europe of the American way of life and standard of living see de Grazia's *Irresistible Empire*. On a smaller scale, some of the same factors were at work in Southeast Asia.

94. Ngai, *Impossible Subjects*. Migration statistics are on pp. 101–3.

95. Ngai, *Impossible Subjects*, chapter 3. The United States had other colonies as well, and Puerto Ricans in the United States prompted similarly ambivalent reactions, but the cases are far from identical. A key difference stemmed from racial classifications, since Puerto Ricans were not "Asian" and therefore were eligible for citizenship.

96. Hoganson, *Consumers' Imperium*, 105–51.

97. Hoganson, *Consumers' Imperium*, 142.

Chapter 4: Depression and the Discovery of Limits

1. Lindblad makes this point well regarding the Netherlands Indies and explores the specific ramifications for the Depression years. See Lindblad, "Structural Origins of the Economic Depression in Indonesia during the 1930s," *Weathering the Storm*, ed. Boomgaard and Brown, 123–42.

2. Some of the most famous studies of Southeast Asia in the 1930s address the relationship between economic distress and political movements. See especially Scott, *Moral Economy of the Peasant*. The essays in Boomgaard and Brown, eds., *Weathering the Storm*, provide excellent analysis, country by country. Booth's essay "Crisis and Response" (295–320) in that collection, and even more her "Night Watchman, Extractive, or Development States?," provide a welcome look at the region as a whole.

3. Wholesale rubber sold for less than three pence a pound in 1932. Drabble, *Malayan Rubber*, 306–7. Boomgaard and Brown call attention to the effect of the contracting production of automobiles in the United States on demand for rubber in the late 1920s as well. See Boomgaard and Brown, "The Economies of Southeast Asia in the 1930s Depression," *Weathering the Storm*, 2.

4. For Burma see Cheng, *The Rice Industry of Burma*, 73. A "basket" was a unit of measure, with a hundred baskets equal to four thousand pounds. For Indochina see *Bulletin économique de l'Indochine: industrie, commerce, finances, statistiques*, part A,

14–15, 83, 128, 208, 278, 362, 442, 512, 592, 658, 724, and 784 (for 1930), 56, 125, 198, 280, and 348 (for 1931). Norland has provided several invaluable studies of the rice economy of French Indochina. Most helpful in this context is her "Rice and the Colonial Lobby," *Weathering the Storm*, ed. Boomgaard and Brown, esp. 204–9.

5. For prices received by peasants see the statement by Tharrawady U Pu, 18 February 1931, Burmese Legislative Council; for land ownership see Cheng, *The Rice Industry of Burma*, 145, 270–71.

6. Foster, "Alienation and Cooperation," 171–75. Ian Brown provides a sensitive assessment of the difficulties of understanding the ways Burmese rice-growers experienced these developments. See his "'Blindness We Mistake for Sight.'"

7. Boomgaard, "Surviving the Slump," *Weathering the Storm*, ed. Boomgaard and Brown, 36–40.

8. Brown, *Economic Change in South-East Asia*, 223. Although helpful for increasing the food supply, the additional rice production only made the situation worse for those growing rice for export, since demand shrank as the supply rose.

9. Brown, *Economic Change in South-East Asia*, 223. Norland argues that in French Indochina rice-growing peasants often came through the Depression relatively well, so long as they maintained their ability to stay on their land. Losing that ability (meaning that they no longer owned or could maintain tenancy) did usually have devastating economic consequences. See Norland, "The Economic Crisis in French Indo-China," *Weathering the Storm*, ed. Boomgaard and Brown, 203.

10. See Foster, "Alienation and Cooperation," chapters 3–4; James C. Scott, *Moral Economy of the Peasant*.

11. Booth, "Four Colonies and a Kingdom," 434–35; Brown, *Economic Change in South-East Asia*, 51–53, 223–24.

12. Ingleson, "Urban Java during the Depression," 305.

13. Ingleson, "Urban Java during the Depression," 296.

14. U.S. vice-consul at Batavia (Sydney Browne) to USDOS, 13 July 1934, 856e.6176/15; "Establishment of Goodyear Tire and Rubber Company Factor at Buitenzorg, Java," CF, RG 59, USNA. M. J. French has argued that Goodyear aimed to evade rubber restriction regulations by exporting finished products (not restricted) rather than raw materials (subjects to maximum quotas). See French, "The Emergence of U.S. Multinational Enterprise," *Economic History Review*, 64–79.

15. Brown, *Economic Change in South-East Asia*, 58; Internal Memo, Division of Far Eastern Affairs (EHD to MFP, SJF, SKH), 5 January 1934, 856d.00/79 CF, RG 59, USNA; Dutch minister of colonies (Colijn) to governor general, Netherlands Indies (de Jonge), 17 September 1933, no. 91 in *DBBPN*, period B, part 3, 146.

16. Southeast Asia's involvement in global patterns of trade may even be said to have been a cause for the arrival of colonizing Europeans. See Reid's classic *Southeast Asia in the Age of Commerce*, vol. 2, esp. chapter 1. Nations such as Thailand which avoided being colonized also were drawn into the world economy, sometimes better controlling the terms of that entry, but the ubiquity of imperialism meant that these

nations always faced the possibility of colonial rule. Imperialism was therefore the structure within which such nations made economic and political decisions.   ˙

17. Stoler, *Carnal Knowledge and Imperial Power*, 37–38.

18. Beb Vuyk's *The Last House in the World* describes one option of the newly destitute Dutch: her unemployed husband moved to the eastern edge of the Indies, a remote place for them, to take on the adventure of running a business there. More often, the Dutch chose what Beb Vuyk and her husband rejected, the "careful existence in Java, in semi-poverty." Vuyk, "The Last House in the World," 5.

19. Brown, *Economic Change in South-East Asia*, 219–21. See also the discussion of sugar in Booth, "Crisis and Response," *Weathering the Storm*, ed. in Boomgaard and Brown, 295–320, and for the Netherland Indies, in Rothe, "Commodity Control in Netherlands India," *Commodity Control in the Pacific Area*, ed. Holland, 280–86.

20. Percentages computed from Whitford, "The Crude Rubber Supply," 614. Liberia was essentially a United States protectorate and rubber producer, but since Firestone controlled rubber production there, and used this rubber for its own business, the situation is not comparable to that of the British, Dutch, and French in their colonies.

21. Edgar Snow wrote an article on the "decline of Western prestige in Asia" and the rise of Japanese prestige: this was much on the mind of United States government officials, who commented on the similarity of Snow's analysis with reports from the United States consul in Batavia in November 1933. See summary by EHD in the Division of Far Eastern Affairs, attached to front of U.S. consul general (K. S. Patton) to USDOS, 14 November 1933, 856d.00/79 CF, RG 59, USNA.

22. For Goodyear Tire see Allen, *The House of Goodyear*, 270–72, and Browne to US-DOS, 13 July 1934, 856e.6176/15 CF, RG 59, USNA. For General Motors see Pound, *The Turning Wheel*, 244, 247–48, 254, 256, and Coert DuBois to USDOS, 23 August 1929, 856d.401/5 CF, RG 59, USNA.

23. Witherow, *Foreign Trade of the United States, Calendar Year 1938*, 102–3. The region identified as "South and Southeast Asia" included India and Ceylon in addition to the Southeast Asian countries. Through 1937 India encompassed Burma. Malaya, the Netherlands Indies, and the Philippines were each more substantial trading partners than India was.

24. Van Royen (Dutch ambassador in Washington) to Dutch foreign minister, 15 October 1929, inv. 334, 2.10.36.051, NNA.

25. Quoted in *Congressional Record*, 71st Cong., 1st sess., vol. 71, part 4, 4492.

26. *Congressional Record*, 71st Cong., 1st sess., vol. 71, part 4, 4496.

27. Ngai, *Impossible Subjects*, 116–20; Salman, *The Embarrassment of Slavery*.

28. Van Royen to Dutch foreign minister, 15 October 1929, inv. 334, 2.10.36.051, NNA, last phrase quoted in English by van Royen. This is close to what Blaine actually said: "America shall not give aid or comfort to those employers and planters in foreign countries whose forced and indentured labor is brought to poverty and degeneration." *Congressional Record*, 71st Cong., 1st sess., vol. 71, part 4, 4488.

29. Dutch Foreign Ministry to Dutch ambassador in Washington, 22 October 1929, (telegram), inv. 334, 2.10.36.051, NNA.

30. The relevant debate occurred on 14 October 1929, as reported in the *Congressional Record*, vol. 71, part 4, 4488–99. The final text of the amendment is found in section 307, Public Law 361, 71st Cong., 2nd sess., chapter 497 (pp. 689–90).

31. *Congressional Record*, vol. 71, part 4, 4488.

32. U.S. consul in Medan, Sumatra, Netherlands Indies (Walter A. Foote), to US-DOS, 14 August 1930, 611.56f6 Tobacco/- CF, RG 59, USNA. I calculated the sum spent on leaf tobacco from this document. Some subsequent documents state a larger figure of US \$11–12 million.

33. Memo, Division of Western European Affairs, USDOS, "Sumatra Wrapper Tobacco and Section 307 of the Tariff Act of 1930," 4 May 1931, 611.56f6 Tobacco/3.5 CF, RG 59, USNA.

34. W. R. Castle (undersecretary of state) to Ogden L. Mills (undersecretary of the treasury), 9 May 1931, 611.56f6 Tobacco 4.5 CF, RG 59, USNA.

35. "Zending der Heeren B. B. M. Rupert, E. Enthoven en H. J. Bool naar de Vereenigde Staten in verband met de moeilijkheden voor den invoer van Sumatra tabak als gevolg van [section] 307 van de Amerikaansche Tariefwet," 18 July 1931, vb. 7-8-31-L14, inv. 363, 2.10.06.051, NNA.

36. Dutch foreign minister to Dutch Minister of Colonies, 7 July 1931, vb. 18-7-31-A13, inv. 363, 2.10.06.051, NNA.

37. Scholars have tended to draw a causal connection between the end of penal sanction labor in the Netherlands Indies and the threat by the United States to prohibit imports, and as the timing of this decision suggests, there is support for that interpretation. Other scholars note other factors at work as well. Margo Groenewoud notes the long history of agitation against penal sanctions in "Towards the Abolition of Penal Sanctions in Dutch Colonial Labor Legislation." Stoler notes that because of the onset of the Depression plantation owners were happy to be relieved of the burden of paying contracted laborers, and so acquiesced in the end of the contract system. See her *Capitalism and Confrontation in Sumatra's Plantation Belt*, 43–45, 88.

38. Castle to Mills, 15 October 1931, 611.56f6 Tobacco/10 CF, RG 59, USNA.

39. Castle to President Herbert Hoover, 15 October 1931, 611.56f6 Tobacco/10 CF, RG 59, USNA.

40. Translated and quoted in report by Laurits S. Swenson (U.S. minister at The Hague) to USDOS, 7 November 1931, 611.56f6 Tobacco/41 CF, RG 59, USNA.

41. Bumper tobacco crops in 1929–31, combined with the worldwide depression, did create serious problems for United States tobacco growers, who saw prices and demand fall precipitously. Washington proved willing to take many other types of actions to protect tobacco growers, including high tariffs and the price support programs of the Agricultural Adjustment Act. See the discussion of United States tobacco in Davis, "Planned Agricultural Adjustment in the United States," *Commodity Control in the Pacific Area*, ed. Holland, 67–70.

42. Salman, *The Embarrassment of Slavery*, esp. 257–64.

43. Minute by G. E. J. Gent (CO), 23 December 1929, "Rubber Restriction, Dutch and English Cooperation with a View to," file 63040, CO 825, UKNA.

44. British Colonial Secretary's Office to Asiatic Planters' Association of Malaya et al., regarding meeting of Sir Cecil Clementi Smith (governor, Straits Settlements) and Jonkheer de Graeff (governor general, Netherlands Indies), 8 September 1930, in Bi-monthly Report of the U.S. Consulate General in Singapore to USDOS, 12 September 1930, 846d.00 PR/19 CF, RG 59, USNA.

45. U.S. consul general Singapore to USDOS, 12 September 1930, 846d.P.R./19 CF, RG 59, USNA.

46. Laurits Swenson (U.S. minister in The Hague) to USDOS, 3 March 1932, 856d.6176/96 CF, RG 59, USNA.

47. Swenson to USDOS, 4 March 1934, 856d.6176/158 CF, RG 59, USNA.

48. Gerrit J. Diekma (U.S. legation in The Hague) to USDOS, 28 July 1930, 856d.6176/75; Swenson to USDOS, 8 December 1933, 856d.6176/118; Patton to USDOS, 5 January 1934, plus the enclosed letter from the United States Rubber Company to the governor general of the Netherlands Indies, 30 November 1933, 856d.6176/139, all in CF, RG 59, USNA. British law had prevented United States rubber companies from establishing plantations in British Malaya, so the only important ones in the region were in the Netherlands Indies.

49. E. G. Holt (chief, Rubber Division, BFDC) to Julius Klein (head, BFDC), 17 March 1929 (254-Rubber), box 1161, entry 1, RG 151, USNA.

50. Swenson to USDOS, 18 November 1933, 856d.6176/113, *FRUS* 1934, vol. 1, 615.

51. For a general discussion see Holland, ed., *Commodity Control in the Pacific Area.* Chapter 12 covers the history of tin restriction and chapter 13 the history of rubber restriction.

52. de Graeff (Dutch minister of colonies) to de Jonge (governor general, Netherlands Indies), 29 December 1931, doc. 271 in *DBBPN*, period B, part 1, 526, for "unsound"; Swenson to USDOS, 21 March 1932, 856d.6176/97 CF, RG 59, USNA, for "no rubber restriction plan."

53. Hull (secretary of state) to Swenson, 23 January 1934, 856d.6176/113 CF, RG 59, USNA. The bottom of this telegram indicates that the instructions to Swenson were approved by the secretary of agriculture, Henry Wallace, and the secretary of commerce, Daniel Roper.

54. Hendrik Colijn (prime minister and minister of colonies, Netherlands) quoted in Swenson to USDOS, 15 December 1933, *FRUS* 1934, vol. 1, 617.

55. Swenson to USDOS, 26 February 1934, *FRUS* 1934, vol. 1, 625; Feis, *Seen from E.A.*, 18–21.

56. For example, Colijn made such statements in January, March, and November 1934. See Swenson to USDOS, 26 January 1934, 856d.6176/134, reporting an interview with Colijn; Swenson to USDOS, 4 March 1934, 856d.6176/158; U.S. minister in the Netherlands (Grenville T. Emmet) to USDOS, 16 November 1934, 856d.6176/309,

reporting conversation with Colijn, all in CF, RG 59, USNA. British officials usually refused to mention a price at all, but for a suggestion of their desires see U.S. consul general in Singapore to USDOS, 15 January 1934, 846d.00 P.R./42 CF, RG 59, USNA, and U.S. chargé in London (Atherton) to USDOS, 16 January 1934, 856d.6176/123 telegram, *FRUS* 1934, vol. 1, 619.

57. Communication from FO to U.S. ambassador in Great Britain (Bingham), encl. in Bingham to USDOS, 23 March 1934, 856d.6176/191 telegram, *FRUS* 1934, vol. 1, 637.

58. Emmet to USDOS, 28 April 1934, 856d6176/230, and Bingham to USDOS, 30 April 1934, 856d.617/232, both in *FRUS* 1934, vol. 1, 657–59.

59. For examples of these complaints see Bingham to USDOS, 23 February 1934, 856d.6176/137, and Simon to Bingham, 26 April 1934, encl. in Bingham to USDOS, 27 April 1934, 856d.6176/245, both in *FRUS* 1934, vol. 1, 624, 655.

60. Drabble, *Malayan Rubber*, 306–7.

61. U.S. chargé in The Hague (Warden Wilson) to USDOS, 15 November 1935, 856d.6176/344 CF, RG 49, USNA. See also A. L. Viles (president, Rubber Manufacturers Association) to William Phillips (undersecretary of state), 11 September 1935, enclosing the association's confidential member bulletin "Investigation of Rubber Situation in the Middle East," 4 September 1935, found in 800.6176/13, CF, RG 59, USNA. As discussed earlier, sometimes during the interwar years the term "Middle East" was used to refer to the region we now call Southeast Asia.

62. For British efforts to raise price of rubber see U.S. chargé in The Hague (Warden McK. Wilson) to USDOS, 23 September 1936, 800.6176/28; for efficiency of plantations see president, Rubber Manufacturers Association (A. L. Viles) to undersecretary of state (William Phillips), attn. H. S. Feis, 3 April 1935, 800.6176/9, and memo of conversation between Viles and Veatch, 19 May 1938, 800.6176/58, all in CF, RG 59, USNA.

63. Feis makes this point quite explicitly in his *Seen from E.A.*, 20–21.

64. U.S. minister in The Hague (Grenville T. Emmet) to USDOS, 27 January 1937, 856d.6176/387; memo of conversation between Viles, Feis, and Veatch, 26 April 1938, 800.6176/55, both in CF, RG 59, USNA.

65. Senator Royal S. Copeland to Secretary of State Cordell Hull, 9 June 1937, and Hull to Copeland, 22 June 1937, 800.6176/45 CF, RG 59, USNA.

66. Memorandum of conversation between Viles, Feis, and Veatch, 26 April 1938, 800.6176/55, for discussion of United States proposal and memorandum of conversation between Viles and Feis; 8 July 1938, 800.6176/63, for Feis response, both in CF, RG 59, USNA.

67. On opposition of Rubber Manufacturers Association to restriction see memorandum of conversation between Viles, E. G. Holt (head, Rubber Division, Department of Commerce), Feis, and Stinebower, 2 March 1938, 800.6176/51 CF, RG 59, USNA. On official United States policy see secretary of state to chargé in Britain (Johnson), 12 March 1938, 856d.6176/486, *FRUS* 1938, vol. 1, 929.

68. Marshall, *To Have and Have Not*, 42.

69. U.S. ambassador in Britain (Joseph Kennedy) to USDOS, 20 June 1939, 811.24 Raw Materials/182, in *FRUS* 1939, vol. 2, 252–57.

70. The best summary of this period is in McFadyean, ed., *The History of Rubber Regulation*, chapters 10–11.

71. Memorandum of conversation between Veatch and E. G. Holt (Rubber Division, BFDC), 24 August 1934, 856d.6176/296 CF, RG 59, USNA.

72. Kramer, *The Blood of Government*, 392–402.

Chapter 5: Challenges to the Established Order

1. In October 1930 the name was changed to Indochinese Communist Party from Vietnamese Communist Party to conform to Comintern directives. The name Indochinese Communist Party (ICP) is used for the sake of simplicity. See Bernal, "The Nghe-Tinh Soviet Movement," 148–49, and Phan Thiên Châu, "Vietnamese Nationalism," 53–54.

2. Inspecteur des affaires politiques et administratives de l'Annam to résident supérieur en Annam, "Extraits de rapports confidentiels, Commission d'Enquête sur les Événements du Nord-Annam," 1–3 October 1930, d. 2688, c. 334, INF, CAOM. French officials also stressed that communists tortured and killed those who opposed them. The French responded in kind: French troops were ordered to fire on unarmed demonstrators, and persons arrested as rebels were sometimes executed without trial.

3. Gouverneur général de l'Indochine (Pierre Pasquier) to minister of colonies, 21 June 1930, 7 F 4, GGI, CAOM; Pasquier to minister of colonies, 20 September 1930, 7 F 4, GGI, CAOM; "Les Associations antifrançaises et la propagande communiste en Indochine: Les faits du mois de décembre 1930 et de janvier 1931," 7 F 5, GGI, CAOM; "Les associations antifrançaises du mois d'août et de la 1ère quinzaine de septembre 1931," 7 F 5, GGI, CAOM.

4. The preceding account is taken primarily from Bernal, "The Nghe-Tinh Soviet Movement," 151–53, but see also Duiker, *The Rise of Nationalism in Vietnam*, esp. 215–33; Khanh, *Vietnamese Communism*, esp. 151–70; Trân, *Les Soviets du Nghe-Tinh de 1930–1931*, as well as the classic treatments by Popkin, *The Rational Peasant*, and Scott, *Moral Economy of the Peasant*.

5. Deputy secretary of the Government of India to undersecretary of state for India, 26 February 2931, file (fl) 1346-1931, folder (fd) 7347-1930, L/P&J/6/2020, India Office Library, London; Official Report of the Burma Legislative Council Debates, 19 February 1931, 16 February 1931.

6. Governor Charles Innes was in London to attend the first India Round Table Conference. Collis, *Trials in Burma*, 179–80, 210–15.

7. Fl. 1346-1931, fd. 7347-1930, L/P&J/6/2020, India Office Library, London.

8. Official Report of the Burma Legislative Council Debates, 12 February 1931. Innes did not mention whether there were other considerations, such as whether

peasants were even able to reach markets during the chaotic conditions, or whether British troops were taking the three-week period to establish safe conditions for the movement of tax collectors. See also the statement by Gertrude Anderson, an American Baptist missionary, that peasants near Tharrawaddy had been "unable to sell their paddy for fear of being murdered," although she did not specify who was the source of this fear. In Women's American Baptist Foreign Mission Society, *Sixty-first Annual Report* (1932), MRL.

9. Official Report of the Burma Legislative Council Debates, 31 August 1931. The amnesty was announced on 30 June 1931. See also Maung Maung, *From Sangha to Laity*, 95–96.

10. Scott, *Moral Economy of the Peasant*; Herbert, *The Hsaya San Rebellion*; Solomon, *Saya San and the Burmese Rebellion*; Cady, *The United States and Burma*; Official Report of the Burma Legislative Council Debates, 4 November 1931.

11. See chapter 7 (on the Saya San rebellion, and especially the footnotes) in Maung Maung, *From Sangha to Laity*, for details of the newspaper coverage.

12. Scott's *Moral Economy of the Peasant* is the best-known example.

13. For Nghe-Tinh quotes see *New York Times*, 7 May 1930, 16, and *Chicago Daily Tribune*, 15 May 1930, 17. For Saya San see *New York Herald Tribune*, with stories on 25 December and each day from 27 to 31 December. The front-page story appeared on 27 December. The name King Golden Crow was reported by both the *New York Herald Tribune* (31 December 1930, 5) and in several stories in the *New York Times*, including front-page stories on 3 and 4 January 1931.

14. Deputy secretary of the Government of India to undersecretary of state for India, 26 February 1931, fl. 1346-1931, fd. 7347-1930, L/P&J/6/2020; Government of Burma to Home Department, Government of India, 5 January 1931, fl. 462-1931, fd. 7347-1930, L/P&J/6/2020, both in India Office Library, London. British officials were so convinced that this was a "usual" rebellion that the manual used by Military Police with "hints" for dealing with the Burmese rebels had been written in 1914, based on one British officer's experience in Upper Burma in the 1880s. See Herbert, *The Hsaya San Rebellion (1930–1932) Reappraised*, 2–3.

15. Government of Burma, *The Origins and Causes of the Burma Rebellion*. The language in this report echoed closely and sometimes was even identical to the government communiqué of 10 February 1931, issued to declare the Soe Thein GBCA an unlawful association.

16. Fl. 1126-1934, 29 March 1934, fd. 7347-1930, L/P&J/6/2020, India Office Library, London.

17. Résident in Vinh (Guilleminet) to Résident supérieur in Annam, 13 May 1930, d. 2642, c. 327; Résident supérieur in Annam (Le Fol) to gouverneur général, 18 May 1930, d. 2642, c. 327; "Extrait du rapport du chef local des services de police et de sûreté en Annam, Commission d'enquête, 8 May 1930, d. 2688, c. 334; inspecteur des affaires politiques et administratives de l'Annam to résident supérieur in Annam, 1–3 October 1930, d. 2688, c. 334, all in INF, CAOM.

18. Report of the Commission d'enquête, p. 26, d. 1597, INF, CAOM.

19. Report of the Commission d'enquête, 46–53.

20. Report of the Commission d'enquête, 10.

21. U.S. consul at Rangoon (Haering) to USDOS, 30 December 1930, 845.00/698, and 24 January 1931, 845.00/699, both in CF, RG 59, USNA. Haering listed as a prominent source of information for his reports F. B. Leach, the chief secretary of the Government of Burma, who staunchly defended government actions in the Burma Legislative Council. For example, see the debates on 10 February 1931, 25 February 1931, and 16 February 1932. Later United States reports from Winfield Scott, who took over the post in November 1931, and Vice-Consul Reginald S. Kazanjian were not markedly different from Haering's reports.

22. China and Japan did maintain consulates in Burma. Although the United States did trade more with Burma than did France or the Netherlands, the United States consulate also served the large American population in Burma, primarily missionaries but also oilmen working for British companies.

23. French consul general at Calcutta to French Foreign Ministry, 11 February 1931, vol. 49 Burma, sous-série British Possessions, série E Asia-Oceania, Archives de Ministère des Affaires Étrangères, Paris; *Koloniaal tijdschrift*, 1931, 105–8, 532–35, 640–41, and 1932, 86–87, 305–8. For French criticisms see *L'Asie française*, December 1931, 380.

24. The series of the reports by the United States consul Waterman can be found in CF, RG 59 USNA, file nos. 851g.00B/3 to 851g.00B/19.

25. British consul general in Saigon (F. G. Gorton) to FO, "Celebration of Labour Day in Indochina," 4 June 1930 [confidential], W6875, inv. 14906, and 7 May 1931, W6761/300/17, inv. 15644, both FO 371, UKNA.

26. For Dutch and French plans to cooperate against communism see de Jonge (governor general of Netherlands Indies) to de Graaf (minister of colonies), 6 November 1931, document 218 in *DBBPN* period B (1931–40), part 1 (2 January 1931–29 March 1932). Cheah, *From PKI to the Comintern*, 68, 74; Malayan Political Intelligence Bulletins from 1929–36 were found in the French Colonial Archives, 7 F 74, GGI, CAOM. Some issues of the Politiek Politioneel Overzicht (Netherlands Indies Secret Police Political Overview) from the 1930s were also found in 7 F 73, GGI, CAOM. The distribution list indicates that United States officials in the region saw these reports regularly.

27. The effects of colonial interests on the confused and tentative reactions of European countries to the Manchurian incident has received too little attention from scholars of this otherwise well-studied event. The best treatment remains Thorne, *The Limits of Foreign Policy*.

28. U.S. minister in The Hague (Laurits S. Swenson) to USDOS, 28 November 1931 (confidential for the secretary and undersecretary), 793.94/3149 CF, RG 59, USNA.

29. See discussion in chapter 2.

30. It is also possible that the Dutch were paying close attention to the disputes

within the Japanese government about the future of Japanese imperial policy. The classic treatments are Beasley, *Japanese Imperialism*, esp. chapter 12, and Nish, *Japanese Foreign Policy, 1869–1942*.

31. French consul in Manila (M. G. Willoquet) to Foreign Affairs Ministry, 31 January 1932, d. 561, c. 46, INF, CAOM.

32. SKH (Stanley K. Hornbeck) to Bill (William R. Castle), 17 December 1931, folder September–December 1931, box 453, Hornbeck Papers.

33. "The Philippine Islands: Question of Withdrawal of American Sovereignty and Responsibility—from the Point of View of U.S. Foreign Policy and International Relations," prepared by Stanley K. Hornbeck, in fd. Philippines, box 491, Hornbeck Papers. See also a public airing of the variety of opinions by United States officials in *Congressional Digest*, 10 (May 1931).

34. The skeptical reader was likely in the State Department, since I found this document in State Department files. Colonel Stanley H. Ford (Military Intelligence Division) to Chief of Staff (War Department), 6 May 1930, 811b.01/133½ CF, RG 59, USNA.

35. Stanley K. Hornbeck, "Problem of Philippine Independence: International Aspects," 13 May 1930, folder Philippines, box 491, Hornbeck Papers. This memo is an internal working paper in preparation for a possible State Department contribution to debate in Congress over the Hawes-Cutting bill, which came out of Senate committee in the spring of 1930 but was not acted upon that year.

36. Henry L. Stimson (secretary of state) to secretary of war, 21 October 1931, 811b.01/149A, confidential file, CF, RG 59, USNA. Stimson had long favored retention, both before and after his term as governor general in the Philippines.

37. Kramer, *The Blood of Government*, 392–427.

38. J. T. Pratt (FO), "Japanese Action at Shanghai," undated memorandum, prob. 31 January 1932, F655/1/10; J. T. Pratt, "The Shanghai Situation, February 1," 1 February 1932, F1263/1/10, both in *DBFP*, 2nd ser., vol. 9, 267, 281. Pratt would have been horrified to know that within fifteen years Britain would both go to war with Japan and "retire" from India.

39. V. Wellesley, 1 February 1932, F654/1/10, *DBFP*, 2nd ser., vol. 9, 283–91.

40. R. Lindsay (in Washington) to J. Simon (British foreign minister), 28 February 1932, F1832/1/10, *DBFP*, 2nd ser., vol. 9, 649–50.

41. Despite the near-certainty in European and United States diplomatic circles that Japan's actions in Manchuria were the beginning of a concerted policy of expansion, that was by no means agreed upon in Japan. Expansion had a variety of meanings in Japanese discussions of the 1930s, and only after mid-decade were calls for expansion southward heard frequently, and even then primarily by the Japanese navy. See the discussion by Peattie in Introduction, 22, and "Japanese Attitudes toward Colonialism, 1895–1945," esp. 119–27, *The Japanese Colonial Empire*, ed. Myers and Peattie. See also Nish's careful exploration in his *Japanese Foreign Policy in the Interwar Period*, esp. chapters 5–6.

42. Memo prepared by the War Department, "Yunnan: A French Sphere of Influence," 17 November 1933, 751.93/37 CF, RG 59, USNA.

43. Note de la sous-direction d'Asie-Océanie, 2 October 1933, *Documents diplomatiques françaises*, 2nd ser., vol. 4, 470–71.

44. Minister of colonies (Colijn) to minister of foreign affairs (de Graeff), 9 February 1934, document 209, *DBBPN*, period B, part 3, 349.

45. Governor general of the Netherlands Indies (de Jonge) to minister of colonies (de Graaf), 7 March 1933, document 272, *DBBPN*, period B, part 2, 524. For the time being de Jonge's confidence was well placed. Despite attempts by some Japanese naval officers to begin planning for actions to control those Southeast Asian oil resources by the mid-1930s, top Japanese officials were still more interested in East Asia, and in not provoking the European powers. See Nish, *Japanese Foreign Policy in the Interwar Period*, 112.

46. U.S. consul general at Batavia (K. S. Patton) to USDOS, 14 November 1933, 856d.00/79 CF, RG 59, USNA. Trade with Southeast Asia was an important but not overwhelming part of Japan's overseas trade. During the 1930s imports from Southeast Asia accounted for about 9 percent of Japan's imports, while exports to Southeast Asia accounted for about 10 percent of the total, with the Netherlands Indies alone responsible for one-third of that figure. A spike in the export figure in the early 1930s, as Beasley notes, "gave an important stimulus to Japanese expectations." Beasley, *Japanese Imperialism*, 223.

47. Patton to USDOS, 14 November 1933, 856d.00/79 CF, RG 59, USNA.

48. F. T. A. Ashton-Gwatkin (League of Nations and Western Department, FO), "Far East: Changing Situation," 3 August 1933, F5189/5189/61, *DBFP*, 2nd ser., vol. 20, 48–52. See also the discussions in McKercher, *Transition of Power* and Andrews, *The Writing on the Wall*.

49. Vansittart minute of 3 April, on F. Lindley (Tokyo) to Simon, 1 March 1934, F1761/373/23, *DBFP*, 2nd ser., vol. 20, 169.

50. Ashton-Gwatkin, "Far East: Changing Situation," 3 August 1933, *DBFP*, 50.

51. Memo from SKH (FE) to secretary of state, 21 January 1932, 811b.01/159 CF, RG 59, USNA.

52. Memo from SKH (FE) to secretary of state, 21 January 1932, 811b.01/159 CF, RG 59, USNA.

53. Golay, *Face of Empire*, 317.

54. "Our General Policy in and toward the Far East," 17 May 1934, by JEJ, folder U.S. Policy 1931–1934, box 423, Hornbeck Papers.

55. "Our General Policy in and toward the Far East," 17 May 1934, by JEJ, folder U.S. Policy 1931–1934, box 423, Hornbeck Papers.

56. Hornbeck to secretary of state, 16 March 1935 (strictly confidential), folder Department of State: Far Eastern Bureau, Correspondence 1934–1938, Hornbeck Papers.

57. For discussion of the Five Power Treaty see LaFeber, *The Clash*, 180; for the

neutralization proposal, "Question of Proposing Neutralization of the Philippine Islands and of Proposing Convocation of a General Conference on the Far East," 30 December 1936 (confidential), folder Conference on Questions of Far East and Pacific, box 128, Hornbeck Papers.

58. Hornbeck to Assistant Secretary (Francis) Sayre, 21 October 1936 (confidential), folder Philippine Islands, Neutralization of, box 344, Hornbeck Papers.

59. "Draft Memorandum Prepared in the Department of State on the Neutralization of the Islands of the Pacific," 16 February 1937, 700.0011 Pacific/25½, *FRUS* 1937, vol. 3, 954–71.

60. "Memorandum by President Roosevelt to the Secretary of State," 1 March 1937, 700.0011 Pacific/28, *FRUS* 1937, vol. 3, 973–74.

61. "Memorandum by Mr. Norman H. Davis of a Conversation with the British Deputy Under Secretary of State for Foreign Affairs (Cadogan)," 22 April 1937, 890.00/47, *FRUS* 1937, vol. 3, 975–78; Eden to R. Lindsay (British minister in Washington), 16 April 1937, *DBFP*, doc. 70, p. 107. Davis was in London because he had recently headed the United States delegation to the London Naval Conference.

62. Eden to Lindsay, 3 May 1937, *DBFP*, doc. 76, p. 113. It is somewhat surprising that Roosevelt even pursued the matter this far, since in the London Naval Conference of 1935–36 Japan's foreign minister Hirota Koki had floated the idea of a new agreement between Japan, Britain, and the United States based on the non-fortification clause in the Washington naval treaties. At the time this idea was swiftly rejected. See Nish, *Japanese Foreign Policy 1869–1942*, 208.

63. Extract from Minutes of the 4th Meeting of Principal Delegates to the Imperial Conference, 1937, 22 May 1937, *DBFP*, doc. 86, pp. 126–31; U.S. ambassador to Japan (Grew) to USDOS, 28 May 1937, 700.0011 Pacific/15, *FRUS* 1937, vol. 3, 979–82.

64. See Golay, *Face of Empire*, 350–54, 392–95. Interestingly, Quezon, who had been completely unmoved by neutralization proposals to this point, in 1937 began to realize how difficult it would be for the Philippines to defend itself against an increasingly ambitious Japan. He reminded Roosevelt during a visit to Washington in 1937 of the commitment by the United States.

65. Mrázek, *Sjahrir*, 102–5.

66. Abdullah, *Schools and Politics*, 209.

67. Abdullah, *Schools and Politics*, 221; Ingleson, *Road to Exile*, 204–7.

68. Mrázek, *Sjahrir*, 122–31. Sukarno and Hatta were sent to Boven Digoel, the same island internment camp to which the PKI rebels had been sent in 1927. The student strike in Burma, beginning at Rangoon University and sparking sympathy strikes throughout the country, had a similar effect on the Burmese and English. See Kyaw Ēi, *The Voice of Young Burma*, 64–80.

69. Discussed in Ricklefs, *A History of Modern Indonesia since c. 1300*, 191–92.

70. U.S. consul general in Batavia (K. S. Patton) to USDOS, 21 August 1933, 856d.00/78 CF, RG 59, USNA.

71. Patton to USDOS, 14 November 1933, 856d.00/79 CF, RG 59, USNA.

72. Patton to USDOS, 15 June 1932, 856d.00/74 CF, RG 59, USNA.

73. U.S. consul general in Batavia (Walter A. Foote) to USDOS, 29 January 1937, 856d.00/96, and Foote to USDOS, 2 August 1937, 856d.01/101, both in CF, RG 59, USNA. The January despatch was summarized in the Division of Western European Affairs, an unusual level of interest for despatches from colonial Southeast Asia.

74. Duiker, *The Rise of Nationalism in Vietnam*, 179. Cao Dai wanted to restore Prince Cuong De of the Vietnamese royal family. Although traditional, the French were still very much opposed.

75. Duiker, *The Rise of Nationalism in Vietnam*, 234–55; Khanh, *Vietnamese Communism*, 205–17.

76. U.S. consul in Saigon (Quincy F. Roberts) to USDOS, 31 January 1926, 851g.00/40 CF, RG 59, USNA.

77. Roberts to USDOS, 29 August 1936, 851g.00 P.R./1 CF, RG 59, USNA.

78. Roberts to USDOS, 15 October 1936, 851g.00/P.R./1 CF, RG 59, USNA.

79. Roberts to USDOS, 29 August 1936, 851g.00 P.R./1 CF, RG 59, USNA.

80. Taylor, "The Relationship between Burmese Social Classes and British-Indian Policy on the Behavior of the Burmese Political Elite," 126.

81. Cady, *History of Modern Burma*, 352–53. The Scheduled Areas were minority-occupied areas, mostly in upper Burma. These areas were incorporated into independent Burma in 1947 but remain a source of tension for the country.

82. Khin Yi, *The Dobama Movement in Burma*, 22–23, 34–40; Cady, *History of Burma*, 334.

83. Taylor, "The Relationship between Burmese Social Classes and British-Indian Policy on the Behavior of the Burmese Political Elite," 228–29. The legislature could not even regulate the language used in its sessions: before 1937 legislators had been allowed to address the council in Burmese or English. After 1937 they were required to speak English if they knew it. Not surprisingly, the law rankled. If Burmese members did not know English, they were permitted to speak in their native language. The measure may have been designed in part to save the cost of translating for "official" members, who were British and spoke no Burmese. There are complaints in the records of the Burma Legislative Council about the cost of translations.

84. Rangoon (Austin C. Brady) to Washington, 6 October 1937, 845C.00 P.R./6 CF, RG 59, USNA. The wife was not named, but this lacuna may be due more to the conventions of State Department reporting than to an early-twentieth-century tendency to erase the identity of women. In official reports usually only elected or appointed officials were mentioned by name. Even civil servants interviewed or referred to in these reports were identified only by title.

85. Brady to USDOS, 7 January 1939, 845c.00/22 CF, RG 59, USNA.

86. Brady to USDOS, 5 June 1939, 845c.00/33 CF, RG 59, USNA.

Conclusion

1. Three who have influenced my work are Anderson, *Imagined Communities*, Mrázek, *Engineers of Happy Land*, and especially Thongchai Winichakul, *Siam Mapped*.

2. The constructed nature of Southeast Asia is taken as a given in discussions of the issue of regionalism. See Hirschman et al., eds., *Southeast Asian Studies in the Balance*, esp. the papers by Charles F. Keyes and Benedict R. Anderson. Even those who attempt to critique the limitations that such constructions have placed on scholarship seem trapped in a perception of the Second World War and the early cold war as the source of this political entity. An especially perceptive but still problematic piece is Rafael, "Regionalism, Area Studies, and the Accidents of Agency."

3. Officials from Thailand participated in many of these political and economic organizations as well, often mediated by the European and American "advisors" in each Thai government ministry.

4. Paul Kramer, in *The Blood of Government*, notes how powerfully this idea about preparing Filipinos for self-rule operated to encourage Filipino élites to adapt to United States political institutions and style, and how most Americans could not, because of their ideas about race, perceive that Filipinos might indeed have achieved the status envisioned in the empire of the mind. American ideas about race may well have functioned to prevent Americans from accepting that any Southeast Asians could for the foreseeable future govern themselves well, but Americans still believed that they believed in Southeast Asians' eventual capability. See Kramer, *The Blood of Government*, 287–89.

5. This phrase is discussed in chapter 3.

6. Many examples exist. Perhaps most useful, because the collection offers a critique of this idea while reinforcing it, are the two important volumes of historiography edited by Hogan. *America in the World: The Historiography of American Foreign Relations since 1941* appeared first, is much more substantial in length and breadth of coverage, and suggests lively debates over important subjects. *Pathways to Power: The Historiography of American Foreign Relations to 1941* is shorter and filled with cries for more attention to the period before the Second World War. Even the titles suggest that the United States acted in the world to a substantially greater degree after 1941.

7. Among the many examples see Borstelman, Apartheid's Reluctant Uncle; Bradley, Imagining Vietnam and America; Fraser, Ambivalent Anti-Colonialism.

Bibliography

Archival Sources

BRITAIN

India Office Library, London

L/P&J
L/MIL

National Archives, Kew

Colonial Office 273, 825
Foreign Office 371

FRANCE

Centre des Archives d'Outre-Mer, Aix-en-Provence

Gouvernement Général d'Indochine
Indochine Nouveau Fonds
Affaires Politiques

Ministre des Affaires Etrangères, Paris

Série E Asie-Océanie

NETHERLANDS

Nationaal Archief, The Hague

Ministry of Colonies
    Geheim Mailrapporten
    Openbaar Mailrapporten
    Geheim Verhalen
    Openbaar Verhalen

UNITED STATES

Hoover Institution, Palo Alto, Calif.

Stanley K. Hornbeck Papers
Ray Lyman Wilbur Papers
Collection Inlichtingsdienst der Deli Planters
Vereeniging den Algemeene Vereeniging van Rubberplanters ter Oostkunst van
  Sumatra

Missionary Research Library, New York

National Archives, College Park, Md.

Bureau of Insular Affairs, Record Group 350
Naval Attachés, Record Group 38
Bureau of Foreign and Domestic Commerce, Record Group 151
Diplomatic and Consular Posts, Record Group 84
Department of State, Record Group 59
  Central Files
  Division of Commercial Affairs
  Division of Current Information
  Entries 535, 538, 593, 623, 624, 648, 653

Rockefeller Archives, Tarrytown, N.Y.

Published Documents and Government Reports

Benda, Harry, and Ruth McVey, eds. *The Communist Uprisings of 1926–1927 in Indo-
  nesia: Key Documents.* Ithaca: Cornell Modern Indonesia Project, 1959.
Bliss, Don C. *Market for Foodstuffs in the Netherlands East Indies.* Trade Information
  Bulletin no. 620. Washington: U.S. Department of Commerce, 1929.
*British Documents on Foreign Affairs: Reports and Papers from the Foreign Office
  Confidential Print,* part II, *From the First to the Second World War,* ser. C, *North
  America, 1919–1939,* vols. 16–17. Frederick, Md.: University Publications of
  America, 1986, 1995.
Bulletin économique de l'Indochine: industrie, commerce, finances, statistiques. Hanoi:
  Gouvernement Général de l'Indochine, 1930, 1931.
Bureau of Foreign and Domestic Commerce, U.S. Department of Commerce. *Motion
  Pictures Abroad.* Washington: U.S. Department of Commerce, 1932–36.
"Burma: A Promising Market for American Goods." *Commerce Reports: A Weekly
  Survey of Foreign Trade* 31 (3 August 1931), 260–61.
Burma, Government of. *The Origins and Causes of the Burma Rebellion (1930–1932).*
  Rangoon: Government of Burma, 1934.
Burma Legislative Council. *Proceedings.* Rangoon: Government of Burma, 1930–39.

Congressional Record. 71st Cong., 1st sess., 1929, vol. 71, pt. 4, 4488–99.

Federal Trade Commission. *Report of the Federal Trade Commission on Foreign Owner-ship in the Petroleum Industry.* Washington: Federal Trade Commission, 1923.

France, Government of. *Documents diplomatiques françaises,* 2nd ser., vol. 4, 1933. Paris: Imprimerie Nationale, 1967.

Golden, N. D. *Short-Subject Film Market in Latin America, Canada, the Far East, Africa, and the Near East.* Trade Information Bulletin no. 544. Washington: U.S. Department of Commerce, 1928.

Great Britain, Department of Overseas Trade. *Report on Economic and Commercial Conditions in the Netherlands East Indies by the British Commercial Agent in Batavia,* ed. G. N. Carey. London: H.M.S.O., 1938.

Great Britain, Foreign Office, Petroleum Department. *Memorandum on the Petroleum Situation for H.M. Ambassador in Washington, D.C.* London: H.M. Stationery Office, Cmd. 1351, 1921.

Great Britain, Government of. *Documents on British Foreign Policy,* 2nd ser., vols. 9 (1932), 20 (1934), 21 (1937). London: Her Majesty's Stationery Office.

International Labour Office. *Intergovernmental Commodity Control Agreements.* Montreal: League of Nations, International Labour Office, 1943.

Kral, J. J. *U.S. Commerce Reports, Supplement.* Trade Information Bulletin 373. Washington: U.S. Department of Commerce, 1925.

League of Nations. *Raw Material Problems and Policies.* Geneva: League of Nations, 1946.

Mann, Lawrence B., and Grace A. Witherlow. *Foreign Trade of the United States in the Fiscal Year 1926–1927.* Trade Information Bulletin 507. Washington: U.S. Department of Commerce, 1927.

Motion Pictures in India. Trade Information Bulletin 614. Washington: U.S. Department of Commerce, 1929.

Netherlands, Government of. *Documenten betreffende de buitenlandse politiek van Nederland,* period A, parts 1–4. The Hague: Nijhoff, 1977.

———. *Documenten betreffende de buitenlandse politiek van Nederland,* period B, parts 1–3 (1931–34). The Hague: Nijhoff, 1985–96.

Netherlands Indies, Government of. *Handbook of the Netherlands East Indies.* Buitenzorg: Departement van Landbouw, Nijverheid en Handel, 1924.

———. *Handbook of the Netherlands East Indies.* Buitenzorg: Departement van Landbouw, Nijverheid en Handel, 1930.

———. *Tien jaar volksraad arbeid, 1918–1928.* Weltevreden: Landsdrukkerij, 1928.

Nu, U. *An Asian Speaks.* Washington: Embassy of the Union of Burma, 1955.

Poeze, Harry A., ed. *Politiek-politioneele overzichten van Nederlandsch-Indie,* vols. 1 (1982), 2 (1983), 3 (1988). The Hague: M. Nijhoff.

Pugh, M. A. *Markets of the Netherlands East Indies,* Trade Information Bulletin 509. Washington: U.S. Department of Commerce, 1927.

Roosevelt, Theodore. *African and European Addresses.* New York: G. P. Putnam's Sons, 1910.

U.S. Department of Commerce. *Commerce Yearbook*, 1925–39. Washington: U.S. Government Printing Office, 1926–40.

U.S. Department of State. *Foreign Relations of the United States*, 1920–23, 1933–37. Washington: U.S. Government Printing Office, 1935–54.

U.S. Public Law 361, 71st Cong., 2nd sess., chap. 497, 1930.

U.S. Senate. *American Petroleum Interests in Foreign Countries, 1945*. Washington: U.S. Government Printing Office, 1946.

Wal, S. L. van der. *Het onderwijsbeleid in Nederlands-Indie, 1900–1940*. Groningen: J. B. Wolters, 1963.

Witherow, Grace A. *Foreign Trade of the United States, Calendar Year 1938*, part II, *Trade by Regions and Countries* (Washington: U.S. Department of Commerce, 1940.

Newspapers and Periodicals

Asie Française, 1926–27, 1930–33

Call of French Indochina, 1924–30

Chicago Daily Tribune, 1926, 1927, 1930–32

Commerce Reports: A Weekly Survey of Foreign Trade, 1925–38

Congressional Digest, 1931

De Standaard, 1919

Film Daily Yearbook, 1925

Indépendance tonkinoise, 1924

De Indische gids, 1930–32

Koloniaal tijdschrift, 1930–33

New York Herald Tribune, 1926, 1927, 1930–32

New York Times, 1926, 1927, 1930–32

Straits Times, August 1922

Secondary Literature

Abalahin, Andrew Jiminez. "Prostitution Policy and the Project of Modernity: A Comparative Study of Colonial Indonesia and the Philippines, 1850–1940." Ph.D. diss., Cornell University, 2003.

Abdullah, Taufik. *Schools and Politics: The Kaum Muda Movement in West Sumatra, 1927–1933*. Ithaca: Southeast Asia Program, 1971.

Abinales, Patricio. "State Authority and Local Power in Southern Philippines, 1900–1972." Ph.D. diss., Cornell University, 1997.

———. "Progressive-Machine Conflict in Early-Twentieth-Century U.S. Politics and Colonial-State Building in the Philippines." *The American Colonial State in the Philippines: Global Perspectives*, ed. Julian Go and Anne L. Foster, 148–81. Durham: Duke University Press, 2003.

Aldrich, Richard J. *The Key to the South: Britain, the United States, and Thailand during the Approach of the Pacific War, 1929–1942*. New York: Oxford University Press, 1993.

Allen, Hugh. *The House of Goodyear: A Story of Rubber and of Modern Business*. New York: Arno, 1976.

Anderson, Benedict. *Imagined Communities: Reflections on the Origin and Spread of Nationalism*. London: Verso, 1983.

———. "Language, Fantasy, Revolution: Java 1900–1950." *Making Indonesia: Essays on Modern Indonesia in Honor of George McT. Kahin*, ed. Daniel S. Lev and Ruth McVey, 26–40. Ithaca: Cornell Southeast Asia Program Publications, 1996.

———. *The Spectre of Comparisons: Nationalism, Southeast Asia and the World*. London: Verso, 1998.

Anderson, Warwick. *Colonial Pathologies: American Tropical Medicine, Race, and Hygiene in the Philippines*. Durham: Duke University Press, 2006. ✔

Andrews, E. M. *The Writing on the Wall: The British Commonwealth and Aggression in the Far East, 1931–1935*. London: Allen and Unwin, 1987.

Antlov, Hans, and Stein Tonnesson, eds. *Imperial Policy and South East Asian Nationalism*. Richmond, Surrey: Curzon, 1995.

Babcock, Glenn D. *History of the United States Rubber Company: A Case Study in Corporate Management*. Bloomington: Indiana University Press, 1966.

Bailyn, Bernard. *Atlantic History: Concept and Contours*. Cambridge: Harvard University Press, 2005.

Bain, H. Foster. *Ores and Industries of the Far East*. New York: Council on Foreign Relations, 1927.

Banner, Hubert S. "The Enchantment of Mountainous Java." *Travel* 51 (September 1928), 47.

Barclay, Paul. "'They Have for the Coast Dwellers a Traditional Hatred': Governing Igorots in Northern Luzon and Central Taiwan, 1895–1915." *The American Colonial State in the Philippines: Global Perspectives*, ed. Julian Go and Anne L. Foster, 217–55. Durham: Duke University Press, 2003.

Beach, Harlan, and John Bartholomew. *World Missionary Atlas*. New York: Institute of Social and Religious Research, 1925.

Beasley, W. G. *Japanese Imperialism, 1894–1945*. Oxford: Oxford University Press, 1991.

Beisner, Robert L. *From the Old Diplomacy to the New, 1865–1900*. Arlington Heights, Ill.: Harlan Davidson, 1986.

Bernal, Martin. "The Nghe-Tinh Soviet Movement." *Past and Present* 92 (August 1981), 148–68.

Bisson, T. A. *American Policy in the Far East: 1931–1940*. New York: Institute of Pacific Relations, 1939.

Blumberger, J. Th. Petrus. *De communistische beweging in Nederlandsch-Indië*. Haarlem, H. D. Tjeenk Willink, 1935.

Boomgaard, Peter, and Ian Brown, eds. *Weathering the Storm: The Economies of Southeast Asia in the 1930s Depression*. Singapore: Institute of Southeast Asian Studies, 2000.

Booth, Anne. "Four Colonies and a Kingdom: A Comparison of Fiscal, Trade, and Exchange Rate Policies in South East Asia in the 1930s." *Modern Asian Studies* 37, no. 2 (2003), 429–60.

———. "Night Watchman, Extractive, or Development States? Some Evidence from Late Colonial South-east Asia." *Economic History Review* 60, no. 2 (2007), 241–66.

———. *Colonial Legacies: Economic and Social Development in East and Southeast Asia*. Honolulu: University of Hawai'i Press, 2007.

Bootsma, N. A. *Buren in de koloniale tijd: De Philippijnen onder Amerikaans bewind en de Nederlandse, Indische, en Indonesische reacties daarop, 1898–1942*. Dordrecht: Foris, 1986.

Borstelmann, Thomas. *Apartheid's Reluctant Uncle: The United States and Southern Africa in the Early Cold War*. New York: Oxford University Press, 1993.

Bradley, Mark. "An Improbable Opportunity: America and the Democratic Republic of Vietnam's 1947 Initiative." *The Vietnam War: Vietnamese and American Perspectives*, ed. Jayne S. Werner and Luu Doan Huynh, 3–23. Armonk, N.Y.: M. E. Sharpe, 1993.

———. "Imagining America: The United States in Radical Vietnamese Anticolonial Discourse." *Journal of American-East Asian Relations*, winter 1995, 299–329.

———. *Imagining Vietnam and America: The Making of Postcolonial Vietnam, 1919–1950*. Chapel Hill: University of North Carolina Press, 2000.

Brandes, Joseph. "Product Diplomacy: Herbert Hoover's Anti-Monopoly Campaign at Home and Abroad." *Herbert Hoover as Secretary of Commerce: Studies in New Era Thought and Practice*, ed. Ellis W. Hawley. Iowa City: University of Iowa Press, 1981.

Brandon, James R. *Theatre in Southeast Asia*. Cambridge: Harvard University Press, 1974.

Breman, Jan. *Koelies, planters en koloniale politiek*. Dordrecht: Foris / KITLV, 1987.

Brimmel, J. H. *Communism in Southeast Asia: A Political Analysis*. Oxford: Oxford University Press, 1959.

Broek, Jan O. M. *Economic Development of the Netherlands Indies*. New York: Institute of Pacific Relations, 1942.

Brown, Ian. "Rural Distress in Southeast Asia during the World Depression of the Early 1930s: A Preliminary Examination." *Journal of Asian Studies* 45, no. 5 (1986), 995–1025.

———. *Economic Change in South-East Asia, c. 1830–1930*. Kuala Lumpur: Oxford University Press, 1997.

———. "'Blindness We Mistake for Sight': British Officials and the Economic World of the Cultivator in Colonial Burma." *Journal of Imperial and Commonwealth History* 33, no. 2 (May 2005), 181–93.

Brumberg, Joan J. *Mission for Life: The Story of the Family of Adoniram Judson*. New York: Free Press, 1980.

Burton, Antoinette, ed. *After the Imperial Turn: Thinking with and through the Nation*. Durham: Duke University Press, 2003.

Cady, John. *History of Modern Burma*. Ithaca: Cornell University Press, 1958.

———. *The United States and Burma*. Cambridge: Harvard University Press, 1976.

Calhoun, Craig, Frederick Cooper, and Kevin W. Moore, eds., *Lessons of Empire: Imperial Histories and American Power*. New York: New Press, 2006.

Chalk, Frank R. "The United States and the International Struggle for Rubber, 1914–1941." Ph.D. diss., University of Wisconsin, 1970.

Cheah, Boon Kheng, ed. *From PKI to the Comintern, 1924–1941: The Apprenticeship of the Malayan Communist Party*. Ithaca: Southeast Asia Program, 1992.

Chen Jian. "The Myth of America's 'Lost Chance' in China: A Chinese Perspective in Light of New Evidence." *Diplomatic History* 21, no. 1 (1997), 77–86.

Cheng, Siok-Hwa. *The Rice Industry of Burma*. Kuala Lumpur: University of Malaysia Press, 1968.

Chester, Edward W. *United States Oil Policy and Diplomacy: A Twentieth Century Overview*. Westport, Conn.: Greenwood, 1983.

Clancy-Smith, Julia, and Frances Gouda, eds. *Domesticating the Empire: Race, Gender, and Family Life in French and Dutch Colonialism*. Charlottesville: University of Virginia Press, 1998.

Clymer, Kenton J. *Protestant Missionaries in the Philippines, 1898–1916: An Inquiry into the American Colonial Mentality*. Urbana: University of Illinois Press, 1986.

Cole, Wayne S. *Roosevelt and the Isolationists, 1932–1945*. Lincoln, University of Nebraska Press, 1983.

Collis, Maurice. *Trials in Burma*. London: Faber and Faber, 1945.

Cooper, Frederick, and Ann Laura Stoler, eds. *Tensions of Empire: Colonial Cultures in a Bourgeois World*. Berkeley: University of California Press, 1997.

Cooper, John Milton. *The Warrior and the Priest: Woodrow Wilson and Theodore Roosevelt*. Cambridge: Belknap, 1983.

Corley, T. A. B. *A History of the Burmah Oil Company*, vol. 1, *1886–1924*. London: Heinemann, 1983.

Corpus, Onofre D. "Western Colonization and the Filipino Response." *Journal of Southeast Asian History* 3 (1962), 1–22.

Costigliola, Frank C. *Awkward Dominion: American Political, Economic, and Cultural Relations with Europe, 1919–1933*. Ithaca: Cornell University Press, 1984.

Couperus, Louis. *The Hidden Force*, trans. Alexander Teixeira de Mattos. Amherst: University of Massachusetts Press, 1990.

Cullather, Nick. *Illusions of Influence: The Political Economy of United States–Philippines Relations, 1942–1960*. Stanford: Stanford University Press, 1994.

Dahm, Bernard. *Sukarno and the Struggle for Indonesian Independence*. Ithaca: Cornell University Press, 1969.

de Grazia, Victoria. *Irresistible Empire: America's Advance through 20th-Century Europe*. Cambridge: Belknap, 2005.

Dorgelès, Roland. "Twentieth-Century 'Savages': The Mois of Indo-China Suddenly Assaulted by the White Man's Civilization." *Asia*, June 1926, 539–42.

Doyle, Michael W. *Empires*. Ithaca: Cornell University Press, 1986.

Drabble, John H. *Malayan Rubber: The Interwar Years*. London: Macmillan, 1991.

Duggan, Stephen, ed. *The League of Nations: The Principle and the Practice*. Boston: Atlantic Monthly, 1919.

Duiker, William J. *The Rise of Nationalism in Vietnam, 1900–1940*. Ithaca: Cornell University Press, 1976.

Dulles, Foster Rhea. "The Anti-Colonial Policies of Franklin D. Roosevelt," *Political Science Quarterly* 70, no. 1 (1955), 1–18.

Elson, Robert E. "International Commerce, the State and Society: Economic and Social Change." *The Cambridge History of Southeast Asia*, vol. 2, *The Nineteenth and Twentieth Centuries*, ed. Nicholas Tarling, 131–95. New York: Cambridge University Press, 1992.

Feis, Herbert. *Seen from E.A.: Three International Episodes*. New York: Alfred A. Knopf, 1947.

Ferguson, Niall. *Empire: The Rise and Demise of the British World Order and the Lessons for Global Power*. New York: Basic, 2003.

———. *Colossus: The Price of America's Empire*. New York: Penguin, 2004.

Fieldhouse, D. K. *The Colonial Empires: A Comparative Survey from the Eighteenth Century*. New York: Delacorte, 1967.

Forbes, W. Cameron. *The Philippine Islands*. Boston: Houghton Mifflin, 1928.

Foster, Anne L. "Alienation and Cooperation: European, Southeast Asian, and American Perceptions of Anti-Colonial Rebellion, 1919–1937." Ph.D. diss, Cornell University, 1995.

———. "French, Dutch, British and U.S. Reactions to the Nghe Tinh Rebellion of 1930–1931." *Imperial Policy and South East Asian Nationalism*, ed. Hans Antlov and Stein Tonnesson, 63–82. Richmond, Surrey: Curzon, 1995.

Fox, Thomas Darryl. "Diplomacy, Revolution, and Power: The United States, Great Britain, and the Destabilization of Southeast Asia, 1873–1948." Ph.D. diss., Ohio State University, 1994.

Fraser, Cary. *Ambivalent Anti-Colonialism: The United States and the Genesis of West Indian Independence, 1940–1964*. Westport, Conn.: Greenwood, 1994.

Frederick, William H. "The Man Who Knew Too Much: Ch. O. Van der Plas and the Future of Indonesia, 1927–1950." *Imperial Policy and South East Asian Nationalism*, ed. Hans Antlov and Stein Tonnesson, 34–62. Richmond, Surrey: Curzon, 1995.

French, M. J. "The Emergence of U.S. Multinational Enterprise: The Goodyear Tire and Rubber Company, 1910–1939," *Economic History Review* 40, no. 1 (February 1987), 64–79.

Friend, Theodore. *Between Two Empires: The Ordeal of the Philippines, 1929–1946.* New Haven: Yale University Press, 1965.

Fuller, Kathryn H. *At the Picture Show: Small-Town Audiences and the Creation of Movie Fan Culture.* Washington: Smithsonian Institution Press, 1996.

Furnivall, J. S. *Netherlands India.* New York: Macmillan, 1944.

Gardner, Lloyd C. *Safe for Democracy: The Anglo-American Response to Revolution, 1913–1923.* New York: Oxford University Press, 1984.

Gardner, Mona. *Menacing Sun.* London: John Murray, 1939.

Go, Julian. "Chains of Empire, Projects of State: Political Education and U.S. Colonial Rule in the Philippines," *Comparative Studies in Society and History* 42 (April 2000), 333–62.

———. "The Chains of Empire: State Building and 'Political Education' in Puerto Rico and the Philippines." *The American Colonial State in the Philippines: Global Perspectives*, ed. Julian Go and Anne L. Foster, 182–216. Durham: Duke University Press, 2003.

———. "The Provinciality of American Empire: 'Liberal Exceptionalism' and U.S. Colonial Rule, 1898–1912." *Comparative Studies in Society and History* 49, no. 1 (2007), 74–108.

———. *American Empire and the Politics of Meaning: Elite Political Cultures in the Philippines and Puerto Rico during U.S. Colonialism.* Durham: Duke University Press, 2008.

Go, Julian, and Anne L. Foster, eds. *The American Colonial State in the Philippines: Global Perspectives.* Durham: Duke University Press, 2003.

Golay, Frank. *Face of Empire: United States-Philippine Relations, 1898–1946.* Madison: Center for Southeast Asian Studies, 1998.

Goncharov, Sergei N., John W. Lewis, and Xue Lita. *Uncertain Partners: Stalin, Mao and the Korean War.* Stanford: Stanford University Press, 1993.

Gouda, Frances. *American Visions of the Netherlands East Indies/Indonesia: US Foreign Policy and Indonesian Nationalism, 1920–1949.* Amsterdam: Amsterdam University Press, 2002.

Gould, James W. *Americans in Sumatra.* The Hague: Nijhof, 1961.

Groenewoud, Margo. "Towards the Abolition of Penal Sanctions in Dutch Colonial Labor Legislation: An International Perspective." *Itinerario* 19, no. 2 (1995), 72–90.

Hardt, Michael, and Antonio Negri, *Empire.* Cambridge: Harvard University Press, 2000.

Harley, John E. *World Wide Influences of the Cinema: A Study of Official Censorship and the International Cultural Aspects of Motion Pictures.* Los Angeles: University of Southern California Press, 1940.

Harloff, A. J. W. "The Influence of the Cinema on Oriental Peoples." *British Malaya*, February 1935, 213–16.

Hemery, Daniel. *Ho Chi Minh: de l'Indochine au Vietnam.* Paris: Gallimard, 1990.

Herbert, Patricia. *The Hsaya San Rebellion (1930–1932) Reappraised.* London: Department of Oriental Manuscripts and Printed Books, British Library, 1982.

Hirschman, Charles, et al., eds. *Southeast Asian Studies in the Balance: Reflections from America.* Ann Arbor: Association for Asian Studies, 1990.

Ho Chi Minh. *Selected Writings, 1920–1969.* Hanoi: Foreign Languages Publishing House, 1977.

Hoff-Wilson, Joan. *Herbert Hoover: Forgotten Progressive.* Boston: Little, Brown, 1975.

Hogan, Michael J. *Informal Entente: The Private Structure of Cooperation in Anglo-American Diplomacy, 1918–1928.* Columbia: University of Missouri Press, 1977.

———. *America in the World: The Historiography of American Foreign Relations since 1941.* New York: Cambridge University Press, 1995.

———. *Pathways to Power: The Historiography of American Foreign Relations to 1941.* New York: Cambridge University Press, 2000.

Hoganson, Kristin L. *Consumers' Imperium: The Global Production of American Domesticity, 1865–1920.* Chapel Hill: University of North Carolina Press, 2007.

Holland, W. L., ed. *Commodity Control in the Pacific Area.* Palo Alto: Stanford University Press for the Institute of Pacific Relations, 1935.

Homan, Gerlof D. "The United States and the Netherlands East Indies: The Evolution of American Anticolonialism." *Pacific Historical Review* 53, no. 4 (1984), 423–46.

Hoover, Herbert. *Memoirs.* New York: Macmillan, 1951–52.

Howard, Randolph L. *Baptists in Burma.* Philadelphia: Judson, 1931.

Ingleson, John. *Perhipunan Indonesia and the Indonesian Nationalist Movement, 1923–1928.* Clayton, Australia: Centre for Southeast Asian Studies, Monash University, 1975.

———. *Road to Exile: The Indonesian Nationalist Movement, 1927–1934.* Singapore: Heineman Educational, 1979.

———. "Urban Java during the Depression." *Journal of Southeast Asian Studies* 19, no. 2 (1988), 292–309.

Iriye, Akira. *After Imperialism: The Search for a New Order in the Far East, 1921–1931.* New York: Antheneum, 1978.

———. *The Cambridge History of American Foreign Relations,* vol. 3, *The Globalizing of America, 1913–1945,* ed. Warren I. Cohen. New York: Cambridge University Press, 1993.

Iriye, Akira, and Warren I. Cohen, eds. *American, Chinese, and Japanese Perspectives on Wartime Asia, 1931–1949.* Wilmington, Del.: SR, 1990.

Isaacs, Harold R. *Scratches on Our Minds: American Images of China and India.* New York: John Day, 1958.

Kahin, George McT. *Nationalism and Revolution in Indonesia.* Ithaca: Cornell University Press, 1952.

Kaplan, Amy, and Donald E. Pease, eds. *Cultures of United States Imperialism.* Durham: Duke University Press, 1993.

Khanh, Huyhn Kim. *Vietnamese Communism, 1925–1945*. Ithaca: Cornell University Press, 1982.

Khin Yi, Daw. *The Dobama Movement in Burma (1930–1938)*. Ithaca: Southeast Asia Program, 1988.

Kimball, Warren F. *The Juggler: Franklin D. Roosevelt as Wartime Statesman*. Princeton: Princeton University Press, 1991.

———. "The Incredible Shrinking War: The Second World War, Not (Just) the Origins of the Cold War." *Diplomatic History* 25, no. 3 (2001), 347–65.

Kleintjes, Philip. *Staatsinstellingen van Nederlandsch-Indië*, vol. 1. Amsterdam: J. H. de Bussy, 1932.

Kornweibel, Theodore. *"Investigate Everything": Federal Efforts to Compel Black Loyalty during World War I*. Bloomington: Indiana University Press, 2002.

Kramer, Paul. *The Blood of Government: Race, Empire, the United States and the Philippines*. Chapel Hill: University of North Carolina Press, 2006.

Kyaw Ēi, U. *The Voice of Young Burma*. Ithaca: Southeast Asia Program, 1993.

LaFeber, Walter. *The New Empire: An Interpretation of American Expansion, 1860–1898*. Ithaca: Cornell University Press, 1963.

———. *The American Search for Opportunity, 1865–1913*, vol. 2 of *The Cambridge History of American Foreign Relations*, ed. Warren I. Cohen. New York: Cambridge University Press, 1993.

———. "Betrayal in Tokyo," *Constitution* 6, no. 2 (fall 1994), 4–10.

———. *The Clash: U.S.–Japanese Relations throughout History*. New York: W. W. Norton, 1997.

Lardizabal, Amparo S. *Pioneer American Teachers and Philippine Education*. Quezon City: Phoenix, 1991.

Larson, George. *Prelude to Revolution: Palaces and Politics in Surakarta, 1912–1942*. Dordrecht: Foris, 1987.

Lawrence, James Cooper. *The World's Struggle with Rubber, 1905–1931*. New York: Harper and Bros., 1931.

Lawrence, Mark Atwood. *Assuming the Burden: Europe and the American Commitment to War in Vietnam*. Berkeley: University of California Press, 2005.

Leffler, Melvyn P. *The Elusive Quest: America's Pursuit of European Stability and French Security, 1919–1933*. Chapel Hill: University of North Carolina Press, 1979.

Levin, N. Gordon, Jr. *Woodrow Wilson and World Politics: America's Response to War and Revolution*. London: Oxford University Press, 1968.

Lewis, Cleona, assisted by Karl T. Schlotterbeck. *America's Stake in International Investments*. Washington: Brookings Institution, 1938.

Linn, Brian McAllister. *Guardians of Empire: The U.S. Army and the Pacific, 1902–1940*. Chapel Hill: University of North Carolina Press, 1997.

Little, Douglas. *Malevolent Neutrality: The United States, Great Britain, and the Origins of the Spanish Civil War*. Ithaca: Cornell University Press, 1985.

Logevall, Fredrik. *Choosing War: The Lost Chance for Peace and the Escalation of the War in Vietnam*. Berkeley: University of California Press, 1999.

Louis, William Roger. *British Strategy in the Far East, 1919–1939*. Oxford: Clarendon, 1971.

———. *Imperialism at Bay, 1941–1945: The United States and the Decolonization of the British Empire*. Oxford: Clarendon, 1977.

Lowry, Edward G. "Trade Follows the Film." *Saturday Evening Post*, 7 November 1925, 12–13.

Malaka, Tan. *From Jail to Jail*, trans. Helen Jarvis. Athens: Ohio University Press, 1991.

Manela, Erez. *The Wilsonian Moment: Self-Determination and the International Origins of Anticolonial Nationalism*. New York: Oxford University Press, 2007.

Marcosson, Isaac F. "The Crisis in Rubber." *Saturday Evening Post*, 5 June 1926.

Marr, David, *Vietnamese Anticolonialism, 1885–1925*. Berkeley: University of California Press, 1971.

———. *Vietnamese Tradition on Trial, 1920–1945*. Berkeley: University of California Press, 1981.

Marshall, Jonathan. *To Have and Have Not: Southeast Asian Raw Materials and the Origins of the Pacific War*. Berkeley: University of California Press, 1995.

Maung Maung, U. *From Sangha to Laity: Nationalist Movements of Burma, 1920–1940*. New Delhi: Manohar, 1980.

May, Glenn Anthony. *Social Engineering in the Philippines: The Aims, Execution, and Impact of American Colonial Policy, 1900–1913*. Westport, Conn.: Greenwood, 1980.

———. "The Business of Education in the Colonial Philippines, 1909–1930." Colonial Crucible: Empire in the Making of the Modern American State, ed. Alfred W. McCoy and Francisco A. Scarano, 151–62. Madison: University of Wisconsin Press, 2009.

McCoy, Alfred W. and Francisco A. Scarano, eds. *Colonial Crucible: Empire in the Making of the Modern American State*. Madison: University of Wisconsin Press, 2009.

McFadyean, Andrew, ed. *The History of Rubber Regulation, 1934–1943*. London: George Allen and Unwin, 1944.

McHale, Shawn Frederick. *Print and Power: Confucianism, Communism, and Buddhism in the Making of Modern Vietnam*. Honolulu: University of Hawai'i Press, 2004.

McKercher, Brian J. C. *The Second Baldwin Government and the United States, 1924–1929: Attitudes and Diplomacy*. New York: Cambridge University Press, 1984.

———. *Transition of Power: Britain's Loss of Global Pre-eminence to the United States, 1930–1945*. New York: Cambridge University Press, 1999.

McMahon, Robert J. *Colonialism and Cold War: The United States and the Struggle for Indonesian Independence, 1945–1949*. Ithaca: Cornell University Press, 1981.

———. *The Limits of Empire: The United States and Southeast Asia since World War II*. New York: Columbia University Press, 1999.

———. "Towards a Pluralist Vision: The Study of American Foreign Relations as International History and National History." *Explaining the History of American Foreign Relations*, ed. Michael J. Hogan and Thomas G. Paterson, 35–50. Cambridge: Cambridge University Press, 2004.

McVey, Ruth. *The Rise of Indonesian Communism*. Ithaca: Cornell University Press, 1965.

Means, Natalie. *Malaysia Mosaic: A Study of Fifty Years of Methodism*. Singapore: Methodist Book Room, 1935.

Merz, Charles. "When the Movies Go Abroad." *Harpers Magazine*, January 1926, 159.

Mook, Hubertus J. van. *The Netherlands Indies and Japan: Battle on Paper, 1940–1941*. New York: W. W. Norton, 1944.

Mrázek, Rudolf. *Sjahrir: Politics and Exile in Indonesia*. Ithaca: Southeast Asia Program, 1994.

———. "Sjahrir at Boven Digoel: Reflections on Exile in the Dutch East Indies." *Making Indonesia: Essays on Modern Indonesia in Honor of George McT. Kahin*, ed. Daniel S. Lev and Ruth McVey, 41–65. Ithaca: Cornell Southeast Asia Program Publications, 1996.

———. *Engineers of Happy Land: Technology and Nationalism in a Colony*. Princeton: Princeton University Press, 2002.

Murray, Martin J. *The Development of Capitalism in Colonial Indochina (1870–1940)*. Berkeley: University of California Press, 1980.

Myers, Ramon H., and Mark R. Peattie, eds. *The Japanese Colonial Empire, 1895–1945*. Princeton: Princeton University Press, 1984.

Ngai, Mae M. *Impossible Subjects: Illegal Aliens and the Making of Modern America*. Princeton: Princeton University Press, 2004.

Ngo Vinh Long. *Before the Revolution: The Vietnamese Peasants under the French*. New York: Columbia University Press, 1991.

Nguyen Hong. "Days of Childhood." *The Light of the Capital: Three Modern Vietnamese Classics*, ed. Greg Lockhart, trans. Monique Lockhart. New York: Oxford University Press, 1996.

Nish, Ian. *Japanese Foreign Policy, 1869–1942*. Boston: Routledge, 1977.

———. *Japanese Foreign Policy in the Interwar Period*. Westport, Conn.: Praeger, 2002.

Nu, U. *U Nu: Saturday's Son*. New Haven: Yale University Press, 1975.

Oblas, Peter. "Treaty Revision and the Role of the American Foreign Affairs Advisor, 1909–1925." *Journal of the Siam Society* 60, no. 1 (1976), 171–86.

Oshikawa, Noriaki. "*Patjar Merah Indonesia* and Tan Malaka: A Popular Novel and a Revolutionary Legend." *Reading Southeast Asia*, ed. Takashi Shiraishi, 9–40. Ithaca: Cornell Southeast Asia Program, 1990.

Phan Thiên Châu. "Vietnamese Nationalism, 1919–1940." *Chuông Việt*, 1966, 51–55.

Popkin, Samuel. *The Rational Peasant: The Political Economy of Rural Society in Viet-nam*. Berkeley: University of California Press, 1979.

Post, Peter, and Elly Touwen-Bouwsma, eds. *Japan, Indonesia and the War*. Leiden: KITLV, 1997.

Pound, Arthur. *The Turning Wheel: The Story of General Motors through Twenty-Five Years, 1908–1933*. Garden City, N.Y.: Doubleday, Doran, 1934.

Quirk, Robert E. *An Affair of Honor: Woodrow Wilson and the Occupation of Veracruz*. New York: W. W. Norton, 1967.

Rafael, Vincente L. "Regionalism, Area Studies, and the Accidents of Agency." *American Historical Review* 104, no. 4 (1999), 1208–20.

Reed, Peter M. "Standard Oil in Indonesia, 1898–1928." *Business History Review* 32 (autumn 1972), 311–37.

Reid, Anthony. *Southeast Asia in the Age of Commerce, 1450–1680*. New Haven: Yale University Press, 1988, 1993.

Reynolds, David. *The Creation of the Anglo-American Alliance, 1937–1941: A Study in Competitive Co-operation*. Chapel Hill: University of North Carolina Press, 1982.

Ricklefs, M. C. *A History of Modern Indonesia since c. 1300*. Stanford: Stanford University Press, 1993.

Roff, William. *The Origins of Malay Nationalism*. New Haven: Yale University Press, 1967.

Rose, Mavis. *Indonesia Free: A Political Biography of Mohammad Hatta*. Ithaca: Southeast Asia Program, 1987.

Rosenberg, Emily. *Spreading the American Dream: American Economic and Cultural Expansion, 1890–1945*. New York: Hill and Wang, 1982.

——. *Financial Missionaries to the World: The Politics and Culture of Dollar Diplo-macy, 1900–1930*. Cambridge: Harvard University Press, 1999.

——. *A Date Which Will Live: Pearl Harbor in American Memory*. Durham: Duke University Press, 2003.

Rotter, Andrew. *The Path to Vietnam: Origins of the American Commitment to South-east Asia*. Ithaca: Cornell University Press, 1987.

Ruscio, Alain, ed. *Ho Chi Minh: textes, 1914–1969*. Paris: L'Harmattan, 1990.

Salman, Michael. *The Embarrassment of Slavery: Controversies over Bondage and Nationalism in the American Colonial Philippines*. Berkeley: University of California Press, 2001.

Scott, James C. *Moral Economy of the Peasant: Rebellion and Subsistence in Southeast Asia*. New Haven: Yale University Press, 1976.

Seldes, Gilbert. *The Movies Come from America*. London: B.T. Batsford, 1937.

Shiraishi, Takashi. *An Age in Motion: Popular Radicalism in Java, 1912–1926*. Ithaca: Cornell University Press, 1990.

——. "A New Regime of Order: The Origin of Modern Surveillance Politics in Modern Indonesia." *Southeast Asia over Three Generations*, ed. James T. Siegel and Audrey R. Kahin, 47–74. Ithaca: Southeast Asia Program Publications, 2003.

Sklar, Robert. *Movie-Made America: A Cultural History of American Movies.* New York: Vintage, 1994.

Smith, Robert F. "Republican Policy and Pax Americana, 1921–1932." *From Colony to Empire: Essays in the History of American Foreign Relations,* ed. William A. Williams, 253–92. New York: J. Wiley, 1972.

Solomon, Robert L. *Saya San and the Burmese Rebellion.* Santa Monica: Rand Corporation, 1969.

Specter, Ronald H. *In the Ruins of Empire: The Japanese Surrender and the Battle for Postwar Asia.* New York: Random House, 2007.

Stanley, Peter W. *A Nation in the Making: The Philippines and the United States, 1899–1921.* Cambridge: Harvard University Press, 1974.

Steinberg, David Joel, ed. *In Search of Southeast Asia: A Modern History.* Honolulu: University of Hawaii Press, 1987.

Stoler, Ann Laura. *Capitalism and Confrontation in Sumatra's Plantation Belt, 1870–1979.* New Haven: Yale University Press, 1985.

———. "Tense and Tender Ties: The Politics of Comparison in North American History and (Post) Colonial Studies." *Journal of American History* 88, no. 3 (December 2001), 829–66.

———. *Carnal Knowledge and Imperial Power: Race and the Intimate in Colonial Rule.* Berkeley: University of California Press, 2002.

Sukarno. *Sukarno: An Autobiography as Told to Cindy Adams.* Indianapolis: Bobbs-Merrill, 1965.

"Survey of Ten Years in Moslem Lands." *International Review of Missions* 12 (January 1923), 40–43.

Tai, Hue Tam Ho. *Radicalism and the Origins of the Vietnamese Revolution.* Cambridge: Harvard University Press, 1992.

Taylor, Arnold. *American Diplomacy and the Narcotics Traffic, 1900–1939: A Study in International Humanitarian Reform.* Durham: Duke University Press, 1969.

Taylor, Robert. "The Relationship between Burmese Social Classes and British-Indian Policy on the Behavior of the Burmese Political Elite, 1937–1942." Ph.D. diss., Cornell University, 1974.

Thamsook, Numnonda. "The American Foreign Affairs Advisers in Thailand, 1917–1940." *Journal of the Siam Society* 64, no. 1 (1976), 75–96.

Thelen, David. "Of Audiences, Borderlands and Comparisons: Toward the Internationalization of American History." *Journal of American History* 79, no. 2 (September 1992), 432–62.

———. "The Nation and Beyond: Transnational Perspectives on United States History." *Journal of American History* 86, no. 3 (December 1999), 965–75.

Thongchai Winichakul. *Siam Mapped: A History of the Geo-Body of a Nation.* Honolulu: University of Hawaii Press, 1994.

Thorne, Christopher. *The Limits of Foreign Policy: The West, the League and the Far Eastern Crisis of 1931–1933.* New York: Putnam, 1972.

———. *Allies of a Kind: The United States, Britain, and the War against Japan, 1941–1945.* Oxford: Oxford University Press, 1978.

Tr'ân, Huy Liêu. *Les Soviets du Nghe-Tinh de 1930–1931.* Hanoi: Éditions en Langues Étrangères, 1960.

Tyrrell, Ian. "Making Nations / Making States: American Historians in the Context of Empire." *Journal of American History* 86, no. 3 (December 1999), 1015–44.

———. "Empire in American History." *Colonial Crucible: Empire in the Making of the Modern American State,* ed. Alfred W. McCoy and Francisco A. *Scarano,* 541–56. Madison: University of Wisconsin Press, 2009.

Vandenbosch, Amry. *The Dutch East Indies: Its Government, Problems and Politics.* Berkeley: University of California Press, 1942.

Von der Mehden, Fred. *Religion and Nationalism in Southeast Asia.* Madison: University of Wisconsin Press, 1968.

Vuyk, Beb. "The Last House in the World." *Two Tales of the East Indies,* trans. Friedericy Vuyk. Singapore: Periplus, 2000.

Walker, J. Samuel. *Prompt and Utter Destruction: Truman and the Use of Atomic Bombs against Japan.* Chapel Hill: University of North Carolina Press, 1997.

Walker, William O., III. *Opium and Foreign Policy: The Anglo-American Search for Order in Asia, 1912–1954.* Chapel Hill: University of North Carolina Press, 1991.

Wanger, Walter. "120,000 American Ambassadors." *Foreign Affairs,* October 1939, 45–59.

Weait, R. H. "The Orient and the Cinema." *British Malaya,* March 1934, 231–32, 245.

Whitford, Harry N. "The Crude Rubber Supply: An International Problem." *Foreign Affairs* 2 (1924), 612–21.

Wiatt, W. E. *Burma: A Review of the Pioneer Foreign Mission Field of Northern Baptists.* New York: Northern Baptist Convention, Board of Missionary Cooperation, 1930.

Wilde, A. Neijtzell de. "De Nederlandsche-Indische politie." *Koloniaal tijdschrift* 13 (1924), 113–80.

Wilkins, Mira. *The Maturing of Multinational Enterprise.* Cambridge: Harvard University Press, 1974.

Williams, Michael C. *Sickle and Crescent: The Communist Revolt of 1926 in Banten.* Ithaca: Cornell Modern Indonesia Project, 1982.

———. *Communism, Religion, and Revolt in Banten.* Monographs in International Studies, Southeast Asia Series, vol. 86. Athens: Ohio University Press, 1990.

Williams, William Appleman. "The Legend of Isolationism in the 1920s." *Science and Society* 18 (winter 1954), 1–20.

"De Woelingen in Indochina." *De Indische gids,* 1930, part 2, 584–608.

Wolters, O. W. *History, Culture, and Region in Southeast Asian Perspectives.* Singapore: Institute of Southeast Asian Studies, 1982.

Yergin, Daniel. *The Prize: The Epic Quest for Oil, Money, and Power.* New York: Simon and Schuster, 1992.

Young, Marilyn. *The Vietnam Wars, 1945–1990.* New York: Harper Perennial, 1991.

Index

Page numbers in *italics* refer to illustrations

Anne L. Foster is an assistant professor of history
at Indiana State University.

Library of Congress Cataloging-in-Publication Data

Foster, Anne L., 1965–
Projections of power : the United States and Europe
in colonial Southeast Asia, 1919–1941 / Anne L. Foster.
p. cm. — (American encounters/global interactions)
Includes bibliographical references and index.
ISBN 978-0-8223-4786-6 (cloth : alk. paper) —
ISBN 978-0-8223-4800-9 (pbk. : alk. paper)
1. Southeast Asia—History—20th century.   2. Imperialism.
3. United States—Relations—Southeast Asia.
4. Southeast Asia—Relations—United States.
5. Europe—Relations—Southeast Asia.   6. Southeast
Asia—Relations—Europe.   I. Title.
II. Series: American encounters/global interactions.
DS526.6.F67 2010
303.48′25907309041—dc22
2010004455